COLLEGE REA....

with Active Critical Thinking

Book 2

Fifth Edition

Janet Maker
Los Angeles Trade-Technical College

Minnette Lenier
Los Angeles Pierce College

WADSWORTH PUBLISHING COMPANY
I(T)P® AN INTERNATIONAL THOMSON PUBLISHING COMPANY
Belmont • Albany • Bonn • Boston • Cincinnati • Detroit • London
Madrid • Melbourne • Mexico City • New York • Paris • San Francisco
Singapore • Tokyo • Toronto • Washington

Editorial Assistant: *Royden Tonomura*
Production: *Robin Lockwood*
Composition: *Thompson Type*
Print Buyer: *Barbara Britton*
Copy Editor: *Joan Pendleton*
Interior Design: *Christy Butterfield*
Cover Design: *Harry Voigt*
Cover Photograph: *Mark Mattock/Masterfile*
Printer: *Quebecor Printing/Fairfield*

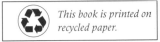

Printed in the United States of America

1 2 3 4 5 6 7 8 9 10

For more information, contact Wadsworth Publishing Company:

Wadsworth Publishing Company
10 Davis Drive
Belmont, California 94002, USA

International Thomson Publishing Europe
Berkshire House 168-173
High Holborn
London, WC1V 7AA, England

Thomas Nelson Australia
102 Dodds Street
South Melbourne 3205
Victoria, Australia

Nelson Canada
1120 Birchmount Road
Scarborough, Ontario
Canada M1K 5G4

International Thomson Editores
Campos Eliseos 385, Piso 7
Col. Polanco
11560 México D.F. México

International Thomson Publishing GmbH
Königswinterer Strasse 418
53227 Bonn, Germany

International Thomson Publishing Asia
221 Henderson Road
#05-10 Henderson Building
Singapore 0315

International Thomson Publishing Japan
Hirakawacho Kyowa Building, 3F
2-2-1 Hirakawacho
Chiyoda-ku, Tokyo 102, Japan

Library of Congress Cataloging-in-Publication Data
College reading with active critical thinking. Book 2 / [compiled by]
    Janet Maker, Minnette Lenier. — 5th ed.
        p.   cm.
    ISBN 0-534-51599-1
    1. College readers.   2. Reading (Higher education)   I. Maker,
Janet.   II. Lenier, Minnette.
PE1122.C572   1997
    428.6—dc20   96-8419

Contents

UNIT IV: CRITICAL READING WITH ACT

Contents by Skills

IMPROVING COMPREHENSION

READING FOR STUDY

SUMMARIZING

CRITICAL READING

Prereading/Subject and Point of View

READING EFFICIENCY

To the Student

As a college student, you will probably spend about one-fourth of your time reading textbooks. The purpose of *College Reading, Book 2* is to teach you the skills necessary to spend your reading time as efficiently as possible and succeed in your classes.

The book is divided into four sections. The first section, *Reading Fundamentals,* reviews the basic skills in vocabulary and comprehension. The second section, *Introduction to Active Critical Thinking (ACT)* begins with an introduction to the six-step ACT method. Then you will read ten selections of interest to college students and analyze them using the ACT method. The next section is *Using ACT for Study.* It begins with an explanation of how to use the ACT method for study reading of textbook material. Then you will practice the method using ten selections from college textbooks on a variety of subjects. The last section is *Critical Reading with ACT.* You will practice the method on persuasive material. The ten selections in this section consist of five pairs of readings. Each pair takes an opposing viewpoint on a controversial issue such as affirmative action or mercy killing.

Each reading selection has test questions. You will use the evaluation checklist in the back of the book to analyze your strengths and weaknesses so that you can improve your skills. The practice in this book will help you understand and remember what you read. It will also help you get better grades in your college classes.

Reading Fundamentals

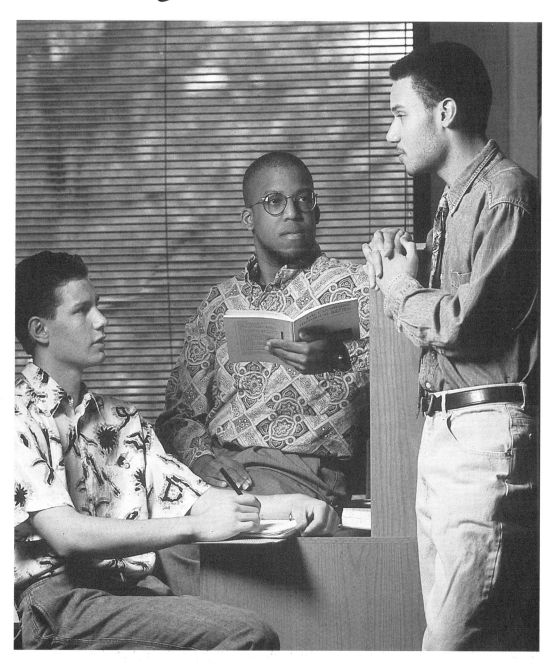

If you are an average full-time college student, you read between eight and ten textbooks per year, or 5,000 pages—not counting any other reading you do for work or for pleasure. Your challenge is to handle this load efficiently and get high grades.

The six-step ACT (Active Critical Thinking) method can help you improve your reading efficiency and your grades. Unit I reviews the basics of vocabulary and comprehension skills. In Unit II you will begin using the ACT method on readings taken from a variety of sources. In Unit III you will use ACT for study reading of textbook material, and in Unit IV you will use ACT for critical reading of persuasive writing. Each reading you do will be followed by a comprehension check, and you will be evaluating your test performance to correct any weaknesses. By the time you have finished this book, you will have the skills to succeed in nearly any college course.

IMPROVING VOCABULARY

One common reason for poor reading speed and comprehension is a poor vocabulary. If you don't understand many of the words in a chapter or article, you will not be able to grasp important concepts without taking the time to look up the words. You can increase your vocabulary by using context clues and the dictionary, and you can remember words through some of the techniques explained below.

Context Clues

You learned most of the words you know by hearing or seeing them in a particular context. When you find a new word in your reading, take a moment to see whether you can figure out its meaning from the sentence or the paragraph that it's in.

In the four sentences that follow, you can figure out the meanings of the difficult words by using four types of context clues: definition clues, contrast clues, example clues, and experience clues. Circle the letter of the definition that comes closest to the meaning of the underlined word.

1. It's usually hard to <u>differentiate</u>, or tell the difference between, identical twins.

   a. confuse

   b. distinguish

   c. talk to

   d. ignore

   The answer is b. The context clue used in this sentence is a **definition clue**. The phrase *or tell the difference* defines the word *differentiate*.

2. Anything from limited to <u>extensive</u> damage can be caused by a hurricane.

   a. major

   b. minor

   c. unusual

   d. new

The answer is a. The context clue used in this case is a **contrast clue**. Extensive damage is contrasted with limited damage.

3. Examples of holidays unique to the <u>heritage</u> of the United States are the Fourth of July and Thanksgiving.

   a. tradition

   b. future

   c. problems

   d. economics

The answer is a. The context clue used is an **example clue**. The sentence gives examples of holidays unique to the heritage of the United States.

4. Most students are <u>elated</u> when final exams are over.

   a. depressed

   b. anxious

   c. angry

   d. joyous

The answer is d. The context clue used is an **experience clue**. Anyone who has ever taken final exams knows that students are happy when they are over.

Dictionary

Sometimes the context does not provide a clue to meaning, or sometimes you cannot understand the ideas being presented without finding out what a word means. In such cases, you will have to use a dictionary. Most people know how to look words up, but very few know how to make the most out of the information that a good dictionary provides.

A dictionary entry has five major parts.

1. main entry

2. pronunciation

3. part or parts of speech

4. etymology (word history)

5. definitions

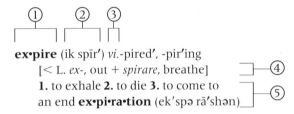

ex•pire (ik spīr′) *vi.*-pired′, -pir′ing
[< L. *ex-*, out + *spirare*, breathe]
1. to exhale **2.** to die **3.** to come to
an end **ex•pi•ra•tion** (ek′spə rā′shən)

When you look up a word in the dictionary, the first thing you see is the **main entry**. The main entry word is divided into syllables, and the syllables are separated by dots.

The **pronunciation** appears in parentheses after the main entry. You can figure out how to pronounce words by using the brief pronunciation guide, which is usually located at the bottom of every other page. A full explanation of pronunciation is usually found at the beginning of a dictionary. Here is a brief pronunciation guide.

> **cat, āte, fäther; pen, ēvil; if, kīte; nō, ôr, fo͞od, book; boil, house; up, turn; chief, shell; thick, *the*; zh, treasure; ŋ, sing; ə for *a* in *about*; ' as in *able* (ā′b′l)**

It is sometimes necessary to use the pronunciation guide because you can't always tell how to pronounce a word from its spelling. There are twenty-six letters in English representing about forty-four sounds, depending on one's dialect. For example, the letter *a* is pronounced differently in the words *cat* (kat), *father* (fä′ther), *ago* (ə gō′), *all* (ôl), and *late* (lāt).

One sound that is common in English is the **schwa sound**. It is written ə and is pronounced "uh." It occurs in unstressed syllables. A stressed syllable is pronounced in a louder voice than an unstressed syllable. For example, in the word *ago* (ə gō′), the stress is on the second syllable. The schwa sound can be spelled with any vowel letter, but it is always pronounced the same way.

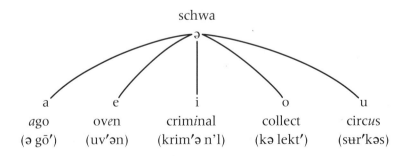

When you look up a word in the dictionary, you should always take the time to figure out its pronunciation. If you can pronounce a word to yourself, you are more likely to remember it. For example, let's go back to the word *expire*. The pronunciation is presented in the dictionary as ik spīr'.

First syllable (ik):	i	appears in the guide as the vowel sound in *it*
	k	does not appear in the guide, because it can be pronounced only one way
		The syllable *ik* rhymes with *sick*.
Second syllable (spīr):	s	does not appear in the guide because it has only one pronunciation
	p	does not appear in the guide because it has only one pronunciation
	ī	appears in the guide as the vowel sound in *kite*
	r	does not appear in the guide because it has only one pronunciation
		The syllable *spīr* rhymes with *fire*.

The accent mark on the second syllable (spīr') means that the second syllable is stressed.

For practice in using the dictionary pronunciation guide, translate the following movie titles into English spelling. (The answers to these three questions appear upside down at the bottom of the page.)

cat, āte, fäther; pen, ēvil; if, kīte; nō, ôr, fo͞od, book; boil, house; up, turn; chief, shell; thick, *the*; zh, treasure; ŋ, sing; ə for *a* in *about*; ' as in *able* (ā'b'l)

1. joo ras'ik pärk

2. fôr'ist gump

3. lī'ən kiŋ

The **part of speech** appears after the pronunciation in a dictionary entry. Here are a few of the abbreviations you will see in dictionary entries:

n. = noun:	a word that names a person, a place, or a thing
v. = verb:	a word that shows an action or a state of being

vt. or *tr. v.* = transitive verb:	an action word that affects a person or thing: "Jim dropped the pencil." A transitive verb requires a direct object to complete its meaning.
vi. = intransitive verb:	an action word that does not affect a person or thing: "The apple fell to the ground."
adj. = adjective:	a word that modifies a noun
adv. = adverb:	a word that modifies a verb, an adjective, or another adverb

If you know parts of speech, you can use words correctly in a sentence. For practice, circle the letter before the correct part of speech of the underlined words in the following sentences. Use the dictionary if you need help. (The answers appear upside down at the bottom of the page.)

1. The man was a work <u>addict</u> who often spent twelve hours a day at the office.

   a. *v.*, ə dikt′

   b. *n.*, ad′ikt

2. People living under a cruel dictator will often try to <u>rebel</u>.

   a. *n.*, reb′′l

   b. *v.*, ri bel′

3. Going to school at night to get a degree can be a difficult <u>project</u>.

   a. *n.*, präj′ekt

   b. *v.*, prə jekt′

   The **etymology**, or origin of the word, appears in brackets after the part of speech.

   ex•pire (ik spīr′) *vi.*-pired′, -pir′ing [< L. *ex-*, out + *spirare*, breathe] **1.** to exhale **2.** to die **3.** to come to an end

The etymology for *expire* says that the word comes from the Latin word parts *ex* (meaning "out") and *spirare* (meaning "to breathe"). The symbol < (meaning "comes from") and the letter L. (the abbreviation for *Latin*) are defined in the front of the dictionary, along with other symbols and abbreviations.

Taking the time to read the etymology is important in vocabulary building. For example, if you know that *spir* means "to breathe," you will have an important clue to an entire word family:

Word	Meaning
ex<u>pir</u>e	end, die (breathe out)
con<u>spir</u>acy	plot (breathe together)
re<u>spir</u>ation	act of breathing (breathe back)
a<u>spir</u>e	to be ambitious (breathe to)
<u>spir</u>it	soul (breath)
in<u>spir</u>e	motivate (breathe in)
e<u>spr</u>it de corps	group spirit (breath of body)
per<u>spir</u>e	sweat (breathe through)
tran<u>spir</u>e	happen (breathe across)
<u>spr</u>ightly	lively (full of breath)
<u>spir</u>e	tapering point (breath)

Word parts are so important in vocabulary development that a separate section of this unit is devoted to discussing them (also see Appendix C).

Definitions form the next part of a dictionary entry. Many words have more than one definition. You must choose the one that best fits the context in which the word is used. For example, the following entry shows that the word *expire* has three definitions:

> **ex•pire** (ik spīr′) *vi.*-pired′, -pir′ing [< L. *ex-*, out + *spirare*, breathe **1.** to exhale **2.** to die **3.** to come to an end

In the sentence "He confessed to the crime before he expired," definition 2 is the one that is meant.

The following words also have more than one meaning. Read each sentence, and identify the dictionary meaning that best describes how the underlined word is used. Write the number of the definition in the space provided. Be sure to choose the definition that matches the part of speech written under the blank. (The answers appear upside down at the bottom of the page.)

    _____ **1.** You can <u>express</u> shades of meaning that aren't even possible in other
       v.   languages.

> **ex•press** (ik spres′) *vt.* [< L. *ex,* out + *premere,* to press] **1.** to squeeze out (juice, etc.) **2.** to put into words, state **3.** to reveal, show **4.** to signify or symbolize **5.** to send by express −*adj.* **1.** expressed, stated, explicit **2.** exact **3.** specific **4.** fast and direct (an *express* bus, highway, etc.] **5.** related to express −*adv.* by express −*n.* **1.** an

express train, bus, etc. **2.** *a)* service for transporting things rapidly *b)* the things sent by express

_____   **2.**   John is in the sophomore <u>class</u>.
n.

class (klas) *n.* [< L. *classis*] **1.** a number of people or things grouped together because of likeness; kind; sort **2.** social or economic rank [the working *class*] **3.** *a)* a group of students taught together *b)* a group graduating together **4.** grade or quality **5.** [Slang] excellence, as of style –*vt.* to classify –*vi.* to be classified

_____   **3.**   I'll have to hurry to <u>catch</u> the train.
vt.

catch (kach) *vt.* caught, catch'ing [< L. *capere*, take] **1.** to seize and hold, capture **2.** to take by a trap **3.** to deceive **4.** to surprise **5.** to get to in time [to *catch* a bus] **6.** to lay hold of; grab [*catch* a ball] **7.** to become affected with [he *caught* a cold] **8.** to understand **9.** to get entangled **10.** [Colloq.] to see, hear, etc. –*vi.* **1.** to become held, fastened, etc. **2.** to take hold, as fire **3.** to keep hold, as a lock –*n.* **1.** a catching **2.** a thing that catches **3.** something caught **4.** one worth catching as a spouse **5.** a snatch or fragment **6.** a break in the voice **7.** [Colloq.] a tricky qualification, to catch at, to seize desperately

Whenever you read a definition in the dictionary, you should do two things to make sure you really understand it. First, put the definition into your own words. Second, make up a sentence using the word. Practice by defining the word *expire* and using it in a sentence. (The answers appear upside down at the bottom of the page.)

Definition: _____

Sentence: _____

Before each reading selection in this book, there is a preview of difficult words that appear in the reading. Use the pronunciation guide at the bottom of each Vocabulary Preview to figure out how to pronounce the words. Read the definitions before you read each selection. Then you will be more likely to know what the words mean when you see them.

Word Parts

You have seen how the dictionary etymology of the word *expire* helped you discover its meaning. The etymology also helped you discover the meaning of a whole group of words based on *spire*. Another way to understand thousands of new words is to gain a knowledge of basic word parts.

ANSWERS

Definition: to come to an end

Sentence: I had to move because my lease expired.

There are three types of word parts: prefixes, roots, and suffixes. **Prefixes** are syllables added at the beginning of words to change their meaning. For example, the word *mispronounce* means "pronounce wrong," because the meaning of *mis* is "wrong." **Roots** form the bases of words. *Spir*, meaning "to breathe," is a root used with different prefixes to form many words. **Suffixes** are syllables added at the end of words to change their meaning or their part of speech. An example of a suffix that changes a word's meaning is the suffix *less*, which means "without." *Useless* means "without use." An example of a suffix that changes a word's part of speech is the suffix *ize*. Adding the suffix *ize* to the noun *ideal* changes it to the verb *idealize*. (Appendix C contains lists of prefixes and root words.)

For practice, write the correct word part from the following list in each blank of the numbered exercises. Make sure that the words match their definitions. Use the underlined words as clues. (The answers appear upside down at the bottom of the page.)

Prefixes	Roots	Suffixes
con = together	fus = pour, melt	or = someone who or something that
pro = forth, forward	tract = draw, pull	
re = back	mit = send	ion = state of
de = away	vok = call, speak	
sub = under		

Word	Definition
1. pro __ __ __ ion	state of <u>pouring</u> forth
2. re __ __ __ e	to <u>call</u> back
3. con __ __ __ __ __	to shrink or <u>draw</u> together
4. detract __ __	<u>someone who</u> belittles or draws from you
5. __ __ __ voke	to call <u>forth</u>
6. con __ __ __ ion	state of disorder (<u>melting</u> together)
7. re __ __ __	to <u>send</u> (back)
8. __ __ voke	to cancel or call <u>back</u>

ANSWERS

Word parts: 1. fus, 2. vok, 3. tract, 4. or, 5. pro, 6. fus, 7. mit, 8. sub, 9. tract, 10. sub

9. sub __ __ __ __ __   to take away (<u>pull</u> from under)

10.   __ __ __ mit   yield (send <u>under</u>)

Word Memory

You will learn hundreds of new words in your college classes, but you may have a problem remembering them all. Pronouncing the word, checking the etymology, putting the definition in your own words, and using the word in a sentence are all aids to memory. In addition, there are two more ways to remember words: using word association and using flash cards.

Word association means linking the new word with one you already know. For example, to remember that *striations* refers to thin lines or grooves, you could associate it with the word *stripes*. Or to remember that *inexplicable* means "not able to be explained," you could remember the phrase *not explainable*.

For practice with word association, make up a word or phrase that you could use to remember each of the following words. (Some possible word associations appear upside down at the bottom of the page.)

1. commentary (käm′ən ter′ē): series of explanatory remarks

    _____

2. transfixed (trans fikst′): motionless

    _____

3. aghast (ə gast′): feeling great horror or dismay

    _____

4. ad lib (ad′lib′): to make up and perform without any preparation

    _____

5. insight (in′sīt): clear understanding of the nature of things

    _____

Another way to memorize a word is to put it on a **flash card.** Write the word and its pronunciation on one side of the card, and write the definition and a sentence using the word on the other side. Your cards should look like these sample cards.

ANSWERS

Word association:
1. comments 2. fixed 3. ghastly 4. At liberty (freed from a script) 5. Seeing into

Front	Back
non sequitur (nän sek′ wi tər)	an inference that does not follow from the premises His speech was full of non sequiturs.

You can test yourself by looking at the front of the card and trying to give the definition. When you are sure you can remember a word, you can retire the card. Carry ten to twenty cards with you so that you can use spare moments (such as when you are standing in line or eating lunch by yourself) to memorize vocabulary. That way you won't have so much work to do the night before an exam.

PARAGRAPH COMPREHENSION

Literal Comprehension

The most important skills in literal comprehension of paragraphs are understanding the subject, the main idea, and supporting details.

Subject   A good paragraph is a group of sentences that explain one central idea, called the subject, or topic, of the paragraph. You can find the subject of a paragraph by asking yourself who or what the whole paragraph is about. Read the following paragraph, and then circle the letter that identifies its subject:

> Newfoundland is Canada's newest province and its oldest. It is the newest because it was the last to join the Dominion, in 1949. But it is also the oldest in that it was the first to be discovered. Scientists have found the remains of a Viking camp almost 1,000 years old on the province's northern shore. Even modern Europeans discovered Newfoundland before they discovered the rest of Canada. John Cabot discovered the southern portion of the province only 5 years after Columbus landed in the West Indies and discovered America. Sir Humphrey Gilbert claimed Newfoundland for England in 1583.

The subject of the paragraph is

   a.   Newfoundland's age.

   b.   Newfoundland.

   c.   Vikings in Newfoundland.

   d.   provinces of Canada.

The answer is a. Choices b and d are too broad, and choice c is too narrow to cover the entire paragraph.

Now read the following paragraph, and circle the letter that identifies its subject:

> Computers will never be able to play the perfect game of chess. A chess player has about thirty moves to choose from on each turn, and the opponent has about thirty possible responses to each of these moves. Therefore, there are about 1,000 variations to consider for each complete move. Because each complete move allows another 1,000 potential moves, a computer would have to consider 10^{75} (1 and 75 zeros) moves to play a short twenty-five move game. Even if a computer could calculate a million moves each second, it would require 10^{69} seconds to complete the game. Since the beginning of our solar system 4.5 billion years ago, only 10^{18} seconds have elapsed.

The subject of the paragraph is

   a. chess.

   b. computers and chess.

   c. chess strategies.

   d. time involved in chess games.

The answer is b. Answers a and d are too broad, and c is off the subject.

Main Idea   Every paragraph should have a main idea, or a central point. The main idea of a paragraph is usually a complete sentence. To find the main idea, ask yourself what the subject is and what the author is saying about the subject.

Now look again at the paragraph about Newfoundland. Circle the letter that identifies its main idea:

   a. Newfoundland is a province in Canada.

   b. Newfoundland is the newest and oldest province in Canada.

   c. Newfoundland was discovered by Vikings.

   d. Newfoundland was discovered before other Canadian provinces.

The answer is b. Choice a is too broad, and choices c and d are too narrow.

Look again at the paragraph about chess and computers. Which of the following is its main idea?

   a. A good chess game takes a very long time.

   b. Playing chess requires a great deal of strategy.

   c. Computers will never be able to play chess perfectly.

   d. Computers cannot equal the human brain at chess.

The answer is c. Choices a and b don't deal with computers, and d is not implied in the paragraph.

Supporting Details   A good paragraph has details that support the main idea. The supporting details explain, clarify, or justify the main idea. Supporting details can be reasons, facts, examples, or testimony.

In the paragraph about Newfoundland, the main idea is supported by **facts**—things that have actually happened or that are true. Facts can include numbers, scientific laws, historical information, and so forth. The paragraph about Newfoundland is supported by historical facts.

In the paragraph about chess and computers, the main idea is supported by **reasons.** The author explains why computers will never be able to play perfect chess games.

Sometimes an author uses one or more **examples,** or samples, to support the main idea. Read the paragraph and fill in the blanks.

Yellowstone National Park has unusual natural attractions. It has a massive cliff of black volcanic glass. It also has geysers that release 15,000 gallons of hot water into the air hour after hour. Finally, it has bubbling mudpots and boiling springs that sometimes reach 150°F.

Subject _____

Main idea _____

Example 1 _____

Example 2 _____

Example 3 _____

The subject is the natural attractions in Yellowstone National Park. The main idea is that Yellowstone National Park has unusual natural attractions. The examples are (1) cliff of black volcanic glass, (2) geysers, and (3) mudpots and boiling springs.

To give **testimony** as support for the main idea means to give opinions or findings of people other than the author. Read the paragraph and fill in the blanks.

According to the *Guinness Book of World Records,* people with the highest IQs are often ordinary. They do not generally have remarkable intuition or freedom from prejudice. They often have rather ordinary jobs, and they do not necessarily excel in the academic world. They are said to have these shortcomings because they are often irritated by the repetition of what to them is obvious.

Subject _____

Main idea _____

Testimony by _____

The subject is people with the highest IQs. The main idea is that they are often ordinary. The testimony is by the *Guinness Book of World Records*.

Finding Main Ideas   In the paragraphs above, the main idea is located in the first sentence. Main ideas are usually, but not always, found in the first sentence of paragraphs. One way to locate the main idea is to look for such **signal words** as *therefore, thus, in other words,* and *most important.*

See if you can locate the main idea and signal words in the following paragraph:

> The main idea can fall in several places within the paragraph. For example, it can, and usually does, begin the paragraph. The author clearly states her most important idea and then spends the rest of the paragraph clarifying, expanding, proving, or explaining it.

The main idea is in the first sentence, and *for example* signals a supporting detail.

Now locate the main idea and signal words in this next paragraph:

> An author could also begin a paragraph by giving examples of an idea. Or she might choose to describe a scene or a historical event. At other times, the writer might begin by using a quotation from another person. In this case, the author begins with supporting details and then moves to a general conclusion. In other words, she puts the main idea at the end of the paragraph.

The main idea is in the last sentence, signaled by *in other words.* Signal words indicating supporting details in this paragraph are *also, or, at other times,* and *in this case.*

Locate the main idea and signal words in the next paragraph:

> The author who chooses to begin a paragraph with examples might not always place the main idea at the end. The main idea could be found toward the middle of the paragraph. In this case, the author follows the main idea with more supporting details. How much support precedes or follows the main idea depends on the author's purpose.

In this example, the main idea is in the second sentence. *In this case* signals a detail.

Now use what you have learned to locate the main idea and signal words in the next paragraph:

> The Amazon River is the widest river in the world, with one-fifth of all the fresh water on earth moving through its mouth. In length it is second only to the Nile, and if stretched across the United States, it would reach from New York to Los Angeles. In addition, the Amazon covers the largest area of any river. Therefore, it can be argued that the Amazon is the mightiest river on Earth.

The main idea is in the last sentence, signaled by *therefore.* The other sentences are supporting details. One of them is preceded by the signal words *in addition.*

Inferential Comprehension

Implied Main Idea   In the preceding paragraphs the main idea is stated somewhere in the paragraph. In some paragraphs, however, the main idea is implied rather than stated. You have to read between the lines to infer (reason out) the main idea. To do this, look at the supporting details and try to think of a statement that they all point to. This statement is the implied main idea. Read the following paragraph, and fill in the blanks.

> Osiris, Egyptian god of the underworld, was often portrayed in mummy wrappings. Isis, frequently represented with a cow's head or horns, was the nature goddess. Ra was the sun god, whose symbol was the pyramid. Amon was often represented as a ram or with a ram's head.

Subject _____

Main idea _____

Supporting detail 1 _____

Supporting detail 2 _____

Supporting detail 3 _____

Supporting detail 4 _____

Type of supporting details _____

The subject is ancient Egyptian gods. The main idea is that there were several Egyptian gods. The supporting details are (1) Osiris, (2) Isis, (3) Ra, and (4) Amon. They are examples.

Valid and Invalid Inferences   Implied main idea is one type of inferential comprehension. Another type is judging whether an inference is valid or invalid. A valid inference is supported by what the author has implied; an invalid inference is not. Use the paragraph about Egyptian gods to complete the following exercise. Mark each inference V if it is valid or I if it is invalid.

_____   **1.**   Osiris was more important than Ra.

_____   **2.**   Egyptian gods represent the spirits of animals.

_____   **3.**   Egyptians believed in an underworld.

_____ **4.** Egyptians had one principal god and several minor ones.

_____ **5.** The cow was sacred to the Egyptians.

The only valid inference is 3; you can infer this because Osiris was the god of the underworld. All the other statements are not implied in the paragraph.

Read the next paragraph and fill in the blanks.

Thomas Alva Edison invented or improved on the telegraph, phonograph, stock ticker, microphone, telephone, light bulb, battery, motion picture projector, and many other things. He held more than 1,300 U.S. and foreign patents and was the first American director of a research laboratory for inventors. His various companies later combined to become General Electric.

Subject _____

Main idea _____

Supporting detail 1 _____

    Minor detail a _____

    Minor detail b _____

    Minor detail c _____

    Minor detail d _____

    Minor detail e _____

    Minor detail f _____

    Minor detail g _____

    Minor detail h _____

Supporting detail 2 _____

Supporting detail 3 _____

Supporting detail 4 _____

Type of supporting details _____

The subject is Thomas Alva Edison. The main idea is that he was an important figure in American technology. The supporting details are that (1) he invented or improved upon many things having to do with electricity (telegraph, phonograph, stock ticker, microphone, telephone, light bulb, battery, and motion picture projector), (2) he held more than 1,300 U.S. and foreign patents, (3) he was the first director of a research laboratory for inventors, and (4) his various companies later combined to become General Electric. The supporting details are historical facts.

Mark each statement V if it is a valid inference. Mark I if it is invalid.

————— **1.** Edison was a great American inventor.

————— **2.** Edison was as intelligent as Einstein.

————— **3.** Edison was a good businessman.

————— **4.** Edison was more interested in science than in money.

————— **5.** Edison set up a school to train young scientists.

Statement 1 is implied by the fact that Edison invented so many things. Statement 3 is implied by the fact that he obtained patents, directed a research laboratory, and founded General Electric. The other statements are not implied in the paragraph.

Read the next paragraph and fill in the blanks.

The first horselike creature lived 700 million years ago and was only about 11 inches high. It had four toes on each forefoot and three on each hind foot. By 45 million years ago the creature had doubled in size and had three toes on all four feet. By 10 million years ago it had doubled in size again, and its feet had a single toe forming a hoof. The true horse, *Equus,* appeared in North America about a million years ago. It migrated to Asia and later became extinct in America. It was finally reintroduced by European settlers.

Subject ——————————————————————————————

Main idea ——————————————————————————————

Supporting detail 1 ——————————————————————————

Supporting detail 2 ——————————————————————————

Supporting detail 3 ——————————————————————————

Supporting detail 4 ——————————————————————————

Type of supporting details ——————————————————————

The subject is the evolution of the horse. The main idea is that the horse evolved over 700 million years. The supporting details are how the horse looked (1) 700 million years ago, (2) 45 million years ago, (3) 10 million years ago, and (4) a million years ago. The supporting details are facts.

Mark V if the statement is a valid inference. Mark I if it is invalid.

_____   **1.**   There was a land bridge to Asia about a million years ago.

_____   **2.**   Europeans were the first to domesticate wild horses.

_____   **3.**   Prehistoric horses were larger than modern horses.

_____   **4.**   The modern horse has been around for 70 million years.

_____   **5.**   Horse toes evolved into hooves.

Statement 1 can be inferred by the fact that the horses migrated from North America to Asia. Statement 5 can be inferred from the number of toes on prehistoric horses. None of the other statements are implied in the paragraph.

Critical Comprehension

Point of View, Argument, and Support   Authors usually have one of three purposes for writing: to inform, to entertain, or to persuade. An author who is trying to persuade us of something is writing from a certain point of view. The point of view in a persuasive paragraph is like the main idea in an informative paragraph; it is the main point the author is trying to make. It can be either stated or implied. The point of view is supported by arguments, which are like the major supporting details. Minor details consist of support for the arguments.

Read the paragraph and fill in the blanks:

> Antioch College in Ohio instituted a brilliant policy to stop sexual abuse on campus. If any student wants to touch another student (usually on a date), he or she must ask first. For example, "May I kiss you?" If things heat up, the student must ask before he or she proceeds to each new level of intimacy. This puts a complete stop to sexual aggression and the familiar claim that when she said "no" she really meant "yes."

Subject _____

Point of view _____

Argument _____

Type of support (facts, examples, testimony, reasons) _____

The subject is the Antioch policy. The point of view is that it is brilliant. The argument is that it stops sexual aggression and the problems of misinterpretation. The supporting details are reasons.

Read the paragraph and fill in the blanks.

> The Antioch policy is ridiculous. Having to discuss such things is so embarrassing that it would take all the fun out of dating.

Subject _____

Point of view _____

Argument _____

Type of support _____

The subject is the Antioch policy. The main idea is that the policy is ridiculous. The argument is that it would take all the fun out of dating. The type of support is reasons.

UNIT II

Introduction to Active Critical Thinking

In Unit II you will start to use the six-step ACT (Active Critical Thinking) method.

Step 1: Preread

Preceding each reading in this book is a preview of the difficult vocabulary words. Going over them in advance assures that they won't interfere with your comprehension when you read the selections.

Psychologists have learned that the mind works in some ways like a library. A library stores information by filing it in categories. You retrieve the information in a library by looking it up under the same categories. In order for your mind to store (learn) and retrieve (remember) information, it must also be filed in categories. The prereading step gives you the categories in advance. This increases your comprehension and speed as you read.

You will use the structure of the reading to get the main ideas in advance. If the selection has informative headings, then all you have to do is read those. If there are no headings, you may have to read the first sentence of each paragraph to get most of the main ideas. If there are illustrations, you should read the captions and try to understand the illustrations. This step should take between 15 seconds and one minute, depending on the structure of the reading. You will be asked to identify the subject and the main idea, just as you did with the paragraphs in Unit I.

Next, you will think about what you already know about the subject. In psychology, this is called "activating your schema." The idea is that you already know something about most subjects. When you read, you should use your experience—what you already know to help you put what you are learning from the page in the right category in your mind. Using your experience will help you realize that A is like B, that C is a result of D, and that E and F cannot both be true, for instance. The more experience you can bring to your reading, the deeper your comprehension will be. You will also be asked to think about what you don't know about the subject, and you will think of some questions that might be answered by reading the selection. This will activate your curiosity, which will also deepen your comprehension.

Step 2: Read

In this book you will always read just to comprehend, without underlining or highlighting. This is because your underlining will be much better if you go back after reading and do it as a separate step. In this book, you will practice underlining or highlighting in Units III and IV.

Step 3: Analyze What You Read

This is where study techniques come in. Underlining is one. The study technique we practice in Unit II is called making graphic organizers. A graphic organizer is a type of picture. It can be an outline, a chart, an idea map, or any other type of drawing. Because of the way the brain works, we cannot remember large blocks of words, but we can remember pictures.

Step 4: Remember What's Important

The reason you memorize information is so that you can recall it when you need it. If you will not be needing it, you don't have to memorize. But in college, you usually have to do something, whether it's write a paper or pass a test, with the information you read. The best way to memorize is not to reread your textbook or listen to taped lectures. The most effective way is to test yourself on what you are trying to remember until you reach the level of memory you need. In Unit II, you will put everything you are trying to remember into the format of your graphic organizer.

Step 5: Make Use of What You Read

This step refers to your output. In college courses, you will be expected to take tests, participate in class discussions, write papers, and possibly give oral reports. In this book, there is a Comprehension Check after each reading. There is also an exercise in which you use the words from the Vocabulary Preview. Both of these activities can be used as tests.

Step 6: Evaluate Your Active Critical Thinking Skills

If you took a test or other evaluation for Step 5, you will find out how well you did. If you were not satisfied with your performance, you should review the six steps of ACT. Did you read the material actively and understand it? Did you make a graphic organizer? Did you test yourself on your graphic organizer enough to remember it? With ACT, a poor grade should not be a reason to become discouraged. It should be seen as a chance to figure out how to improve, so you will do better next time. In this book we have provided an Evaluation Guide on page 465.

1

How to Improve Your Vocabulary

Vocabulary Preview

addict (ad'ikt): one unable to give up a habit, such as using drugs

differentiate (dif ə ren'shē āt'): to make unlike; to show the difference between

context (kän'tekst): parts just before and after a word or passage that influence its meaning

extensive (ik sten'siv): having a great or far-reaching area or scope

heritage (her'ə tij'): a tradition handed down from one's ancestors or the past

origin (ôr'ə jin): beginning; source; root

emancipate (i man'sə pāt'): to free from confinement

corroborate (kə räb'ə rāt'): to support or confirm

literal (lit'ər əl): following the exact words of the original

elated (i lāt'id, ē lāt'id): raised the spirits of; made very proud or happy

cat, āte, fäther; pen, ēvil; if, kīte; nō, ôr, fo͞od, book; boil, house; up, turn; chief, shell; thick, *the*; zh, treasure; ŋ, sing; ə for *a* in *about*; ' as in *able* (ā'b'l)

Step 1: Preread

Preview the following selection by reading the title, author's name (he is a famous actor), and the headings. Answer the following questions without looking back at the reading.

1. What is the subject?

   _____

2. What is the main idea?

   _____

3. Take a moment to think about how to improve vocabulary. Think about what you know, what you don't know, and what you might find out from reading the selection. Make up three questions that might be answered by reading it.

   a. _____

b. _____

c. _____

Step 2: Read

 Read the selection without underlining.

Write your starting time here: _____

How to Improve Your Vocabulary

Tony Randall

Words can make us laugh, cry, go to war, fall in love. Rudyard Kipling called words the most powerful drug of mankind. If they are, I'm a hopeless addict—and I hope to get you hooked, too!

Whether you're still in school or you head up a corporation, the better command you have of words, the better chance you have of saying exactly what you mean, of understanding what others mean—and of getting what you want in the world.

English is the richest language—with the largest vocabulary on earth. Over 1,000,000 words!

You can express shades of meaning that aren't even *possible* in other languages. (For example, you can differentiate between "sky" and "heaven." The French, Italians and Spanish cannot.)

Yet, the average adult has a vocabulary of only 30,000 to 60,000 words. Imagine what we're missing!

Here are five pointers that help me learn—and remember—whole *families* of words at a time.

They may not *look* easy—and won't be at first. But if you stick with them you'll find they *work*!

What's the first thing to do when you see a word you don't know?

I. Try to Guess the Meaning of the Word from the Way It's Used

You can often get at least *part* of a word's meaning—just from how it's used in a sentence.

That's why it's so important to read as much as you can—different *kinds* of things: magazines, books, newspapers you don't normally read. The more you *expose* yourself to new words, the more words you'll pick up *just by seeing how they're used*.

For instance, say you run across the word "manacle":

"The manacles had been on John's wrists for 30 years. Only one person had a key— his wife."

You have a good *idea* of what "manacles" are—just from the context of the sentence.

But let's find out *exactly* what the word means and where it comes from. The only way to do this, and to build an extensive vocabulary *fast*, is to go to the dictionary. (How lucky, you *can*—Shakespeare *couldn't*. There *wasn't* an English dictionary in his day!)

So you go to the dictionary. (NOTE: Don't let dictionary abbreviations put you off. The front tells you what they mean, and even has a guide to pronunciation.)

2. Look It Up

Here's the definition for "manacle" in *The American Heritage Dictionary of the English Language*.

> **man-a-cle** (man′ə kəl) *n.* Usually plural. **1.** A device for confining the hands, usually consisting of two metal rings that are fastened about the wrists and joined by a metal chain; a handcuff. **2.** Anything that confines or restrains. – *tr. v.* **manacled,-cling,-cles. 1.** To restrain with manacles. **2.** To confine or restrain as if with manacles; shackle; fetter. [Middle English *manicle*, from Old French, from Latin *manicula*, little hand, handle, diminutive of *manus*, hand.]

The first definition fits here: A device for confining the hands, usually consisting of two metal rings that are fastened about the wrists and joined by a metal chain; a handcuff.

Well, that's what you *thought* it meant. But what's the idea *behind* the word? What are its *roots*? To really understand a word, you need to know.

Here's where the detective work—and the *fun*—begins.

3. Dig the Meaning Out by the Roots

The root is the basic part of the word—its heritage, its origin. (Most of our roots come from Latin and Greek words at least 2,000 years old—which come from even earlier Indo-European tongues!)

Learning the roots: (1) Helps us *remember* words. (2) Gives us a deeper understanding of the words we *already* know. And (3) allows us to pick up whole families of *new* words at a time. That's why learning the root is the *most important part of going to the dictionary*.

Notice the root of "manacle" is *manus* (Latin) meaning "hand."

Well, that makes sense. Now, other words with this root, <u>man</u>, start to make sense, too.

Take <u>man</u>ual—something done "by hand" (<u>man</u>ual labor) or a "handbook." And <u>man</u>age—to "handle" something (as a <u>man</u>ager). When you e<u>man</u>cipate someone, you're taking him "from the hands of" someone else.

When you <u>man</u>ufacture something, you "make it by hand" (in its original meaning).

And when you finish your first novel, your publisher will see your—originally "handwritten"—<u>man</u>uscript.

Imagine! A whole new world of words opens up—just from one simple root!

The root gives the *basic* clue to the meaning of a word. But there's another important clue that runs a close second—the *prefix*.

4. Get the Powerful Prefixes Under Your Belt

A prefix is the part that's sometimes attached to the front of a word. Like—well, *prefix*! There aren't many—fewer than 100 major prefixes—and you'll learn them in no time at all just by becoming more aware of the meanings of words you already know. Here are a few. (Some of the "How-to" vocabulary-building books will give you the others.)

prefix		meaning	examples	literal sense
Latin	Greek			
com, con, co, col, cor	sym, syn, syl	with, very, together	conform sympathy	"form with" "feeling with"
in, im, il, ir	a, an	not, without	innocent amorphous	"not wicked" "without form"
contra, counter	anti, ant	against, opposite	contravene antidote	"come against" "give against"

Now, see how the *prefix* (along with the context) helps you get the meaning of the italicized words:

- "If you're going to be my witness, your story must *corroborate* my story." (The literal meaning of *corroborate* is "strength together.")

- "You told me one thing—now you tell me another. Don't *contradict* yourself." (The literal meaning of *contradict* is "say against.")

- "Oh, that snake's not poisonous. It's a completely *innocuous* little garden snake." (The literal meaning of *innocuous* is "not harmful.")

Now, you've got some new words. What are you going to do with them?

5. Put Your New Words to Work at Once

Use them several times the first day you learn them. Say them out loud! Write them in sentences.

Should you "use" them on *friends*? Careful—you don't want them to think you're a stuffed shirt. (It depends on the situation. You *know* when a word sounds natural—and when it sounds stuffy.)

How about your *enemies*? You have my blessing. Ask one of them if he's read that article on pneumonoultramicroscopicsilicovolcanoconiosis. (You really can find it in the dictionary.) Now, you're one up on him.

So what do you do to improve your vocabulary?

Remember: (1) Try to guess the meaning of the word from the way it's used.

(2) Look it up. (3) Dig the meaning out by the roots. (4) Get the powerful prefixes under your belt. (5) Put your new words to work at once.

That's all there is to it—you're off on your treasure hunt.

Now, do you see why I love words so much?

Aristophanes said, "By words, the mind is excited and the spirit elated." It's as true today as it was when he said it in Athens—*2,400 years ago*!

I hope you're now like me—hooked on words forever.

1000 words

Write your ending time here: _____

Subtract your starting time: _____

Total time: _____

Check the Rate Chart in the back of the book to find out how many words per minute you have read, and then record your score on the Progress Chart.

Step 3: Analyze What You Read

 Make Graphic Organizers

It is often easier to understand and remember what we read when we put it into some kind of picture. Following is an outline of the selection you just read:

How to Improve Your Vocabulary

  I.   Try to guess the meaning of the word from the way it's used.

  II. Look it up.

 III. Dig the meaning out by the roots.

 IV. Get the powerful prefixes under your belt.

  V. Put your new words to work at once.

An outline is a type of picture, but a concept or idea map is easier to remember because it is even more visual. Following is a blank concept map. Write the title in the circle, and write the Roman numeral headings in the rectangles.

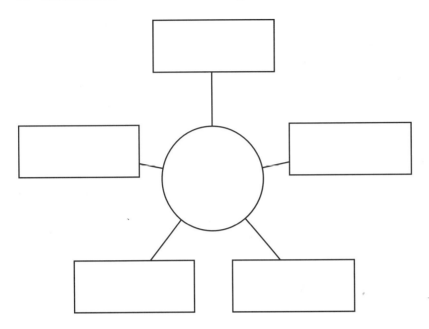

Step 4: Remember What's Important

 Using your concept map, test yourself or have someone else test you on the ways to improve vocabulary. Keep testing until you think you can remember everything you need to know.

Step 5: Make Use of What You Read

 When you are ready, complete the following Comprehension Check. Do not look back at the reading.

Step 6: Evaluate Your Active Critical Thinking Skills

After your test has been graded, answer the questions on the chart on page 465.

COMPREHENSION CHECK

Multiple Choice

Circle the letter before the best answer to each of the following questions.

1. English
   a. is not based on any other language.
   b. is at least 2,000 years old.
   c. has more words than any other language.
   d. cannot differentiate shades of meaning like most European languages.

2. The first thing you should do when you see an unfamiliar word is to
   a. look up the meaning in the dictionary.
   b. look for the roots.
   c. look for the prefixes.
   d. try to figure out the word's meaning from its context.

3. Randall says you become a word detective when
   a. the word has more than one meaning.
   b. you can look up the meaning in the dictionary.
   c. you begin to trace a word's origin.
   d. you use the word's context to find the meaning.

4. There are
   a. more than 100 major prefixes.
   b. about 100,000 words in the English language.
   c. about half a million words in the average adult's vocabulary.
   d. fewer than 100 major prefixes.

5. Randall was probably asked to write this article because he
   a. is an actor.
   b. is recognized as an expert in word usage.
   c. was a college professor.
   d. is a college graduate.

6. Word memory is improved by
   a. learning the roots.
   b. remembering the context in which the word was used.
   c. using the words in speaking and writing.
   d. all of the above.

7. According to the article,
   a. dictionaries have existed since before Shakespeare's time.
   b. you can learn new words without using the dictionary.
   c. the most important part of using the dictionary is learning the pronunciation of words.
   d. Aristophanes spoke English.

8. The author feels that
   a. people with large vocabularies are more successful in life.
   b. guessing the meaning of an unknown word is a bad habit.
   c. the average adult who speaks English knows most of the words in the language.
   d. a word's prefixes and roots will translate into the same definition as in the dictionary.

Short Answer

9. Why does Randall say that learning the root is the most important part of going to the dictionary?

   _____

   _____

   _____

10. What is the main idea of the prefix chart Randall uses in making his fourth point in the reading?

    _____

    _____

Essay

Describe the five ways to improve vocabulary.

_____

_____

_____

_____

_____

_____

_____

_____

VOCABULARY IN CONTEXT

Write the best word from this list in the blank in each sentence below:

addicting   differentiate   context   extensive   heritage

origin   emancipating   corroborated   literal   elated

1. The base of the Great Pyramid in Egypt could hold ten football fields because it

    is so _____ .

2. The _____ of the word *assassin* came from the drug hashish,
    which one extreme religious group in Persia always smoked before terrorizing
    and killing its victims.

3. For years, criminals have escaped conviction for crimes they have committed

    because other people have falsely _____ their alibis.

4. Until recently, it was not realized that Valium, the most widely prescribed drug
    in the United States, was psychologically and sometimes physically

    _____ .

5.   The _____ of a sentence will tell you which meaning a person is using when he or she says "That's baloney."

6.   Abraham Lincoln is credited with _____ the slaves in 1863, but actually he freed the slaves only in those states that had left the Union and over which he had no control.

7.   Nose prints, not paw prints, are used by breeders and trainers to

    _____ prize dogs because, like human fingerprints, nose prints are all different.

8.   Before writing *Roots*, Alex Haley spent years researching his African

    _____ .

9.   People are usually _____ when they receive a promotion or pay raise at work.

10. The _____ meanings of the individual words do not help define an expression like "Drop in any time."

VOCABULARY REVIEW

Dictionary Definitions

> *For explanation see pp. 2–8*

Here are the dictionary entries for five words used in the reading. Above each entry is the sentence that the word was used in. In the blank before the sentence, put the number of the definition that fits the way the word is used. The abbreviation under each blank tells you which part of speech the word is, so you can more easily find the proper definition.

_____   1.   "Here are five <u>pointers</u> that help me learn—and remember—whole
n.   families of words at a time."

point'er *n.* **1.** a long, tapered rod for pointing to things **2.** an indicator on a meter, etc. **3.** a large, lean hunting dog with a smooth coat **4.** [Colloq.] a helpful hint or suggestion

_____   2.   "The more you <u>expose</u> yourself to new words, the more words you'll
v.   pick up *just by seeing how they're used.*"

ex·pose (ik spōz') *vt.*-posed', -pos'-ing [see EXPOUND] **1.** to lay open **2.** to reveal; exhibit; make known **3.** *Photography* to subject (a sensitized film or plate) to actinic rays

_____ **3.** "A <u>device</u> for confining the hands, usually consisting of two metal rings
n.   that are fastened about the wrists and joined by a metal chain; a handcuff."

de·vice (di vīs') *n.* [see DEVISE **1.** a thing devised; plan, scheme, or trick **2.** a mechanical contrivance **3.** an ornamental design, esp. on a coat of arms—**leave to one's own devices** to allow to do as one wishes

_____ **4.** "Take manual—something done 'by hand' (<u>manual</u> labor) . . ."
adj.

man·u·al (man'yoo wəl) *adj.* [<L. *manus,* a hand] **1.** made or worked by hand [*man- ual* typewriter] **2.** involving skill or hard work with the hands – *n.* **1.** a handy book for use as a guide, reference, etc. **2.** prescribed drill in the handling of a weapon

_____ **5.** ". . . the better <u>command</u> you have of words, the better chance you
n.   have of saying exactly what you mean, of understanding what others mean—and of getting what you want in the world."

com·mand (kə mand') *vt.* [< L. *com-,* intens. + *mandare,* entrust] **1.** to give an order to; direct **2.** to have authority over; control **3.** to have for use [to *command* a fortune] **4.** to deserve and get [to *command* respect] **5.** to control (a position); overlook – *vi.* to have authority – *n.* **1.** order; direction **2.** controlling power or position **3.** mastery **4.** a military or naval force, or district, under a specified authority

Pronunciation Practice

For practice with the pronunciation guide, do the exercises below.

cat, āte, fäther; pen, ēvil; if, kīte; nō, ôr, fōod, book; boil, house; up, turn; chief, shell; thick, *the*; zh, treasure; ŋ, sing; ə for *a* in *about*; ' as in *able* (ā'b'l)

1. Translate these famous book titles into English spelling.

    a. *thə* sun ôl'sō rīz'əz—Ernest Hemingway

    _____

    b. ə tāl uv tōo sit'ēz—Charles Dickens

    _____

   c. prīd and prej′ə dis—Jane Austen

_____

   d. *thə* good ʉrth—Pearl Buck

_____

   e. *thə* tīm mə shēn′—H. G. Wells

_____

2. Say each word below out loud and listen for the sounds. Then circle the words that contain the sound of schwa (ə).

   differentiate   context   origin   literal   elate

3. Say each word below out loud and listen for the sounds. Then circle the words that contain long vowel sounds (ā, ē, ī, ō, ū).

   addict   extensive   heritage   emancipate   corroborate

2

Unlock Your Own Creativity

Vocabulary Preview

obsolete (äb′sə lēt′): no longer in use; out of date

trivial (triv′ē əl): commonplace, insignificant, unimportant

entrée (än′trā): the main course of a meal

germinate (jʉr′mə nāt′): to start developing; sprout, as from a seed

metaphors (met′ə fôrz′): figures of speech in which one thing is spoken of as if it were another

realm (relm): an area of rule, as a kingdom or region

colleagues (käl′ēgz): fellow workers

additive (ad′ə tiv): something extra that is added to a product

ambiguity (am bə gyo͞o′ə tē): lack of clearness; the quality of having more than one possible meaning

self-esteem (self ə stēm′): self-respect; belief in oneself

cat, āte, fäther; pen, ēvil; if, kīte; nō, ôr, fo͞od, book; boil, house; up, tʉrn; chief, shell; thick, *the*; zh, treasure; ŋ, sing; ə for *a* in *about*; ' as in *able* (ā′b'l)

Step I: Preread

Preview the following selection by reading the title and the headings numbered 1 to 8. Answer the following questions without looking back at the reading.

1. What is the subject?

_____

2. What is the main idea?

_____

3. Take a moment to think about what you know about creativity, what you don't know, and what you might find out from reading the selection. Make up three questions.

   a. _____

b. _____

c. _____

Step 2: Read

 Read the selection without underlining.

Write your starting time here: _____

Unlock Your Own Creativity

Roger von Oech

IF I HELD UP A SHEET OF WHITE PAPER and put a black dot on it with my pen, what would you see? I've used this demonstration on thousands of adults in the seminars I run, and invariably I get the same answer: "A black dot." When I tried it on a kindergarten class, a forest of hands shot up. "A Mexican hat," piped one kid. "Naw, that's a burnt hamburger," said another. "A squashed bug," observed a third.

When young, we're naturally creative because we let our minds run free. But as we're taught to follow the rules, our thinking narrows. For much of life this can be a blessing: it wouldn't do to create a new way home from work if it meant driving down the wrong side of the freeway.

But in many areas of our lives, creativity can be a matter of survival. Things are changing too fast to get along simply with old ideas. When I was working for IBM ten years ago, half of what any technical engineer had learned became obsolete in only three years; it happens even sooner now. And what about our home lives? With, for instance, more and more women opting for careers and independence, couples have to be more creative about their relationships to avoid conflicts.

Fortunately creativity isn't all that mysterious. One important creative trait was well-defined by Nobel Prize-winning physician Albert Szent-Györgyi when he said, "Discovery consists of seeing what everybody has seen and thinking what nobody has thought."

How do we start "thinking what nobody has thought"? Usually it takes a whack on the head, like Newton supposedly had when an apple striking his skull awakened him to the laws of gravity. Whacks can range from something as major as losing a job to something as trivial as wanting an unusual entrée for a dinner party. We're more likely to respond creatively—which is to say, come up with a new idea—if we've already been chipping away at the "mental locks" that close our minds.

What are these locks? As I said in my book *A Whack on the Side of the Head*, for the most part they are our uncritical acceptance of eight common statements:

1. *"Find the right answer."* Almost from the first day of school, we're taught that there's one right answer to every problem. But many important issues are open-ended. Take the question "What do I do now that I've lost my job?" The obvious right answer is: "Look for another job." There is also a second right answer: "Go back to school and learn a new trade." Or a third: "Start your own business."

    The mere act of looking for a second answer will often produce the new idea you need. As French philosopher Emile Chartier said: "Nothing is more dangerous than an idea when it is the only one we have."

2. *"That's not logical."* Hard, logical thinking can be death to a new idea because it eliminates alternatives that seem contradictory. New ideas germinate faster in the loose soil of soft thinking, which finds similarities and connections among different things or situations.

    In my workshops, I ask people to create metaphors to unlock their thoughts. A manager had been thinking logically about what was wrong with his company, but couldn't get a grip on it until he came up with this metaphor: "Our company is a galley ship without a drummer. We've got some people rowing at full beat, some at one-half beat, and some deadbeats." This man made himself the missing "drummer," with the result that the operation smoothed out.

3. *"Follow the rules."* To get an idea, you often have to break rules that no longer make sense. My friend Nolan Bushnell, the founder of Atari Inc. and inventor of the first video game, is a dedicated rule breaker. Once Bushnell was trying to make pinball games more fun. For a long time he followed the rule that the playing field had to be 26 inches wide. Only when he threw away that rule and made the field 30 inches was he able to increase the game's possibilities.

4. *"Be practical."* To grow, ideas initially need the wide realm of the possible, rather than the narrow one of the practical. You can enter this realm by asking, "What if . . .?"

    An engineer in a chemical company startled his colleagues by asking, "What if we put gunpowder in our house paint? When it starts peeling in a few years, we just put a match to it and blow it off." The house might blow up with such a paint, but this engineer was talking to "idea" men who brushed aside the impracticality and started thinking. Eventually they came up with the idea of an additive that could later be activated and cause paint to be easily stripped off walls. The company is now developing the process.

5. *"Don't be foolish."* One of the best ways of unleashing creativity was demonstrated in an Israeli high school. Before they were given a standard creativity test, 141 tenth-graders were treated to a recording of a popular comedian. Those who heard it did significantly better than the control group, which was not so entertained. Humor can show us the ambiguity of situations, revealing a second and often startling answer.

    Being foolish is a form of play. If necessity is the mother of invention, play is its father. When faced with a problem, let yourself play, risk being foolish. And write down the ideas that then come to you.

6. *"Don't make mistakes."* If you're piloting a jetliner, you'd better keep this lock on your mind. When looking for new ideas, however, you need the attitude of Carl

Yastrzemski. In 1979, after the Boston Red Sox star collected his 3000th hit, a reporter asked, "Hey, Yaz, aren't you afraid all this attention will go to your head?"

"Well," Yastrzemski said, "in my career I've been up to bat over ten thousand times. That means I've been unsuccessful over seven thousand times. That fact alone keeps me from getting a swelled head."

Success and failure, he knew, are part of the same process. And mistakes can simply be stepping stones in the creative process. As IBM founder Thomas J. Watson once said, "The way to succeed is to double your failure rate."

7. *"That's not my area."* Fresh ideas almost invariably come from outside one's field of specialization. I tell people to become hunters. The successful hunter ranges widely, keeps a sharp eye out, and knows his prey when he sees it.

A friend of mine worked in a lab experimenting with a new solar material, gallium arsenide. Her job was to make precision cuts in the material with a high-speed wafer saw. Every time she did so, the material cracked. At home, she was watching her husband make wooden cabinets and noticed that, when he wanted to make precision cuts on certain types of wood, he *reduced* his saw's speed. She tried that on the gallium arsenide and it worked.

Creative people have to be generalists, interested in everything and aware that what they learn in one field might prove useful in another. We're all generalists at home—chefs, decorators, teachers, gardeners, handymen—and home is where to start being creative. The average homemaker is confronted daily with more creative opportunities than the middle manager in a company sees in a month.

8. *"I'm not creative."* Most of us retain the idea that creativity is only for artists and inventors. And when we put ourselves down as not creative, we set in motion a self-fulfilling prophecy. A person who thinks he's not creative in his everyday life won't try a creative solution to an important problem.

A major oil company brought in a team of psychologists to find out why some people in its research and development department were more creative than others. After three months of study, the psychologists came up with this difference: the creative people *thought* they were creative and the less creative people didn't think they were.

Self-esteem is essential to creativity because any new idea makes you a pioneer. Once you put an idea into action, you're out there alone taking risks of failure and ridicule.

As management consultant Roy Blitzer has said, "The only person who *likes* change is a wet baby." But we need change—the type of change that comes only through the creative thinking of all the people, not just the geniuses.

1400 words

Write your ending time here: _____

Subtract your starting time: _____

Total time: _____

Check the Rate Chart in the back of the book to find how many words per minute you have read, and then record your score on the Progress Chart.

Step 3: Analyze What You Read

 Make Graphic Organizers

Fill in the following outline:

Mental Locks

I. _____

II. _____

III. _____

IV. _____

V. _____

VI. _____

VII. _____

VIII. _____

Step 4: Remember What's Important

 Using your outline, test yourself or have someone test you on the mental locks to creativity. Keep testing until you think you can remember them.

Step 5: Make Use of What You Read

 When you are ready, complete the following Comprehension Check. Do not look back at the reading.

Step 6: Evaluate Your Active Critical Thinking Skills

After your test has been graded, answer the questions on the chart on page 465.

COMPREHENSION CHECK

Multiple Choice

Circle the letter before the best answer to each of the following questions.

1. Creativity is lost in part by
   a. the loss of memory capacity as we grow older.
   b. the natural maturation process.
   c. becoming too serious as adults.
   d. being taught to follow rules.

2. Creativity aids in
   a. our survival in the business world.
   b. the relationships between couples.
   c. finding new answers to old problems.
   d. all of the above.

3. Which of the following is one of the author's "mental locks"?
   a. finding too many answers to a problem.
   b. saying it's outside your field.
   c. breaking all the rules.
   d. finding an answer too quickly.

4. Which of the following methods does the author use in his seminars to help his clients unlock creative abilities?
   a. creating poems.
   b. writing.
   c. creating metaphors.
   d. making a list of goals.

5. The author implies that creativity is
   a. inborn and cannot be developed.
   b. found only in children.
   c. lost during the educational process.
   d. found more in women than in men.

6. When the author says "usually it takes a whack on the head" to unlock creativity, he means that creativity is

   a. often the result of a physical accident.

   b. often triggered by some kind of surprising experience.

   c. not a normal function of the brain.

   d. all of the above.

7. The author feels that creative people

   a. like to watch sports more than other people do.

   b. are more willing to take risks than others.

   c. never use logical thinking to solve problems.

   d. are more likely to be accident prone.

8. When the author says "new ideas germinate faster in the loose soil of soft thinking," he means that

   a. logical thinkers make more mistakes.

   b. creative thinkers like planting things outdoors.

   c. creative thinkers cannot make decisions.

   d. creative thinkers are more flexible in their thoughts.

Short Answer

9. Why does the author say that creativity can be a matter of survival?

   _____

   _____

10. Why does the author say that self-esteem is essential to creativity?

   _____

Essay

What does the author think is the way to start thinking creatively?

_____

_____

_____

VOCABULARY IN CONTEXT

Write the best word from this list in the blank in each sentence below:

obsolete   trivial   entrée   germinate   metaphor   realm

colleagues   additives   ambiguities   self-esteem

1. Health-conscious people often decide to limit the number of times per week they have beef as an _____ with a meal.

2. Typewriters were made almost _____ in the modern office by the invention of word processing.

3. One of the _____ of the English language is a sentence such as "Visiting relatives can be boring." The word *visiting* can be a verb form or an adjective, and each use gives the sentence a different meaning.

4. Remembering _____ facts that others never knew became the basis for one of the most popular games in 1986 and 1987.

5. Having an income of $1 million a year is beyond the _____ of most people's ability.

6. Your business _____ can become good friends or your worst enemies.

7. Your _____ can be reflected in the confidence with which you dress and talk.

8. Seeds should _____ indoors in very cold weather so that the young shoots won't freeze.

9. "He's a bear before he drinks his coffee in the morning" is a _____ .

10. The amount and kind of food _____ , such as chemical colorings, are carefully regulated by the federal government.

VOCABULARY REVIEW

Dictionary Definitions

For explanation see pp. 2–9

For practice in finding the correct meaning of a word in the dictionary, select the correct meaning of the following three words from the reading. Above each entry is a sentence using the word. In the blank before the sentence, put the number of the definition that fits the way the word is used. The abbreviation under each blank tells you which part of speech the word is, so you can more easily find the proper definition.

_____
n.
1. When an audience wants to show an actor how much they enjoyed his performance, they will give him a big <u>hand</u> and perhaps a standing ovation.

hand (hand) *n.* [<OE.] **1.** the part of the arm below the wrist, used for grasping **2.** a side or direction [at my right *hand*] **3.** possession or care [the land is in my *hands*] **4.** control [to strengthen one's *hand*] **5.** an active part [take a *hand* in the work] **6.** a promise to marry **7.** skill **8.** one having a special skill **9.** manner of doing something **10.** handwriting **11.** applause **12.** help [to lend a *hand*] **13.** a hired worker [a farm *hand*] **14.** a source [to get news at first *hand*] **15.** anything like a hand, as a pointer on a clock **16.** the breadth of a hand **17.** *Card Games a)* the cards held by a player at one time *b)* a round of play – *adj.* of, for, or controlled by the hand – *vt.*

_____
n.
2. Being the <u>head</u> of a large corporation such as IBM means that you not only have to run the company but also represent that company at community affairs.

head (hed) *n.* [<OE. *heafod*] **1.** the part of the body containing the brain, and the jaws, eyes, ears, nose, and mouth **2.** the mind; intelligence **3.** *pl.* **head** a unit of counting [ten *head* of cattle] **4.** the main side of a coin **5.** the uppermost part or thing; top **6.** the topic or title of a section, chapter, etc. **7.** the foremost or projecting part; front **8.** the part designed for holding, striking, etc. [the *head* of a nail] **9.** the membrane across the end of a drum, etc. **10.** the source of a river, etc. **11.** froth, as on beer **12.** the pressure in an enclosed fluid, as steam **13.** a position of leadership or honor **14.** a leader, ruler, etc. – *adj.* **1.** most important; principal **2.** at the top or front **3.** striking against the front [*head* current] – *vt.* **1.** to be the chief of; command **2.** to lead; precede **3.** to cause to go in a specified direction – *vi.* to set out; travel [to *head* eastward]

———— **3.** There is usually only one <u>right</u> answer to objective questions on a test.
adj.

right (rīt) *adj.* [< OE. *riht,* straight] **1.** with a straight or perpendicular line **2.** up-right; virtuous **3.** correct **4.** fitting; suitable **5.** designating the side meant to be seen **6.** mentally or physically sound **7.** *a)* designating or of that side toward the east when one faces north *b)* designating or of the corresponding side of some-thing *c)* closer to the right side of one facing the thing mentioned – *n.* **1.** what is right, just, etc. **2.** a power, privilege, etc., belonging to one by law, nature, etc. **3.** the right side **4.** the right hand **5.** [*often* R-] *Politics* a conservative or reaction-ary position, party, etc. (often with *the*) – *adv.* **1.** straight; directly [go *right* home] **2.** properly; fitting **3.** completely **4.** exactly [*right* here] **5.** according to law, jus-tice, etc. **6.** correctly **7.** on or toward the right side **8.** very; in certain titles [the *right* honorable] – *vt.* **1.** to put upright **2.** to correct **3.** to put in order

Pronunciation Practice

For practice with the pronunciation guide, translate the names of these famous comedi-ans into English spelling.

cat, āte, fäther; pen, ēvil; if, kīte; nō, ôr, fo͞od, book; boil, house; up, tᴜrn; chief, shell; thick, *the*; zh, treasure; ŋ, sing; ə for *a* in *about*; ' as in *able* (ā'b'l)

1. wo͞op'ē gōld' bᴜrg

_____

2. rich'ərd prī'ər

_____

3. jer'ē sīn'feld

_____

4. rä'bin wil'yəmz

_____

5. jā le'nō

_____

6. ed'ē mᴜr'fē

_____

Etymology

By looking at a word's etymology in the dictionary, you can find the meaning of its prefixes. Here are ten words from the reading that contain common prefixes. The prefixes, their meanings, and other words that can help you remember the meanings are also provided.

Word	Prefix	Meaning of Prefix	Another Word
independence	in, im	not	incapable
respond	re	back	return
uncritical	un	not	unstable
eliminates	e, ex	out	edit
contradictory	contra	against	contrary
connections	con, com	with, together	conform
mistake	mis	wrong, not	misbehave
similarities	sim, sym, syn, syl	same, together	simultaneous
ambiguity	ambi, amphi	both	amphibian
prophecy	pro	before, forward	project

Using these prefixes, match the following difficult words to their definitions.

_____ **1.** indelible   **a.** send out; let out

_____ **2.** resilient   **b.** without conditions

_____ **3.** unconditional   **c.** cannot be erased

_____ **4.** emit   **d.** having a common center with another

_____ **5.** contrapuntal   **e.** forecast, especially of outcome of a disease

_____ 6. concentric

_____ 7. misnomer

_____ 8. symbiosis

_____ 9. ambidextrous

_____ 10. prognosis

f. the living together in close union of two dissimilar organisms

g. able to use both hands

h. against the beat (the point of rhythm)

i. wrong name

j. able to bounce back

3

The Many Miracles of Mark Hicks

Vocabulary Preview

portfolios (pôrt fō′lē ōz′): selections of representative works, as of artists

quadriplegic (kwäd′rə plē′jik): one who is totally paralyzed from the neck down

intrigued (in trēgd′): interested

severed (sev′ərd): cut in two

disarming (dis är′miŋ): removing suspicion, fear, or hostility

impassioned (im pash′ənd): filled with strong feeling

documentary (däk′yə men′tə rē): a motion picture or a television show that presents factual material in a dramatic way

excruciating (iks krōō′shē āt′iŋ): intensely painful

transpose (trans pōz′): to transfer or shift the position of

lithographs (lith′ə grafs′): prints made by a method that uses the repulsion between grease and water

wry (rī): humorous in a twisted or sarcastic way

aspirated (as′pə rāt′id): sucked or drawn in, as by inhaling

prestigious (pres tij′əs): having the power to impress as the result of having success or wealth

integrity (in teg′rə tē): the quality or state of being of high moral principle; uprightness, honesty, and sincerity

bantered (ban′tərd): joked or teased good-naturedly

cat, āte, fäther; pen, ēvil; if, kīte; nō, ôr, fōōd, book; boil, house; up, turn; chief, shell; thick, *the*; zh, treasure; ŋ, sing; ə for *a* in *about*; ′ as in *able* (ā′b′l)

Step 1: Preread

Preview the following selection by reading the title, the first paragraph, and the last paragraph. Answer the following questions without looking back at the reading.

1. What is the subject?

2. What is the main idea?

_____

3. Take a moment to think about what it would be like to be a quadriplegic and an artist. Think about what you know about it, what you don't know, and what you might find out from reading the selection. Make up three questions that might be answered by reading it.

a. _____

b. _____

c. _____

Step 2: Read

 Read the selection without underlining.

Write your starting time here: _____

The Many Miracles of Mark Hicks

JAN STUSSY

EIGHT YEARS AGO, I WAS REVIEWING THE art portfolios of applying students in my studio classroom on the campus of the University of California at Los Angeles. My secretary approached me with a special request from a quadriplegic student who wished to join my class in life drawing. "He draws by holding the pencil in his teeth," she said.

"That's crazy!" I replied. "It's tough enough to learn with skilled hands, but to try to draw with your mouth is . . . impossible. My answer is *No*!"

When I turned back to the portfolios of the waiting students—accepting some and rejecting others on the merits of their ability as draftsmen—my secretary added another student's portfolio to the pile. The work was above average in skill, and the drawings intrigued me. "Yes," I said, "I'll accept this student."

Before I could say another word, the quadriplegic flashed past me in his wheelchair, turned and stopped—facing the suddenly quiet class and a red-faced professor.

I tried not to look at him as I explained to the class (but mostly to him) that the work was going to be very hard for all of them (*especially* him) and now was the time to withdraw if anyone (*anyone!*) had second thoughts. Two students left, but those serious eyes from the wheelchair didn't even blink. I dismissed the class and asked the young man to remain.

In a soft, quiet voice, 23-year-old Mark Hicks told me that when he was 12 he fell from a tree house in his back yard in Manhattan Beach, Calif. "It was nobody's fault," he said calmly. "I just fell." The accident severed his spinal column, causing permanent paralysis from the neck down.

Mark had drawn before his accident. Slowly, he began to sketch again (and later taught himself to paint with oils) by holding the tools clenched in his teeth. He developed very strong jaw muscles. "If all my muscles were as strong as my jaws," he remarked with disarming good humor, "I could lift up this building."

Perfecting his drawing was, for Mark, like learning to fly. Through it, he could escape from his body into the make-believe world of his mind. He worked with a tutor at home to complete high school, then went to a junior college to major in art and to develop his skill as a draftsman.

Mark did not think of himself as pitiful, so he was not embarrassed. He simply was what he was. He accepted his limitations and worked beyond his capacities, setting an example and inspiring other students. True, I was his teacher—but in a larger sense, he was mine.

His impact on me and the class was so dramatic and useful that I resolved to capture him on film. I wanted to show other people how courage and spirit can achieve great things in spite of all odds. I had never made a film, but if Mark could draw, I could make a movie.

In September 1973 I wrote an impassioned letter to my dean telling him how I wanted to make a short documentary so others could share what we found in Mark. The dean was so moved that he sent a check for $6000 from funds earmarked for special projects. It was the first of many improbable miracles.

Mark knew a student, John Joseph, in the U.C.L.A. cinema department, who wanted to make a film for his senior project. We joined forces.

Four other talented students soon joined us. We rented cameras, tripods, sound equipment and lights, and shot Mark as he lived his life. No real story, no firm plot. We filmed his father getting him out of bed, sitting him in his chair and brushing his teeth. We followed his mother cooking food and feeding it to him. We shot his attendant putting him into his van and driving him to school. We photographed him in my life-drawing class, going to exhibits, parties and back to the hospital.

The high point of the movie came about when my gallery director—unaware that Mark made his pictures with his teeth—saw his paintings and offered to give Mark a one-man exhibition. We followed Mark's van to San Francisco and documented the opening of his show, the reception party and the highly successful exhibit. Mark sat among his pictures enjoying one of the happiest moments of his life. "I reached my goal," he said. "And I did it sitting down."

At that point we ran out of money and film. In our enthusiasm, we had spent the entire $6000 and had shot 64 rolls of expensive color film. Not a dime was left to develop it. It was excruciating to have that huge stack of film and not be able to see what we had done. It was, said Mark, "like being pregnant, forever."

Hat in hand and trembling nervously, I called on Paul Flaherty, chief executive at the Technicolor laboratory. When I told him about Mark and the film project, he offered to develop and print 15 rolls as a charitable gesture. So, I sent 30. If the miracle was going to work, we might just as well go for 30.

About a month later, Flaherty called: "That film is very, very good. Can I meet Mark?"

We wheeled Mark in the next day. After 35 minutes of conversation, Flaherty promised to develop the remaining 34 rolls—again for free. The miracles were holding.

But we were still broke. We had editing to do and sound tapes to transpose and music to score and inserts and titles to make and a final print to get. We needed more money. I wrote a letter describing our project and offering one of Mark's lithographs for a $200 donation, or a set of one of his and one of mine for $500. I mailed it to everyone I ever knew. The money began to roll in, and we went back to work.

When it came time for a title, we recalled a wry observation Mark made in the movie and chose *Gravity Is My Enemy*. (It was perhaps the only enemy he ever had.)

Then the money problem struck again. The rough cut was finished but we needed a major miracle to get the final and expensive print and negative made. We had begged and borrowed from everyone. It looked like the miracles had finally run out.

At that dark moment, Mark died.

He had aspirated some food into his lung while swallowing and was unable to cough it up. It could have happened a dozen times before. But it didn't happen until he had finished his film and seen a rough cut.

Mark was gone, but we had come this far because of him and we could not stop now. We had to show others what he had been. About three weeks after Mark's funeral, I took our scratchy work print to Ray Wagner, then a vice president of M-G-M. Halfway through he turned on the lights and, with tears running down his face, told me he would make a free final print. Mark's miracles were still operating.

We sent the finished film to the prestigious San Francisco Film Festival. To our surprise it took first place in the documentary-films competition, winning the Golden Gate Award, the top festival prize. This made it automatically eligible to be nominated for an Academy Award—and to our astonishment, it *was*. Yet another miracle!

Although we knew we hadn't a chance of winning the Oscar, it was well worth the price of our rented tuxedos for John Joseph and me to attend the glamorous Academy Awards. As I sat through the opening presentations my mind drifted back to Mark and how much I wished he could be sharing the nomination with us. Despite the realities, I really wanted that Oscar—for Mark and U.C.L.A. and for everyone who had made the film possible. Most of all, I wanted it to prove to other students who want to make movies that if you do it with feeling and integrity . . . you can win.

My mouth was dry as the moment approached for the presentation in our category. Time passed in slow motion as Kirk Douglas and Raquel Welch bantered before opening the envelopes. Then I heard Raquel say: "And the winner is—*Gravity* . . ."

I have no recollection of walking up that long aisle of applauding movie stars and reaching the podium. I meant to thank everyone, but I froze.

Then, as in a dream, I heard myself saying, "Just finishing our film was a miracle—and this award is another. But the greatest miracle of all was Mark Hicks. He showed us how to live life as a hero. It's Mark's film and his award. He can't be here tonight; he has left his wheelchair and is running free somewhere in God's Heaven." Then, I took the golden Oscar, held it over my head and concluded: "Mark, *this* is for you."

1500 words

Write your ending time here: _____

Subtract your starting time: _____

Total time: _____

Check the Rate Chart in the back of the book to find out how many words per minute you have read, and then record your score on the Progress Chart.

Step 3: Analyze What You Read

 Make Graphic Organizers

Although this reading is nonfiction, its structure is like that of a story. Therefore, we will organize it according to the structure of stories: setting, characters, plot, and theme. Fill in the chart.

The Many Miracles of Mark Hicks

Setting: (Where and when does it take place?)	
Characters: (Who is in the story?)	
Plot: (What happens in the story?)	
Theme: (What can we learn about life from the story?)	

Step 4: Remember What's Important

 Using your chart, test yourself or have someone else test you on the reading. Keep testing until you think you can remember it.

Step 5: Make Use of What You Read

 When you are ready, complete the following Comprehension Check. Do not look back at the reading.

Step 6: Evaluate Your Active Critical Thinking Skills

 After your test has been graded, answer the questions on the chart on page 465.

COMPREHENSION CHECK

Multiple Choice

Circle the letter before the best answer to each of the following questions.

1. John Joseph was

    a. another art instructor.

    b. Mark's attendant.

    c. a cinema student at UCLA.

    d. the person who presented the Academy Award.

2. Mark had injured himself

    a. in an auto accident.

    b. by falling from a tree.

    c. during an art class.

    d. while making a film.

3. At first, the art teacher thought that Mark

    a. should take the class to improve his drawings.

    b. did not like him very much.

    c. couldn't draw very well.

    d. would not be able to pass the class.

4. The person who wrote the story for the movie was

    a. the art instructor.

    b. Mark.

    c. John Joseph, a cinema student.

    d. nobody; there was no real story or plot.

5. You can infer from the article that

    a. an Academy Award can be won by an amateur.

    b. Mark did not know many people.

    c. Mark became rich as an artist.

    d. Mark's parents blamed themselves for the accident.

6. You can infer from the article that Mark

    a. was a good filmmaker.

    b. was an angry young man.

    c. felt good about himself.

    d. was a person who gave up easily.

7. The gallery director probably

    a. could tell that Mark was handicapped by the drawings.

    b. would not have let Mark show his paintings if he had known that Mark was handicapped.

    c. was surprised to find out that Mark was handicapped.

    d. took the paintings because he felt sorry for Mark.

8. The film about Mark

    a. was sad for the people who made it.

    b. cost Mark his life.

    c. was much more expensive than the art teacher thought it would be.

    d. looked amateurish.

Short Answer

9. The author says, "True, I was his teacher, but in a larger sense he was mine." What did the art teacher learn from Mark?

    _____

10. What message did the art teacher hope was communicated to film students by winning the Academy Award for *Gravity Is My Enemy*?

    _____

    _____

Essay

Explain the story, "The Many Miracles of Mark Hicks," as if you were telling it to someone who had not heard it before.

_____

_____

_____

_____

_____

_____

_____

_____

_____

_____

VOCABULARY IN CONTEXT

Write the best word from this list in the blank in each sentence below:

portfolios   **quadriplegics**   **intrigued**   **severed**   **disarming**

impassioned   **documentary**   **excruciating**   **transposed**

lithographic   **wry**   **aspirating**   **prestigious**   **integrity**   **banter**

1. It is now possible to sew a _____ finger back on.

2. Dancers sometimes have to go on stage even when they have

   _____ pain in their legs.

3. _____ smoke can make people cough.

4. A Nobel Prize is one of the most _____ awards that a person
   can win.

5. Instead of just presenting the facts, lawyers often make _____
   speeches that play on the jury's emotions.

6. A police officer's testimony used to be unquestioned, but today people doubt

   the _____ of the police.

7. The invitation to attend a wrestling match _____ me, and I
   decided to go.

8. "Gravity is my enemy" was a _____ observation made by Mark Hicks.

9. There is a lot of good-natured _____ at a class reunion.

10. The musician _____ the song into an easier key for him to sing.

11. Actors carry _____ of pictures to show producers the various types of characters they can portray.

12. The doctor's _____ manner put her patient at ease.

13. _____ have great difficulty doing the simple tasks we take for granted.

14. A great deal of research should be done before making

    a _____ film.

15. After a certain number of prints, _____ plates are destroyed so that no unauthorized prints can be made.

VOCABULARY REVIEW

Dictionary Definitions

For explanation see pp. 2–9

For practice in finding the correct meaning of a word in the dictionary, select the correct meaning of the following seven words from the reading. Above each entry is a sentence using the word. In the blank before the sentence, put the number of the definition that fits the way the word is used. The abbreviation under each blank tells you which part of speech the word is, so you can more easily find the proper definition.

_____   1.   When I turned back to the portfolios of the waiting students—accept-
adv.   ing some and rejecting others on the merits of their ability as drafts-
                 men—my secretary added another student's portfolio to the pile.

back (bak) *n.* [< OE. *bæk*] **1.** the rear part of the body from the nape of the neck
    to the end of the spine. **2.** the backbone **3.** a part that supports or fits the back
    4. the rear part or reverse of anything **5.** *Sports* a player or position behind the
    front line – *adj.* **1.** at the rear **2.** remote **3.** of or for the past [*back* pay] **4.** back-
    ward – *adv.* **1.** at, to, or toward the rear **2.** to or toward a former condition, time,
    activity, etc. **3.** in reserve or concealment **4.** in return or requital [pay him *back*]
    – *vt.* **1.** to move backward **2.** to support **3.** to bet on **4.** to provide or be a back for

_____ **2.** Before I could say another word, the quadriplegic <u>flashed</u> past me in
v.   his wheelchair, turned and stopped—facing the suddenly quiet class
          and a red-faced professor.

flash (flash) *vt.* [ME. *flashen,* to splash] **1.** to send out a sudden, brief light **2.** to
     sparkle **3.** to come or pass suddenly **4.** to send (news, etc.) swiftly – *n.* **1.** a
     sudden, brief light **2.** a brief moment **3.** a sudden, brief display **4.** a brief news
     item sent by radio, etc. **5.** a gaudy display – *adj.* happening swiftly or suddenly—
     flash'er *n.*

_____ **3.** It's Mark's <u>film</u> and his award.
n.

film (film) *n.* [OE. *filmen*] **1.** a fine, thin skin, coating, etc. **2.** a flexible cellulose
     material covered with a substance sensitive to light and used in photograph **3.** a
     haze or blur **4.** a motion picture – *vt., vi.* **1.** to cover or be covered as with a film
     2. to photograph or make a motion picture (of)

_____ **4.** He developed very <u>strong</u> jaw muscles.
adj.

strong (strôŋ) *adj.* [OE. *strang*] **1.** *a)* physically powerful *b)* healthy; sound **2.** morally
     or intellectually powerful [a *strong* will] **3.** firm; durable [a *strong* fort] **4.** power-
     ful in wealth, numbers, etc. **5.** of a specified number [troops 50,000 *strong*] **6.**
     having a powerful effect **7.** intense in degree or quality [*strong* coffee, a *strong*
     light, *strong* colors, etc.]

_____ **5.** He <u>developed</u> very strong jaw muscles.
v.

de•vel•op (di vel'əp) *vt.* [< Fr. *dé-* apart + OFr. *voloper,* to wrap] **1.** to make fuller,
     bigger, better, etc. **2.** to show or work out by degrees; disclose **3.** *Photog.* to put (a
     film, etc.) in chemical solutions to make the picture visible **4.** to come into being
     or activity; occur or happen

_____ **6.** He <u>simply</u> was what he was.
adv.

sim•ply (sim'plē) *adv.* **1.** in a simple way **2.** merely [*simply* trying] **3.** completely
     (*simply* overwhelmed]

_____ **7.** The dean was so <u>moved</u> that he sent a check for $6,000. . . .
v.

move (mo͞ov) *vt.* moved, mov'ing [<L. *movere*] **1.** to change the place or position of
     2. to set or keep in motion **3.** to cause (*to do, say,* etc.) **4.** to arouse the emotions,
     etc. of **5.** to propose formally, as in a meeting **6.** to change one's residence **7.** to
     make progress **8.** to take action **9.** to make a formal application (*for*) **10.** to evac-
     uate: said of the bowels **11.** *Commerce* to be sold: said of goods – *n.* **1.** act of
     moving **2.** an action toward some goal **3.** *Chess, Checkers,* etc. the act of moving a
     piece, or one's turn to move

Pronunciation Practice

For practice with the pronunciation guide, translate these holidays into English spelling.

cat, āte, fäther; pen, ēvil; if, kīte; nō, ôr, fo͞od, book; boil, house; up, turn; chief, shell; thick, *the*; zh, treasure; ŋ, sing; ə for *a* in *about*; ' as in *able* (ā'b'l)

1. sānt pa'triks dā

    _____

2. val'ən tīnz'dā

    _____

3. thə fôr*th*' əv joo lī'

    _____

4. mə môr'ē əl dā

    _____

5. no͞o'yirz ēv

    _____

6. fä'*th*ərz dā

    _____

Etymology

By looking at a word's etymology in the dictionary, you can find the meaning of its roots. Here are six words from the reading that contain common roots. The roots, their meanings, and other words that can help you remember the meanings are also provided.

Word	Root	Meaning of Root	Another Word
1. quadriplegic	quad	four	quadrangle
2. request	ques	to ask or to seek	question
3. resolve	solv	to explain	solve
4. impassioned	pass	feeling	passion

5. <u>photo</u>graphed   photo   of or produced   photocopy
                                              by light

6. trans<u>pos</u>e   pos   put or place   pose

Using these roots, match the following difficult words to their definitions:

_____ **1.** quadrennial

_____ **2.** inquest

_____ **3.** absolve

_____ **4.** impassive

_____ **5.** photic

_____ **6.** juxtapose

a. to free from guilt (explain why someone is not guilty)

b. to put side by side

c. showing or having no feelings

d. having to do with the effect of light upon, or the production of light by, organisms

e. occurring once every four years

f. an official inquiry, usually to seek out the cause of a sudden and unexpected death

4

Superstitions: Just Whistling in the Dark

Vocabulary Preview

irrational (i rash′ə n′l): unreasonable, not logical

philosophers (fi läs′ʉ fərz): people who study philosophy or the principles of conduct, thought, knowledge, and the nature of the universe

Norse (nôrs): West Scandinavian: Norwegian, Icelandic

wrath (rath): intense anger

rationalized (rash′ən ə līzd′): explained or interpreted; made reasonable

incorruptibility (in′kə rup′tə bil′ə tē): state of being unable to be spoiled or made immoral

consternation (kän′stər nā′shən): great shock or fear

episode (ep′ə sōd′): event or series of events complete in itself

distorted (dis tôrt′id): twisted out of shape; misrepresented

aversion (ə vʉr′zhən): strong dislike

cat, āte, fäther; pen, ēvil; if, kīte; nō, ôr, f͞ood, book; boil, house; up, turn; chief, shell; thick, *the*; zh, treasure; ŋ, sing; ə for *a* in *about*; ′ as in *able* (ā′b′l)

Step 1: Preread

Preview the following selection by reading the title and the headings. Run your eyes quickly down the page to get a general idea of what is under each heading. Answer the following questions without looking back at the reading.

1. What is the subject?

   _____

2. What is the main idea?

   _____

3. Take a moment to think about superstitions. Think about what you know, what you don't know, and what you might find out from reading the selection. Make up three questions.

a. _____

b. _____

c. _____

Step 2: Read

 Read the selection without underlining.

Write your starting time here: _____

Superstitions: Just Whistling in the Dark

DON BOXMEYER

WHY DO YOU SUPPOSE THE BOSS IS SO grumpy?

"Dunno. Maybe he got up on the wrong side of the bed."

"He'd probably feel better if you got him a cup of coffee."

"Right. Knock on wood."

One of these fellows is superstitious. He probably goes out of his way to avoid meeting black cats. He doesn't walk under ladders, step on sidewalk cracks or open umbrellas indoors, and he worries a lot if he breaks a mirror.

That makes him a trifle silly and just like almost everybody else.

A superstition is a belief based wholly on fear and not in harmony with any known law of science. How do you know the number 13 is unlucky? You just know it. How do you know that spilling salt is unlucky? It just is.

Irrational? Yes and no.

Superstitions, wrote Rabbi D. R. Brasch in his book, "How Did It Begin?" have reasons, backgrounds and practical explanations. They belonged to the social life of both the civilized and the savage.

Here are some examples.

The Unlucky Number 13

In some European countries, you can't live in house No. 13. It does not exist. No. 12 is followed by No. 12½ and then No. 14. Many office buildings in this country skip the 13th floor. Some airlines and sports arenas omit 13 as a seat number. A true triskaidekaphobiac would not start a journey on the 13th of any month (on Friday the 13th he stays right in bed with the covers pulled way up over his head), will not buy or use 13 of anything, will not wear a number 13 on a uniform or eat with 12 others.

Why? Historically, 13 represents the number of men present at the Last Supper. Greek philosophers and mathematicians scorned the number 13 as being "imperfect," and in Norse mythology, 12 gods were present when the evil spirit Loki busted a party at a good address in Valhalla and killed Balder, a very popular god.

Walking Under Ladders

This superstition has a practical application. You could get a bucket of paint on the head. But custom says if you walk under a ladder, the wrath of the gods will be on you in any case and what you ought to do is quickly cross your fingers and make a wish.

Historians have rationalized that the ladder, leaning against a wall, forms a triangle signifying the Holy Trinity. To pass through such sacred space is a punishable offense. It's flat dangerous to play with such supernatural forces; a bucket of paint on the head is nothing compared to what could be in store.

Getting out of Bed on the Wrong Side

It is written that to get out of bed on the left side is to subject your day to misfortune and misery. You are supposed to rise from the right and place your right foot on the floor first. If you err, go back to bed until you can do it correctly. This superstition has to do with the ancient belief that right was right and left was wrong.

Spilling Salt

If this happens to you, you're supposed to take a pinch of salt and toss it over your left shoulder into the face of the devil.

This superstition is rooted in the ancient and biblical importance of salt. Salt purifies; hence it became the symbol of incorruptibility. Salt on the table became the emblem of justice, and to upset it became a forewarning of injustice.

In a famous Last Supper painting by Leonardo da Vinci, the faces of Jesus and the Apostles vividly show consternation and grief. Why? Historians say because someone just dumped the salt shaker over.

Who did it? Judas, of course. But there is no confirmation of this episode; Brasch said da Vinci merely used the old superstition to dramatize his painting.

Breaking a Mirror

This is good for seven years of bad luck or it could cause a death in the family. If a mirror breaks, legend instructs you to get the pieces out of the house posthaste and bury them in the ground.

Before the invention of mirrors, man gazed at his reflection in pools, ponds and lakes. If the image was distorted, disaster was sure to strike. (Sometimes a sneaky enemy would ruin his foe's day by pitching a pebble into the water.)

Gradually water gave way to shiny metal and then glass, but man still was convinced any injury to the reflection would be visited upon the real thing, just as he thought that . . . piercing the eyes of an enemy in a picture would cause the enemy to go blind. And the seven years? It is thought that the figure stems from Roman belief that a man's body physically rejuvenated itself every seven years and he became, in effect, a new man.

Meeting a Black Cat

Custom dictates that if your path is crossed by a black cat, you're really going to be in for it unless you return home immediately.

To the Egyptians, the cat was a god and anyone who killed one was punished. Come the Middle Ages, however, and the cat was linked to witches and Satan. Everyone knows what happens when you cross the devil.

Whistling

This is a professional superstition; newsmen are not supposed to whistle in the newsroom, and actors do not whistle in the dressing room. It probably goes back to the sailor's deep aversion to whistling except at very special times.

In the days of sail, seamen believed it was possible to call up a storm by the accidental use of magic—like duplicating the noise of wind in the rigging. Whistling on board was to invite bad luck, except when the ship was becalmed, and then only by an expert who would know in which precise direction to send the whistle as an order for wind.

1000 words

Write your ending time here: _____

Subtract your starting time: _____

Total time: _____

Check the Rate Chart in the back of the book to find how many words per minute you have read, and then record your score on the Progress Chart.

Step 3: Analyze What You Read

   Fill in the following chart:

Superstition	Background/Explanation
1. The unlucky number 13	
2. Walking under ladders	
3. Getting out of bed on the wrong side	
4. Spilling salt	

5. Breaking a mirror	
6. Meeting a black cat	
7. Whistling	

Step 4: Remember What's Important

 Using your chart, test yourself or have someone else test you on the superstitions. Keep testing until you think you can remember what you need to know.

Step 5: Make Use of What You Read

 When you are ready, complete the following Comprehension Check. Do not look back at the reading.

Step 6: Evaluate Your Active Critical Thinking Skills

 After your test has been graded, answer the questions on the chart on page 465.

COMPREHENSION CHECK

Multiple Choice

Circle the letter before the best answer to each of the following questions.

1. The author thinks people who believe in superstitions are
   a. abnormal.
   b. logical.
   c. a bit silly.
   d. correct.

2. From the reading we can infer that superstitions
   a. are no longer believed.
   b. have been believed in every period of time.
   c. are religious in origin.
   d. are dangerous.

3. A triskaidekaphobiac
   a. stays home on Friday the thirteenth.
   b. believes the number thirteen has religious importance.
   c. thinks the number thirteen is lucky.
   d. thinks numbers determine our fate.

4. If you break a mirror, you are supposed to
   a. stay indoors that day.
   b. bury the pieces.
   c. throw the pieces into a river, ocean, or lake.
   d. throw a piece over your shoulder.

5. Whistling is a superstition that started with
   a. sailors.
   b. soldiers.
   c. artists.
   d. chefs.

6. The author implies that

    a. superstitions are based on scientific fact.

    b. superstitious people do silly things.

    c. educated people are not superstitious.

    d. superstitions have no place in modern society.

Matching

Match the background to the superstition; write the letter from the second column in the space in the first column.

_____ **7.** The unlucky number 13   **a.** The Holy Trinity

_____ **8.** Meeting a black cat   **b.** Right is right and left is wrong

_____ **9.** Walking under ladders   **c.** Witches and Satan

_____ **10.** Getting out of bed on   **d.** The Last Supper
          the wrong side

Essay

Discuss the background of at least five superstitions.

_____

_____

_____

_____

_____

_____

_____

_____

_____

_____

VOCABULARY IN CONTEXT

Write the best word from this list in the blank in each sentence below:

irrational   philosopher   Norse   wrath   rationalize

incorruptibility   consternation   episodes   distort   aversion

1. Some people have such a strong _____ to cabbage that even the smell of it cooking makes them sick.

2. Thursday was named after the _____ god Thor, the god of thunder.

3. Most _____ of television programs are recorded on videotape for later broadcast rather than presented live.

4. During the Middle Ages, beliefs about witchcraft were so _____ that cows, insects, and birds were convicted of being witches and put to death.

5. You must make someone very angry to incur his or her _____ .

6. Mirrors in carnival fun houses are shaped to _____ people's reflections.

7. Scandals such as Watergate have shaken our faith in the _____ of our political leaders.

8. People _____ their continuing to smoke by pointing to healthy elderly people who have smoked all of their lives.

9. Eighteenth-century patients at St. Bartholomew's Hospital must have

   felt _____ at being asked to pay their funeral expenses when they were admitted.

10. Socrates, probably the best known Greek _____ , never wrote down his own teachings; we know what he said because a student, Plato, took notes.

VOCABULARY REVIEW

Parts of Speech

For explanation see p. 5

For each word below, write its part of speech. Then change it to the new part of speech. Write a sentence using the new word. Use a dictionary if you need help.

Word	Part of Speech	New Part of Speech	New Word
1. rationalize	_____	adjective	_____

Sentence: _____

_____

| **2.** aversion | _____ | adjective | _____ |

Sentence: _____

_____

| **3.** distort | _____ | noun | _____ |

Sentence: _____

_____

| **4.** philosopher | _____ | verb | _____ |

Sentence: _____

_____

| **5.** episode | _____ | adjective | _____ |

Sentence: _____

_____

| **6.** irrational | _____ | adverb | _____ |

Sentence: _____

_____

7. incorruptibility   _____   adjective   _____

Sentence: _____

_____

Word Parts

Here are some common word parts that will help you with this exercise:

Prefixes	Roots	Suffixes
in, im, ir = not	*tort* = twist	*ate* = become
dis = not, apart, very	*phil* = love	*ology* = study of
re = again, back	*sophos* = wise	*ible* = able to be
super = over, beyond	*juven* = young	*er* = one who
a = away	*myth* = legend	*al* = like, of
com, con, cor = together, very, with	*rupt* = break, spoil	*tion, ion* = act of, state of
	vert, vers = turn	
	firm = strong	
	rat = think	

Using these word parts as hints, match the following words to their definitions.

_____ **1.** irrational

_____ **2.** philosopher

_____ **3.** mythology

_____ **4.** supernatural

_____ **5.** incorruptible

_____ **6.** confirmation

_____ **7.** distort

_____ **8.** rejuvenate

_____ **9.** aversion

a. can't be broken down or morally destroyed

b. beyond the natural or ordinary

c. twist

d. feeling of wanting to turn away because of dislike

e. act of proving or making something stronger

f. using illogical thinking

g. a person who studies because of a love of wisdom

h. study of legends

i. to make young again

5

Saved

Vocabulary Preview

convey (kən vā′): carry; communicate by words or actions

articulate (är tik′yə lit): able to express oneself easily and clearly

hustler (hus′lər): [Slang] a person who makes money dishonestly

functional (fuŋk′shə nəl): performing or able to perform a function

emulate (em′yə lāt′): try to equal or surpass

motivation (mōt′ə vā′shən): some inner drive that causes a person to do something or act in a certain way; goal

riffling (rif′liŋ): leafing rapidly through (a book, etc.)

immensely (i mens′lē): greatly; hugely

inevitable (in ev′i tə bəl): cannot be avoided or evaded; certain to happen

circulation (sɥr′kyo͞o lā′shən): the passing of something, as money or news, from person to person or place to place

rehabilitation (re′hə bil′ə tā′shən): bringing back or restoring a person to a constructive role in society

devour (di vour′): to take in greedily with the mouth, eyes, ears, or mind

isolation (i′sə lā′shən): separation; privacy; being alone

engrossing (in grōs′iŋ): taking one's entire attention; very interesting

feigned (fānd): pretended

vistas (vis′təz): views

dormant (dôr′mənt): latent or sleeping

confers (kən fɥrz′): gives or bestows

afflicting (ə flikt′iŋ): causing pain or suffering to someone

alma mater (äl′mə mät′ər): school that one attended

cat, āte, fäther; pen, ēvil; if, kīte; nō, ôr, fo͞od, book; boil, house; up, tɥrn; chief, shell; thick, *the*; zh, treasure; ŋ, sing; ə for *a* in *about*; ' as in *able* (ā′b'l)

Step 1: Preread

Preview the following selection by reading the title and the first sentence of each paragraph. Answer the following questions without looking back at the reading.

1. What is the subject?

    _____

2. What is the main idea?

    _____

3. Take a moment to think about Malcolm X and learning to read and write. Think about what you know, what you don't know, and what you might find out from reading the selection. Make up three questions.

    a. _____

    b. _____

    c. _____

Step 2: Read

Read the selection without underlining.

Write your starting time here: _____

Saved

MALCOLM X

I BECAME INCREASINGLY FRUSTRATED at not being able to express what I wanted to convey in letters that I wrote, especially those to Mr. Elijah Muhammad. In the street, I had been the most articulate hustler out there—I had commanded attention when I said something. But now, trying to write simple English, I not only wasn't articulate, I wasn't even functional. How would I sound writing in slang, the way I would *say* it, something such as, "Look, daddy, let me pull your coat about a cat, Elijah Muhammad—"

Many who today hear me somewhere in person, or on television, or those who read something I've said, will think I went to school far beyond the eighth grade. This impression is due entirely to my prison studies.

It had really begun back in the Charlestown Prison, when Bimbi first made me feel envy of his stock of knowledge. Bimbi had always taken charge of any conversation he was in, and I had tried to emulate him. But every book I picked up had few sentences which didn't contain anywhere from one to nearly all of the words that might as well have been in Chinese. When I just skipped those words, of course, I really ended up with little idea of what the book said. So I had come to the Norfolk Prison Colony still going through only book-reading motions. Pretty soon, I would have quit even these motions, unless I had received the motivation that I did.

I saw that the best thing I could do was get hold of a dictionary—to study, to learn some words. I was lucky enough to reason also that I should try to improve my penmanship. It was sad. I couldn't even write in a straight line. It was both ideas together that moved me to request a dictionary along with some tablets and pencils from the Norfolk Prison Colony school.

I spent two days just riffling uncertainly through the dictionary's pages. I'd never realized so many words existed! I didn't know *which* words I needed to learn. Finally, just to start some kind of action, I began copying.

In my slow, painstaking, ragged handwriting, I copied into my tablet everything printed on that first page, down to the punctuation marks.

I believe it took me a day. Then, aloud, I read back, to myself, everything I'd written on the tablet. Over and over, aloud, to myself, I read my own handwriting.

I woke up the next morning, thinking about those words—immensely proud to realize that not only had I written so much at one time, but I'd written words that I never knew were in the world. Moreover, with a little effort, I also could remember what many of these words meant. I reviewed the words whose meanings I didn't remember. Funny thing, from the dictionary first page right now, that "aardvark" springs to my mind. The dictionary had a picture of it, a long-tailed, long-eared, burrowing

African mammal, which lives off termites caught by sticking out its tongue as an ant-eater does for ants.

I was so fascinated that I went on—I copied the dictionary's next page. And the same experience came when I studied that. With every succeeding page, I also learned of people and places and events from history. Actually the dictionary is like a miniature encyclopedia. Finally the dictionary's A section had filled a whole tablet—and I went on into the B's. That was the way I started copying what eventually became the entire dictionary. It went a lot faster after so much practice helped me to pick up handwriting speed. Between what I wrote in my tablet, and writing letters, during the rest of my time in prison I would guess I wrote a million words.

I suppose it was inevitable that as my word-base broadened, I could for the first time pick up a book and read and now begin to understand what the book was saying. Anyone who has read a great deal can imagine the new world that opened. Let me tell you something: from then until I left that prison, in every free moment I had, if I was not reading in the library, I was reading on my bunk. You couldn't have gotten me out of books with a wedge. Between Mr. Muhammad's teachings, my correspondence, my visitors—usually Ella and Reginald—and my reading of books, months passed without my even thinking about being imprisoned. In fact, up to then, I never had been so truly free in my life.

The Norfolk Prison Colony's library was in the school building. A variety of classes was taught there by instructors who came from such places as Harvard and Boston universities. The weekly debates between inmate teams were also held in the school building. You would be astonished to know how worked up convict debaters and audiences would get over subjects like "Should Babies Be Fed Milk?"

Available on the prison library's shelves were books on just about every general subject. Much of the big private collection that Parkhurst had willed to the prison was still in crates and boxes in the back of the library—thousands of old books. Some of them looked ancient: covers faded, old-time parchment-looking binding. Parkhurst, I've mentioned, seemed to have been principally interested in history and religion. He had the money and the special interest to have a lot of books that you wouldn't have in general circulation. Any college library would have been lucky to get that collection.

As you can imagine, especially in a prison where there was heavy emphasis on rehabilitation, an inmate was smiled upon if he demonstrated an unusually intense interest in books. There was a sizable number of well-read inmates, especially the popular debaters. Some were said by many to be practically walking encyclopedias. They were almost celebrities. No university would ask any student to devour literature as I did when this new world opened to me, of being able to read and *understand*.

I read more in my room than in the library itself. An inmate who was known to read a lot could check out more than the permitted maximum number of books. I preferred reading in the total isolation of my own room.

When I had progressed to really serious reading, every night at about ten P.M. I would be outraged with the "lights out." It always seemed to catch me right in the middle of something engrossing.

Fortunately, right outside my door was a corridor light that cast a glow into my room. The glow was enough to read by, once my eyes adjusted to it. So when "lights out" came, I would sit on the floor where I could continue reading in that glow.

At one-hour intervals the night guards paced past every room. Each time I heard the approaching footsteps, I jumped into bed and feigned sleep. And as soon as the guard passed, I got back out of bed onto the floor area of that light-glow, where I would read for another fifty-eight minutes—until the guard approached again. That went on until three or four every morning. Three or four hours of sleep a night was enough for me. Often in the years in the streets I had slept less than that. . . .

I have often reflected upon the new vistas that reading opened to me. I knew right there in prison that reading had changed forever the course of my life. As I see it today, the ability to read awoke inside me some long dormant craving to be mentally alive. I certainly wasn't seeking any degree, the way a college confers a status symbol upon its students. My homemade education gave me, with every additional book that I read, a little bit more sensitivity to the deafness, dumbness, and blindness that was afflicting the black race in America. Not long ago, an English writer telephoned me from London, asking questions. One was, "What's your alma mater?" I told him, "Books." You will never catch me with a free fifteen minutes in which I'm not studying something I feel might be able to help the black man.

900 words

Write your ending time here: _____

Subtract your starting time: _____

Total time: _____

Check the Rate Chart in the back of the book to find how many words per minute you have read, and then record your score on the Progress Chart.

Step 3: Analyze What You Read

 **Make Graphic Organizers**

Fill in the following chart:

Saved	
Setting: (Where and when does it take place?)	
Characters: (Who is in the story?)	
Plot: (What happens in the story?)	
Theme: (What does the story teach us about life?)	

Step 4: Remember What's Important

Using your chart, test yourself or have someone test you on the reading. Keep testing until you think you can remember everything you need to know.

Step 5: Make Use of What You Read

When you are ready, complete the following Comprehension Check. Do not look back at the reading.

Step 6: Evaluate Your Active Critical Thinking Skills

After your test has been graded, answer the questions on the chart on page 465.

COMPREHENSION CHECK

Multiple Choice

Circle the letter before the best answer to each of the following questions.

1. Malcolm X read to

    a. gain status and power.

    b. become wealthy.

    c. become a great speaker.

    d. help black people.

2. Malcolm X completed

    a. high school.

    b. college.

    c. eighth grade.

    d. junior college.

3. An aardvark is

    a. a termite.

    b. an African bird.

    c. a burrowing mammal.

    d. an armadillo.

4. Malcolm X read in semi-darkness because

    a. he didn't pay his electric bill.

    b. the prison guards were cruel.

    c. there was no window in his room.

    d. he read after "lights out."

5. Malcolm X began reading books after

    a. completing high school.

    b. improving his vocabulary.

    c. getting out of prison.

    d. finishing second grade.

6. Malcolm X copied the dictionary because

   a. he didn't know a better method of vocabulary improvement.

   b. there are no better methods of vocabulary improvement.

   c. he didn't have any other books.

   d. he was bored.

7. Malcolm X's story shows that

   a. illiterate people are stupid.

   b. illiterate people are articulate.

   c. prison helps people reform.

   d. illiterate people can learn.

8. The administration at Norfolk Prison Colony

   a. encouraged prisoners to improve themselves.

   b. forced prisoners to work constantly.

   c. kept prisoners isolated.

   d. allowed prisoners to read whenever they wished.

Short Answer

What conclusion can you draw from this article . . .

9. about the possibility of rehabilitating prisoners?

   _____

10. about the effects of reading on one's life?

   _____

   _____

Essay

Explain the story "Saved" as if you were telling it to someone who had not heard it before.

_____

_____

_____

_____

_____

_____

_____

_____

_____

_____

_____

VOCABULARY IN CONTEXT

Write the best word from this list in the blank in each sentence below:

cosmology   retrieval   retention   distinctive

heredity   neuropsychologist   associative   perception

physiological   senility

1. Scientists are experimenting with new "youth" drugs like Gerovital to

   prevent _____ .

2. The _____ markings on certain animals serve as a form of
   camouflage in their natural habitats.

3. If you were hearing the voices of invisible beings, you might go

   to a _____ .

4. _____ determines the color of our eyes.

5. No one has yet found a _____ cause for mental illness, although
   it has long been suspected that it is not completely psychological.

6. Musicians become skilled at the _____ of small differences in
   sound that most of us can't hear.

7. The _____ of game by some breeds of hunting dogs almost seems to be an inborn ability.

8. The eye's _____ of visual images enables us to see a motion picture as a flowing unit rather than as a series of separate pictures.

9. The principle of _____ memory involves relating new information to what is already known.

10. Einstein's theory on the _____ of the spatial universe is that it curves back on itself and is, therefore, infinite.

VOCABULARY IN CONTEXT

Write the best word from the following list in the blank in each sentence.

Part A

dormant   alma maters   convey   feigned   afflicting

confer   emulate   articulate   immense   vistas

1. Many politicians are so _____ that their speaking ability alone gets them elected to office.

2. Because of the different shades of meaning of words, it is sometimes difficult

   to _____ to others exactly what we mean.

3. Susan had always admired her successful uncle, and when she grew up she

   tried to _____ him.

4. The _____ portions served at the restaurant were impossible to eat.

5. He _____ illness to avoid work.

6. The invention of the printing press opened new _____ for the common person.

7. The seed, planted in the fall, lay _____ until the spring rains.

8. Many universities _____ over 2,000 degrees a year.

9. The most common disease, _____ over 53 percent of the people in the United States, is tooth decay.

10. Until recently, most top business executives claimed Ivy League colleges

    as _____ .

Part B

engrossing   inevitable   riffling   rehabilitation

hustlers   isolation   functional   motivation   circulation

devours

11. People who favor the death penalty usually don't believe in the

    _____ of criminals.

12. Two-dollar bills are no longer in general _____ .

13. My daughter loves fairy tales so much that she _____ the Disney videos of *Snow White, Cinderella,* and *Sleeping Beauty.*

14. Con artists are _____ who take advantage of people.

15. Success in school depends on _____ as well as on ability.

16. You can get a general idea of a book by _____ through its pages.

17. Death and taxes are said to be the only two things that are

    _____ .

18. In order to be _____ in society, you need to know basic mathematics.

19. For those who like them, crossword puzzles are _____ .

20. Solitary confinement is considered a severe punishment because people suffer

    from _____ .

VOCABULARY REVIEW

Dictionary Definitions

For explanation see pp. 2–9

For practice in finding the correct meaning of a word in the dictionary, select the correct meaning of the following six words from the reading. Above each entry is a sentence using the word. In the blank before the sentence, put the number of the definition that fits the way the word is used. The abbreviation under each blank tells you which parts of speech the word is, so you can more easily find the proper definition.

_____ **1.** I became increasingly frustrated at not being able to express what I
n.   wanted to convey in <u>letters</u> that I wrote, especially those to Mr. Elijah Muhammad.

let·ter (let′ər) *n.* [<L. *littera*] **1.** any character of the alphabet **2.** a written or printed message, usually sent by mail **3.** [*pl.*] *a*) literature *b*) learning; knowledge **4.** literal meaning – *vt.* to mark with letters

_____ **2.** When I just <u>skipped</u> those words, of course, I really ended up with little
v.   idea of what the book said:.

skip (skip) *vi., vt.* **skipped, skip′ping** [ME. *skippen*] **1.** to leap lightly (over) **2.** to ricochet or bounce **3.** to pass from one point to another, omitting or ignoring (what lies between) **4.** [Colloq.] to leave (town, etc.) hurriedly – *n.* a skipping; specif., a gait alternating light hops on each foot

_____ **3.** I couldn't even write in a straight <u>line</u>.
n.

line (līn) *n.* [< L. *linea*, lit., linen thread] **1.** a cord, rope, wire, etc. **2.** any wire, pipe, etc., or system of these, conducting fluid, electricity, etc. **3.** a thin, threadlike mark **4.** a border or boundary **5.** a limit **6.** outline; contour **7.** a row of persons or things, as of printed letters across a page **8.** a succession of persons or things **9.** lineage **10.** a transportation system of buses, ships, etc. **11.** the course a moving thing takes **12.** a course of conduct, action, explanation, etc. **13.** a person's trade or occupation **14.** a stock of goods **15.** a piece of information **16.** a short letter, note, etc. **17.** a verse of poetry **18.** [*pl.*] all the speeches of a character in a play **19.** the forward combat position in warfare **20.** *Football* the players in the forward row **21.** *Math.* the path of a moving point – *vt.* **lined, lin′ing 1.** to mark with lines **2.** to form a line along

_____ **4.** Between what I wrote in my tablet, and writing letters, during the <u>rest</u>
n.   of my time in prison I would guess I wrote a million words.

rest (rest) *n.* [OE.] **1.** sleep or repose **2.** ease or inactivity after exertion. **3.** relief from anything distressing, tiring, etc. **4.** absence of motion **5.** what is left **6.** a supporting device **7.** *Music* a measured interval of silence between tones, or a symbol for this – *vi.* **1.** to get ease and refreshment by sleeping or by ceasing from work **2.** to be at ease **3.** to be or become still **4.** to be supported; lie or lean (*in, on,* etc.) **5.** to be found [the fault *rests* with him] **6.** to rely; depend – *vt.* **1.** to cause to rest **2.** to put for ease, etc. [*rest* your head here]

5. Anyone who has read a <u>great</u> deal can imagine the new world that
_____   opened.
adj.

great (grāt) *adj.* [OE.] **1.** of much more than ordinary size, extent, etc. **2.** most important; main **3.** designating a relationship one generation removed [great-grandparent] **4.** [Colloq.] skillful (often with *at*) **5.** (Colloq.) excellent; fine – *n.* a distinguished person

6. Fortunately, right outside my door was a corridor light that <u>cast</u> a glow
_____   into my room.
v.

cast (kast) *vt.* **cast, cast'ing** [<ON. *kasta*] **1.** to throw with force; fling; hurl **2.** to deposit (a ballot or vote) **3.** to direct [to *cast* one's eyes] **4.** to project [to *cast* light] **5.** to throw off or shed (a skin) **6.** to shape (molten metal, etc.) by pouring into a mold **7.** to select (an actor) for (a role or play) – *n.* **1.** a casting; throw **2.** something formed in a mold **3.** a plaster form for immobilizing a limb **4.** the set of actors in a play or movie **5.** an appearance, as of features **6.** kind; quality **7.** a tinge; shade

Word Parts

By looking at a word's etymology in the dictionary, you can find the meaning of its roots. Here are six words from the reading that contain common roots. The roots, their meanings, and other words that can help you remember the meanings are also provided.

Word	Root	Meaning of Root	Another word
1. tele<u>vis</u>ion	vis	see	vision
2. <u>dic</u>tionary	dic	to say	predict
3. pro<u>gress</u>	gress	to go, walk, or step	aggression
4. tele<u>phon</u>ed	phon	sound	phonograph
5. at<u>ten</u>tion	ten	to hold	retention
6. <u>mot</u>ions	mot	to move	locomotive

Using these roots, match the following difficult words to their definitions.

_____ **1.** vis-à-vis

a. a place to <u>walk</u> out (exit)

_____ **2.** abdicate

b. capable of spontaneous <u>movement</u>

_____ **3.** egress

c. to <u>say</u> you're leaving a high position

_____ **4.** cacophony

d. the length of time something is <u>held</u>

_____ **5.** tenure

e. (to <u>see</u> a person) face to face

_____ **6.** motile

f. harsh, jarring <u>sound</u>

6

How to Strengthen Your Memory Power

Vocabulary Preview

cosmological (käz mə lä′jə k′l): relating to the branch of philosophy and science that deals with the study of the universe as a whole and of its form and nature as a physical system.

retrieval (ri trē′v′l): possibility of getting something back or recovering it

retention (ri ten′shən): holding or keeping

distinctive (dis tiŋk′tiv): distinguished from others; characteristic

heredity (hə red′ə tē): passing of characteristics from parent to child by means of genes

neuropsychologist (noo′rō sī käl′ə jist): psychologist who studies the mind and the nervous system

associative (ə sō′shē āt′iv, ə sō′shə tiv): of, characterized by, or causing association, as of ideas

perception (pər sep′shən): mental grasp of objects, qualities, and so on by means of the senses; awareness; comprehension

physiological (fiz′ē ə läj′i k′l): bodily; physical

senility (si nil′ə tē): state typical of or resulting from old age; showing the marked deterioration often accompanying old age, especially confusion or memory loss

cat, āte, fäther; pen, ēvil; if, kīte; nō, ôr, fōod, book; boil, house; up, turn; chief, shell; thick, *the*; zh, treasure; ŋ, sing; ə for *a* in *about*; ' as in *able* (ā′b′l)

Step 1: Preread

Preview the following selection by reading the title and the first sentence of each paragraph. Answer the following questions without looking back at the reading.

1. What is the subject?

_____

2. What is the main idea?

_____

3. Take a moment to think about memory. Think about what you know, what you don't know, and what you might find out from reading the selection. Make up three questions.

a. _____

b. _____

c. _____

Step 2: Read

Read the selection without underlining.

Write your starting time here: _____

How to Strengthen Your Memory Power

Mary Russ

ONE OF ALBERT EINSTEIN's biographers tells a story about an encounter between the physicist and a neighborhood girl that took place as he was walking through slush and snowdrifts on his way to teach a class at Princeton. After they had chatted for a while, the girl looked down at Einstein's moccasins, which were soaking wet. "Mr. Einstein, you've come out without your boots again," she said. Einstein laughed and pulled up his trousers to show his ankles. "And I forgot my socks," he confessed.

Although you probably don't have your head in the clouds of cosmological physics, you undoubtedly experience a fair share of forgetfulness: You are introduced to someone at a party and forget the name before the handshake is over; you walk away from a department-store counter, leaving your umbrella tilted against it; you reach for the car keys only to discover that you have no idea where you left them.

Why is it that our memory sometimes lets us down? To understand this breakdown, it's important first to have an idea of how the whole process works. Memory is a set of mental abilities, more wide-ranging than the one word would seem to imply. It involves the registration, storage and retrieval of information.

Though there is disagreement over how memory actually works, many scientists believe that a memory causes a "trace" in the brain—not a physical mark or groove but rather a chemical change. It also is believed that the function of memory is divided into the two categories of short-term and long-term memory. Short-term has a very low retention rate, usually less than 20 seconds. Long-term memory is relatively permanent and has virtually unlimited capacity.

The nerve changes that take place in the brain are different for each type of memory. In short-term, the processing of a fact or impression involves a speedy but complex chain of events. Suppose you look up the telephone number of the local pizzeria. As you see the number, there are chemical changes on the retina of the eye. This triggers impulses in the brain that persist for a brief time and then die out as they're replaced by other patterns of activity: new facts, sights and sounds that you experience. This dying out is the reason that you forget the number practically immediately after you've dialed it and started talking.

If you don't want the pattern to fade out—if you want the fact or impression to be part of long-term memory—it must in some way be selectively maintained and reestablished as a distinctive pattern. This will happen if the impression is repeated enough or is made more vivid or important to you. For instance, you make yourself remember a good friend's telephone number by rehearsing it in your mind. As a long-term memory it is there for keeps, just waiting for the right cue to retrieve it.

Of course, some of us do a better job at remembering than others. One popular view is that certain people are simply born with better memories than others, but a number of psychologists doubt that heredity is the determining factor. Dr. Barbara Jones, a Massachusetts neuropsychologist, observes, "While heredity has something to do with it, it appears that there are certain personality styles that relate more specifically to memory. People who have more rigid personalities—who rely on routine, are well-organized, and aim toward gaining control of their lives—tend to have very good memories because they depend more on their knowledge of facts."

Is there a way to improve your memory? Can you make certain that essential information doesn't get dumped out of a short-term compartment in 20 seconds? The memory experts say yes.

"Association is the key," says Harry Lorayne, author of *The Memory Book*. You have to relate what you want to remember to something verbal or visual. Lorayne offers an example of how this works: Very few people can accurately remember the shape of foreign countries—except perhaps Italy. That's because most people have come to note that Italy is shaped like a boot. The shape of a boot is something already known and therefore hard to forget.

All human memory is associative. It involves connecting particular concepts, events, facts and principles and weaving them into systematic relation with each other. Enthusiasm, fear or anything which causes a heightening of perception can intensify this process of association. Your interest—or lack of it—in what you are seeing, hearing or learning can make all the difference.

Good organization can also assist your memory, just as an orderly street plan helps you to find your way to a particular corner in a city. Organization involves grouping items by categories and establishing a pattern to make remembering easier. For instance, if you start making a point of placing the car keys on the shelf near the door to the garage, you're not likely to lose track of them.

Failure to pay attention is frequently the real reason why we forget. We blame our memory for something that is really the fault of our concentration. At a party you may forget the names of people you met because during the introductions you were actually concentrating on the impression you were giving—and not the new names. Failure to pay attention is also the most common reason for absentmindedness—you may "forget" where you put your car keys because you were not paying a bit of attention when you put them down.

Certain physiological states can interfere with memory function. Anyone who has ever had too much to drink knows that the morning after it may be difficult to recollect what happened the night before. "People who are drunk are not processing information," says Dr. Laird Cermak, a professor and research psychologist. Since alcohol depresses the brain and the nervous system, it's particularly difficult to learn anything when you've been drinking.

There are also memory disorders that result from accidents, strokes and serious psychological stress. Following a severe head injury that produces a concussion, a person may experience a loss of memory known as amnesia. Such loss can cover periods ranging from a few minutes prior to an accident to weeks or even years before the injury. The more serious the injury, the greater the period of amnesia is likely to be. Occasionally amnesia is permanent, but usually the patient recovers most of the lost memories.

Perhaps the memory loss feared most by people is the one that begins to appear at the onset of old age. Psychologists agree that as we get older there is a very gradual loss of the ability to learn and to recall. As a person grows older, some brain cells die or are destroyed by minute injuries of various kinds. But the memory problems common among many older people should not be confused with senility, and it is dangerous to make general statements about the long-term functional changes which take place as a person ages. Professor Ian Hunter, author of *Memory*, says: "So much depends on the individual, his circumstances and interests, the sort of accomplishments he has acquired and whether he continues to use those accomplishments or not. Some people become old before their time while others continue to function at high levels of achievement into extreme old age."

Doctors are currently working on developing a drug that will help slow down or prevent memory loss due to age. Though there's no miracle pill yet, you can make your memory work better by using some of the techniques of association and organization mentioned above. Here are a few tricks to try:

One of the most famous systems for remembering a list of errands or objects is called the "link" method. According to Lorayne, it works like this: You link together the objects by associating the first to the second, the second to the third, the third to the fourth, and so on. You should make your associations as ridiculous or exaggerated as possible, so that you "see" them in your mind's eye. Let's say that one morning you want to remember to visit a sick friend at the hospital and pick up some postage stamps. Try picturing your friend lying under a giant stamp rather than a blanket. This image will be hard to forget.

Another good trick that will help you remember tasks that must be done is to make a physical change in your environment. This acts as a cue. For instance, Lorayne suggests that if you're worried about burning dinner while you watch TV, put a frying pan on the set to remind you that dinner's in the oven.

When you're introduced to lots of people at a party it can be hard to remember names. Make sure you hear the name when you're introduced. If you didn't get it, ask the person to repeat it. Then say the name over several times in your head. This repetition will help the name to stick.

1600 words

Write your ending time here: _____

Subtract your starting time: _____

Total time: _____

Check the Rate Chart in the back of the book to find out how many words per minute you have read, and then record your score on the Progress Chart.

Step 3: Analyze What You Read

Make Graphic Organizers

We have filled in the main points in the following outline. Go back to the reading and find each one. Some of them have been paraphrased. Write the Roman numeral from the outline in the margin of the reading next to where the point is located. Then locate the subpoints and write the capital letter from the outline next to each subpoint in the reading. Then write the subpoints in the blanks below.

How to Strengthen Your Memory Power

I. Memory is a set of mental abilities

    A. _____

    B. _____

    C. _____

II. Theory that memory causes a chemical trace in the brain

III. Function of memory divided into two categories

    A. _____

        1. _____

        2. _____

    B. _____

        1. _____

        2. _____

IV. Ways to keep short-term memories from fading out

    A. _____

    B. _____

V. People with rigid personalities remember better

VI. Ways to improve memory

    A. _____

       1. _____

         _____

       2. _____

    B. _____

       1. _____

       2. _____

VII. Reasons for forgetting

    A. _____

    B. _____

    C. _____

    D. _____

VIII. Memory tricks

    A. _____

    B. _____

    C. _____

Use your outline to fill in the idea map on the next page. Write the title in the circle. Write the Roman numeral headings in the rectangles. Write the capital letter headings in the triangles, and write the Arabic number headings in the ovals.

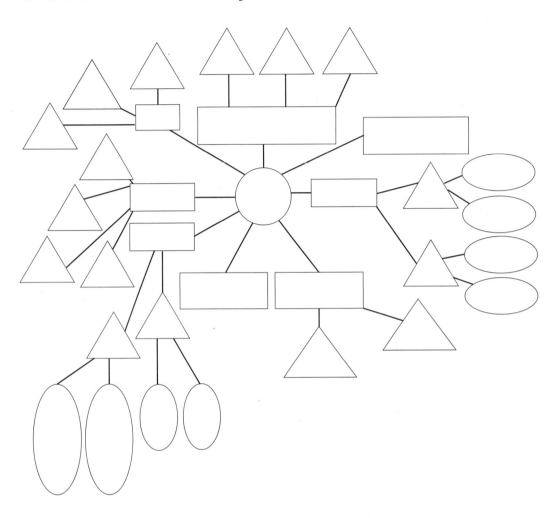

Step 4: Remember What's Important

  Test yourself on the outline or have someone test you. Keep testing until you think you can remember it.

Step 5: Make Use of What You Read

  When you are ready, complete the Comprehension Check. Do not look back at the reading.

Step 6: Evaluate Your Active Critical Thinking Skills

  After your test has been graded, answer the questions on the chart on page 465.

COMPREHENSION CHECK

Multiple Choice

Circle the letter before the best answer to each of the following questions.

1. The type of person who remembers best is
    a. brilliant.
    b. well organized.
    c. very young.
    d. a student.

2. A major reason for forgetting is
    a. low intelligence.
    b. drinking.
    c. amnesia.
    d. failure to pay attention.

3. Scientists believe that memory is
    a. electronic, like a computer.
    b. chemical.
    c. physical, like a mark or groove.
    d. all of the above.

4. Short-term memory lasts
    a. a few hours.
    b. almost forever.
    c. less than thirty seconds.
    d. about thirty minutes.

5. From the story about Albert Einstein, you can infer that he didn't have a good memory for
    a. everyday things.
    b. anything.
    c. numbers.
    d. physics.

6.   Russ implies that the best way to remember a lecture is to

   a. try to copy down everything that's said.

   b. use a tape recorder.

   c. use drugs that aid memory.

   d. repeat the key concepts over and over.

7.   Russ implies that a good way to remember material for tests would be to

   a. organize it in categories.

   b. make visual and verbal associations.

   c. repeat the facts you don't remember over and over.

   d. do all of the above.

8.   Memory experts

   a. are still learning about memory.

   b. believe that the principles of memory are based on cosmological physics.

   c. believe that long-term memories fade within a few days and cannot be retrieved.

   d. have finally identified all the chemicals involved in the memory process.

Short Answer

9.   Give an example of something you can remember using the "link" method. Use a list of at least three items.

   Item   **Mental picture**

   a. _____   _____

   b. _____   _____

   c. _____   _____

10. Give an example of something you can remember by making a physical change in your environment. Explain how the change will work as a cue.

   _____

   _____

Essay

Explain what the reading says about remembering and forgetting. Use a separate piece of paper.

VOCABULARY IN CONTEXT

Write the best word from this list in the blank in each sentence below:

cosmology   retrieval   retention   distinctive   heredity

neuropsychologist   associative   perception   physiological   senility

1. Scientists are experimenting with new "youth" drugs like Gerovital to

   prevent _____ .

2. The _____ markings on certain animals serve as a form of camouflage in their natural habitats.

3. If you were hearing the voices of invisible beings, you might go to

   a _____ .

4. _____ determines the color of our eyes.

5. No one has yet found a _____ cause for mental illness, although it has long been suspected that it is not completely psychological.

6. The _____ of game by some breeds of hunting dogs almost seems to be an inborn ability.

7. Musicians become skilled at the _____ of small differences in sound that most of us can't hear.

8. The eye's _____ of visual images enables us to see a motion picture as a flowing unit rather than as a series of separate pictures.

9. The principle of _____ memory involves relating new information to what is already known.

10. Einstein's theory on the _____ of the spatial universe is that it curves back on itself and is, therefore, infinite.

VOCABULARY REVIEW

For explanation
see pp. 10–11

Word Memory

There are four major ways to memorize new words: (1) make the word meaningful by using it in context, (2) make associations between the new word and a familiar word, (3) use word parts, and (4) use flash cards.

1. *Use the word in context.* Write sentences that make clear the meanings of the following words from this article.

    a. retention _____

    b. distinctive _____

    c. perception _____

2. *Make word associations.* In the space next to each of the following words from this article, write a familiar word that can help you remember the new one.

    a. heredity _____

    b. associative _____

    c. physiological _____

3. *Use words parts.* In the space after each word part below, write in the letter of its definition. Use the dictionary if you need help. The definitions may be used more than once.

    a. *cosmo* = _____   *logy*   = _____   **1.** state or condition of
                                                       2. again
    b. *senil* = _____   *ity*   = _____   **3.** mind
                                                       4. study of
    c. *neuro* = _____   *psycho* = _____   **5.** old
                                                       6. one who
         log   = _____   *ist*   = _____   **7.** nerve
                                                       8. find
    d. *re*   = _____   *trieve* = _____   **9.** universe

4. *Make flash cards.* Find ten words from previous readings in this book that you are having trouble remembering. On the front of a card, write the word and its pronunciation. On the back, write the definition in your own words and use the word in a sentence. Test yourself by looking at the front of the card and trying to restate the

definition and a sentence. The average person needs seven self-testing sessions to thoroughly master a new word.

Analogies

A word analogy is a puzzle in which two sets of words are compared. The two words in the first set have a relationship to each other. You have to recognize the relationship in order to fill in the blank. Analogies use the mathematical symbols :, which means *is to*, and ::, which means *as*.

easy : simple : : _____ : memory

The example reads: *easy* is to *simple* as _____
is to *memory*. You must understand the relationship between *easy* and *simple*. They are synonyms; they mean the same thing. Now look at the Vocabulary Preview for this reading. Which words fit in the blank? What is a synonym for *memory*? The answer is *retention*.

For each analogy below, write the word from the Vocabulary Preview that completes the analogy. Look back at the preview if you need help.

neuropsychologist   associative   perception

physiological   senility   cosmology   retrieval

retention   distinctive   heredity

1. relatively : absolutely : : _____ : ordinary

2. retrieval : recovery : : _____ : awareness

3. retention : forgetting : : _____ : immaturity

4. body : mind : : _____ : psychological

5. inheritance : training : : _____ : environment

7

Don't Tell Jaime Escalante Minorities Can't Meet (High) Standards!

Vocabulary Preview

barrio (bä′rē ō): A chiefly Spanish-speaking community or neighborhood in a U.S. city

Hispanic (hi span′ik): of or relating to Spain or Spanish-speaking Latin America

rigorous (rig′ər əs): strict; severe; hard

demographic (dem′ə graf′ik): having to do with the study of size, growth, density, and distribution of human populations

turmoil (tur′moil): commotion; uproar; confusion

morale (mə ral′): the state of mind of a person or group as shown by confidence, cheerfulness, and discipline

aspirations (as′pə rā′shənz): desires for achievement

cosmetology (käz′mə täl′ə jē): the work of a beautician

culminate (kul′mə nāt′): to reach the highest point or climax

skeptical (skep′ti k′l): not easily convinced; doubting; questioning

commitment (kə mit′mənt): a pledge or promise to do something

feat (fēt): a deed of unusual daring or skill

idiosyncratic (id′ē ə siŋ kra′tik): having to do with a personal peculiarity or mannerism

virtually (vur′choo wə lē): as if in effect, although not in actual fact or name

podium (pō′dē əm): an elevated platform for a lecturer or conductor

cat, āte, fäther; pen, ēvil; if, kīte; nō, ôr, fo͞od, book; boil, house; up, turn; chief, shell; thick, *the*; zh, treasure; ŋ, sing; ə for *a* in *about*; ′ as in *able* (ā′b′l)

Step 1: Preread

Preview the following selection by reading the title and the first sentence of each paragraph. The film *Stand and Deliver* was about Jaime Escalante. Answer the following questions without looking back at the reading.

1. What is the subject?

2. What is the main idea?

_____

3. Take a moment to think about what you know about minority achievement and math. Think about what you know, what you don't know, and what you might find out from reading the selection. Make up three questions.

a. _____

b. _____

c. _____

Step 2: Read

 Read the selection without underlining.

Write your starting time here: _____

Don't Tell Jaime Escalante Minorities Can't Meet (High) Standards!

DAVID SAVAGE

THE SCHOOL DAY STARTS EARLY FOR students of Jaime Escalante, mathematics teacher at Garfield High School in east Los Angeles. By 7 A.M., students from Escalante's trigonometry and calculus classes are stopping by to ask his help on a difficult problem before they head off to their other classes. Some of the students are tenth graders taking math analysis or trigonometry. Others are working on second-year, college-level calculus.

These students work on mathematics afternoons, evenings, on weekends, and, for many, during the summer at a nearby community college. Ask one of them what they think of this demanding schedule, and the likely answer is, "It's fun."

Fun? And this unexpected reaction is just the beginning of the surprises at Garfield High School.

"He makes you want to work hard. He psyches you up to do it," says Frank Quezada, a Garfield senior. "He makes mathematics fun. But you also feel guilty if you don't do the work for him."

The "he" is Escalante—a Bolivian immigrant, who over the past decade has transformed a barrio high school known more for gangs than for good grades into the city's best training ground for young mathematicians. Nearly 100 percent of Garfield's students are Hispanic. And among the 50 high schools in Los Angeles, Garfield is the leader in the number of students who take and pass the College Board's rigorous advanced placement tests in algebra and calculus.

Escalante—whose achievements with his young charges have been recognized by the California State Board of Education, *Reader's Digest* magazine, and President Reagan—succeeds through a combination of drive, inspiration, and humor. And although his success story is unique, it raises an issue that goes beyond one school and one teacher.

That issue—the most difficult one facing California—is what education officials refer to, in a code of sorts, as the "demographic problem." What it boils down to, in more direct terms, is whether minority students can be expected to meet the more rigorous standards of recent education reforms.

By the year 2000, a majority of the state's schoolchildren will be minorities—Hispanic, black, and Asian. Already, Hispanic students make up more than half of the student population in the huge Los Angeles Unified School District, the nation's second largest school system. Whether the measure is grades, test scores, or college degrees, Hispanic and black students crowd at the bottom.

According to the California Commission on Postsecondary Education, for every 1,000 Hispanic ninth graders, only 661 will be graduated from high school. Black students fare only slightly better, with 667 ending up as high school graduates.

Distressingly few of those graduates move further up the educational ladder. Among Hispanic ninth graders, only 17 of that 1,000 will end up as university graduates. The picture for blacks is nearly the same: 16 will earn university degrees.

A clue to Hispanics' and blacks' low achievement record might lie in what Jaime Escalante found when he arrived at Garfield in 1974: Low grades, low morale, and low aspirations were the norm. Failure, however, doesn't fit into Escalante's frame of reference. A decade earlier, Escalante had been a highly successful mathematics teacher in Bolivia; his student teams had won national championships. When Escalante and his wife left the country because of political turmoil, he arrived in the United States unable to speak the language of the majority and with education credentials that were not recognized in California. His first job was as a busboy in a Pasadena coffee shop.

"My English was nothing, zero, an empty set," he recalls. After taking night classes to improve his English, he earned a high-paying job with the Burroughs Corp. as a computer analyst. A high salary, however, didn't satisfy him; his true love was teaching. Escalante took a big pay cut to go to work in the Los Angeles school district. And at Garfield, he found a school where most students took one math class and quit.

"I was ready to quit, too," he says. "All they were taking were Mickey Mouse courses—cosmetology, cooking. I tell them, 'You have a great future ahead—at McDonald's cooking hamburgers.'"

Escalante set out to raise students' sights and show them that minority students can succeed in a demanding academic program. He says he "scrapped the textbooks we were using" and ordered a high-level mathematics series. He spoke to the principal, his fellow math teachers, and even teachers in Garfield's junior high feeder schools about creating a new sequence of math courses that would culminate in a senior year of advanced calculus.

Many were skeptical, and a few resisted the idea of scrapping proficiency math courses in favor of algebra, trigonometry, and calculus. But the toughest sell was the students. What they needed, he told them, was not extraordinary mathematical ability, but *ganas*—a Spanish word that loosely translated means "drive" or "desire to succeed."

Giving his students *ganas*—that is, discipline, desire, determination, and the will to work—says Escalante, is his main task in the first two weeks of the school year.

"I have a heart-to-heart talk with students. We talk about money and about success. Everyone wants to play football, be a big star. I ask them, 'How many Garfield students have become pro football players and make big money?' They don't know the answer, but I do. Zero.

"Then I tell them the money is in computers and physics and chemistry and biology. And they want you out there. But you have to speak their language first, and the language is math."

Though his classes have 50 students or more, Escalante sits down with each tenth grader and goes over a learning contract. The students and their parents must sign the contracts, committing themselves to a program of hard work in school and at home. For most, the commitment is a stiff challenge.

But Escalante has found potential among Garfield students. In May 1982, 14 of his students achieved a top score on the College Board's advanced placement examination in calculus, an extraordinary feat for such a school. The accomplishment was noticed first, however, because the Educational Testing Service (E.T.S.) questioned the scores. Examiners had noted that the students had worked problems in a similar, idiosyncratic way.

Many in the Hispanic community suspected that E.T.S. questioned the scores only because the students came from a barrio school. E.T.S. officials denied the charge.

"We followed the same procedures in this case as in any other. The graders don't know the names or schools of the papers they are grading," says Frank Romero, director of the E.T.S. office in Los Angeles.

Escalante put the controversy to rest by rounding up his students in August and having E.T.S. officials administer the test to them again. Once again, all 12 (two had already left the city) achieved passing scores on the rigorous exam, despite having virtually no time for preparation.

"It was clear that the students did know calculus. It was a credit to Mr. Escalante," said Romero.

Since then, Escalante's program—and its reputation—have grown steadily. Last year, 102 of his seniors took the advanced placement (A.P.) calculus exam, and more than three-fourths got passing grades, an achievement that will earn them a year's worth of college credit in math. This year, he has 150 students enrolled in courses to prepare for the A.P. exams. And his success has created a farm system in the junior high schools of east Los Angeles, as teachers and students upgrade to get ready for Escalante's major league program.

Escalante's high expectations, however, tell only part of the reason for his success. The rest, as with any outstanding teacher, lies in his approach to teaching. In front of his class, Escalante is part tough taskmaster and part comedian. Each class begins with a five-minute quiz. Students pick up the quizzes on their way into the room and work the problems quietly. When Escalante sounds a bell, selected students collect the papers. The teacher has yet to say a word.

But as he moves through a set of problems in rapid-fire style, Escalante the actor emerges. Under his podium, he keeps a collection of dolls and stuffed animals, each of which has a meaning to the students. He wanders through the aisles as he talks, offering a mock karate chop to those who stumble on a question. Their eyes follow him wherever he moves. He can turn suddenly and whisper an answer that can be heard throughout the small auditorium.

"You need the skill of an actor to keep their attention," he says. "You need to show that energy to attract people. The teacher also needs the patience of a doctor to show love to the kids."

1500 words

Write your ending time here: _____

Subtract your starting time: _____

Total time: _____

Check the Rate Chart in the back of the book to find how many words per minute you have read, and then record your score on the Progress Chart.

Step 3: Analyze What You Read

 Make Graphic Organizers

Fill in the following chart:

Don't Tell Jaime Escalante Minorities Can't Meet (High) Standards

Setting: (Where and when does it take place?)	
Characters: (Who is in the story?)	
Plot: (What happens in the story?)	

Theme:
(What does the story
teach us about life?)

Step 4: Remember What's Important

 Using your chart, test yourself or have someone test you on the reading. Keep testing until you think you can remember what you need to know.

Step 5: Make Use of What You Read

 When you are ready, complete the following Comprehension Check. Do not look back at the reading.

Step 6: Evaluate Your Active Critical Thinking Skills

 After your test has been graded, answer the questions on the chart on page 465.

COMPREHENSION CHECK

Multiple Choice

Circle the letter before the best answer to each of the following questions.

1. Escalante emigrated from
    a. East Los Angeles.
    b. Mexico.
    c. Bolivia.
    d. Ecuador.

2. He taught
    a. English.
    b. mathematics.
    c. both English and mathematics.
    d. only advanced calculus classes.

3. Escalante
    a. could not get any job but teaching.
    b. secured a teaching job as soon as he arrived in Los Angeles.
    c. finally got a teaching job after waiting fifteen years.
    d. had to take his teaching credentials again.

4. The students
    a. took an SAT test and failed.
    b. took an advanced calculus test but cheated.
    c. took an advanced calculus test and passed.
    d. never got to take the test because they were Hispanic.

5. An additional 150 students signed up for Escalante's high-level math courses because
    a. he walked around campus with a sign-up list.
    b. their parents insisted.
    c. they were required to do so.
    d. the other students had been so successful.

6. Jaime Escalante's students were able to succeed because

   a. he made them more intelligent.

   b. he recognized their abilities and motivated them.

   c. he restructured the classes so they were no longer difficult.

   d. they took easier versions of the Advanced Placement exams.

7. Because of their success in the math courses

   a. the students got great jobs.

   b. all Escalante's students went to college.

   c. the students increased their belief in themselves.

   d. many of his students became student teachers.

8. From the article we can infer that Jaime Escalante

   a. has a Ph.D. in child psychology.

   b. is a good lecturer.

   c. has children of his own.

   d. hates the American school system.

Short Answer

9. How did Jaime Escalante give his students *ganas*?

_____

10. Why do you think Escalante has his students and their parents sign a learning contract?

_____

_____

Essay

Explain the story "Don't Tell Jaime Escalante Minorities Can't Meet (High) Standards!" as if you were telling it to someone who had not heard it before.

_____

_____

_____

_____

_____

_____

_____

_____

_____

_____

_____

_____

_____

_____

VOCABULARY IN CONTEXT

Write the best word from this list in the blank in each sentence below.

barrio   Hispanic   rigorous   demographic   morale

aspirations   turmoil   cosmetology   culminates   skeptical

commitment   feat   idiosyncratic   virtual   podium

1. Military boot camp includes a very _____ physical training program.

2. The teacher was _____ about whether or not Susan's dog had really eaten her homework.

3. When people get married they make a _____ to honor and respect each other.

4. The heavy rains in Malibu caused mud slides that brought traffic to

   a _____ standstill.

5. People's _____ are often based on what they think they deserve; someone who doesn't think much of himself will not try for a challenging career.

6. Famous _____ artists include Goya and Velázquez from Spain, and Rivera and Orozco from Mexico.

7. Working for bonuses and other prizes helps to increase employees'

    _____ .

8. Rolling over and over while balancing a ball on the nose would be quite a

    _____ for a human, but it's not too hard for a seal.

9. The government of the Soviet Union was in _____ as the individual republics broke away.

10. A great baseball team's season _____ in playing in the World Series.

11. Students who learn _____ make people more beautiful than they were before.

12. Many _____ habits become irritating to others.

13. When a speaker wants to add emphasis, he might pound on

    the _____ he's standing behind.

14. There's often a strong sense of community among Mexican American families

    living in the _____ .

15. The amount of money given to a state by the federal government is often

    determined by _____ studies.

VOCABULARY SKILLS REVIEW

Parts of Speech

For each word below, write the part of speech. Then change it to the new part of speech. Write a sentence using the new word. Use a dictionary if you need help.

Word	Part of Speech	New Part of Speech	New Word
1. rigorous	_____	noun	_____

Sentence _____

_____

| **2.** commitment | _____ | verb | _____ |

Sentence _____

_____

| **3.** virtually | _____ | adjective | _____ |

Sentence _____

_____

| **4.** idiosyncratic | _____ | noun | _____ |

Sentence _____

_____

| **5.** skeptical | _____ | adverb | _____ |

Sentence _____

_____

Analogies

Write the word from the Vocabulary Preview that completes each analogy below.

1. mock : fake : : _____ : strict

2. minority : majority : : _____ : peace

3. huge : tiny : : _____ : sure

4. extraordinary : average : : _____ : begin

5. aspirations: goals : : _____ : pledge

8

Over-the-Counter Addictions

Vocabulary Preview

exert (ig zʉrt′): to put into action

withdrawal (with drôl′): the body's negative mental and physical reactions when a person stops using an addictive drug

substance (sub′stəns): a drug, especially one whose use is regulated by law

pharmacologist (färm′ə käl′ə gist): a scientist dealing with the effect of drugs on living organisms

cold turkey (kōld tʉr′kē): (slang) the abrupt and total stopped usage of a drug by an addict

stimulant (stim′yə lənt): something that rouses or excites to activity or increased activity

psychic (sī′kik): concerning the mind; psychological; mental

die-hard (dī′härd′): a person stubbornly resistant to new ideas, reform, and so on

aftermath (af′tər math′): a result, especially an unpleasant one; aftereffect

abruptly (ə brupt′lē): suddenly; unexpectedly

agitation (aj′ə tā′shən): disturbance or excitement caused by emotional or physical factors

tolerance (täl′ər əns): the natural or developed ability to resist the effects of the continued or increasing use of a drug

binging (binj′iŋ): doing something excessively

bulimia (bə lē′mē ə): an eating disorder characterized by binging and forcing oneself to eliminate large amounts of food

degenerate (di jen′ə rāt′): to lose former, normal, or higher qualities; to decline

generic (jə ner′ik): medication or other product that doesn't have a trademark

tout (tout): to claim to be of great worth; praise

chronic (krän′ik): lasting a long time or coming back often: said of a disease; continuing indefinitely; habitually

habitual (hə bich′oo wəl): much seen, done, or used: usual; done or acquired by habit

plague (plāg): to harrass; trouble; torment

cat, āte, fäther; pen, ēvil; if, kīte; nō, ôr, fo͞od, book; boil, house; up, tʉrn; chief, shell; thick, *the*; zh, treasure; ŋ, sing; ə for *a* in *about*; ' as in *able* (ā′b'l)

Step 1: Preread

 Preview the following selection by reading the title and all the headings. Answer the following questions without looking back at the reading.

1. What is the subject?

    _____

2. What is the main idea?

    _____

3. Take a moment to think about addiction to over-the-counter drugs. Think about what you know, what you don't know, and what you might find out from reading the selection. Make up three questions.

    a. _____

    b. _____

    c. _____

Step 2: Read

 Read the selection without underlining.

Write your starting time here: _____

Over-the-Counter Addictions

Jean Laird

ARE YOU A JUNKIE? MILLIONS ARE AND don't realize it. These innocent addicts are hooked on many of the same remedies you'll find sitting in your medicine chest. Here's how to protect your family.

It Can Happen to Anyone

Most folks wouldn't dream of ignoring the directions that come with a prescription medicine. Yet we adopt a dangerously casual attitude regarding over-the-counter (OTC) drugs. "How dangerous can they be," we reason, "when even a child can buy them?"

In fact, OTC remedies like laxatives and sleeping aids are still drugs, and they exert a powerful effect on our bodies. Used properly, these products are safe and usually very effective. However, when they are misused, these same drugs can turn on us. Even though they might not make you "high," some OTC drugs can be powerfully addicting.

"If you experience physical or psychological withdrawal symptoms after you stop using a substance," notes Joe Graedon, pharmacologist and author, "then you are addicted." The problems connected with these addictions can prove far more hazardous than the ailment you are trying to treat.

Here's how to help you and your family stay on friendly terms with OTC drugs, and what to do when you find yourself or a loved one addicted.

Sleeping Pills

OTC sleep aids are approved by the FDA "for occasional use only." By taking them for an extended period—more than two weeks—you risk becoming dependent on them, warns Gerald Rachanow, deputy director of the FDA's Division of Over-the-Counter Drugs.

These products are actually antihistamines, an allergy medication that causes sleepiness as a side effect. Long-term use of these products can make it difficult to fall asleep without them.

Kicking the Habit

Quit cold turkey, even if that means a few nights of restless sleep. Moderate daily exercise is a natural sleep inducer; avoid caffeine (it's in chocolate and some soft drinks, as well as in coffee and tea) and stimulant medicines (check the label). If your sleep problems persist for more than two weeks, see your doctor.

Diet Pills

Especially popular with teenage girls, OTC diet pills are a $110-million-a-year business. These products do not directly cause weight loss. Instead, they are supposed to reduce appetite, making it easier to stick to a sensible, reduced-calorie diet. Although there is some evidence that these products decrease appetite, they remain controversial. Right in the middle of the diet-aid controversy is phenylpropanolamine (PPA), the active ingredient in many top-selling products. Research indicates that for about one-third of people, PPA causes a temporary increase in blood pressure. Healthy individuals can weather the increase without danger; people with high blood pressure face a much greater risk.

Dr. Michael H. M. Dykes also warns that diet-pill users risk "psychic dependence and other undesirable side effects." Use these products only as long as weight loss continues without side effects (fluttering heart, dizziness, and nausea) and without the need for higher doses, usually four to six weeks.

Kicking the Habit

If you have been taking OTC diet pills for longer than six weeks—or if you experience any side effects—stop using these products immediately. Otherwise, you can safely taper off.

Stimulants

Most die-hard coffee lovers are familiar with the unpleasant aftermath of quitting their brew abruptly. Headaches and agitation are common withdrawal symptoms. The offending agent, caffeine, is also the active ingredient in most OTC stay-awake products. Stop taking these pills abruptly and you'll likely experience the same symptoms.

What's more, according to psychologist Dr. Steven Levy, author of *Managing the Drugs in Your Life,* the body develops a tolerance for caffeine, requiring more and more to get the same stimulating effect. The bigger your caffeine habit, the worse the withdrawal symptoms you will experience.

Kicking the Habit

Most experts recommend tapering off the pills and avoiding other sources of caffeine.

Laxatives

Even with clear warnings on the packages that "frequent or continued use may result in dependency," laxatives are among the most widely abused OTC drugs. The most tragic abusers are young people—mostly women—who use laxatives in a misguided attempt to maintain their weight while binging on high-calorie foods. This practice, called bulimia, can cause severe illness or even death.

Most laxative abusers, however, began taking the products for good reason, but just didn't know when to stop. These folks soon discovered the unpleasant facts of laxative abuse.

Dr. Marvin M. Schuster, gastroenterologist at Johns Hopkins School of Medicine, says the most habit-forming laxatives contain phenolphthalein. This chemical works by irritating the nerves that cause intestinal muscles to contract. "Eventually," Dr. Schuster warns, "these nerve cells can permanently degenerate. The intestine actually becomes partially paralyzed, making constipation worse than it was before you took the laxatives."

Kicking the Habit

Dr. Schuster advises using a bulk-type laxative, which works more naturally than the stimulant types containing phenolphthalein. Common brand names of bulk-type laxatives include Fiberall and Metamucil; or look for less expensive generic and store brands containing psyllium fiber.

Eye Drops

Some eye drops—notably those that tout their ability to reduce redness—contain drugs that constrict the blood vessels in the eyes, which makes the eyes appear whiter. Using eye drops occasionally is safe. However, using these products for more than three days only makes the redness worse. You may find you are having to use them every few hours. Cutting back leaves your eyes redder than they started out.

Kicking the Habit

The best way is to taper off. If you are really worried about chronic eye redness, see a doctor.

Nasal Sprays

Habitual users of nasal spray often find it is very difficult to stop. That's why instructions on nasal sprays warn against use for more than three days. If you get addicted, you'll find you can't breathe through your nose without them; congestion, sneezing, and a runny nose may plague you constantly.

How to Kick the Habit

To wean yourself from nasal spray addiction, Dr. C. Edwin Webb, pharmacist and Director of Professional Affairs of the American Pharmaceutical Association, advises switching from long-lasting, 12-hour brands of spray to short-acting forms, then going on to children's formula, decreasing the number of uses of each product as you go along.

1000 words

Write your ending time here: _____

Subtract your starting time: _____

Total time: _____

Check the Rate Chart in the back of the book to find out how many words per minute you have read and then record your score on the Progress Chart.

Step 3: Analyze What You Read

 Make Graphic Organizers
Fill in the chart.

Type of Drug	Risks	How to Kick the Habit
1.		
2.		
3.		
4.		
5.		
6.		

Step 4: Remember What's Important

 Test yourself or have someone test you on the chart until you think you can remember it.

Step 5: Make Use of What You Read

 When you are ready, complete the Comprehension Check. Do not look back at the reading or the chart.

Step 6: Evaluate Your Active Critical Thinking Skills

 After your test has been graded, answer the questions on the chart on page 465.

COMPREHENSION CHECK

Multiple Choice

Circle the letter before the best answer to each of the following questions.

1. "OTC" stands for
   a. once-toxic chemicals.
   b. the government agency that regulates drugs.
   c. overly taken chemicals.
   d. over-the-counter.

2. The ingredient in sleeping pills that causes sleepiness is actually
   a. an appetite depresser.
   b. an antidepressant.
   c. an allergy medication.
   d. poisonous.

3. Diet pills
   a. are usually effective.
   b. are especially popular with teenage girls.
   c. directly cause weight loss.
   d. contain a form of cocaine.

4. Long-term use of laxatives can result in
   a. heart attacks.
   b. loss of appetite.
   c. an increase in blood pressure.
   d. partial paralysis of the intestine.

5. You can infer from the reading that
   a. the author wants these drugs taken off the market.
   b. the author feels that most people don't realize how dangerous these drugs can be.
   c. doctors should prescribe all sleeping medications.
   d. people should not buy over-the-counter drugs because they are too dangerous.

6. The author implies that

    a. it is easy to stop using over-the-counter medication.

    b. you should see a doctor before using over-the-counter drugs.

    c. people are more careless with over-the-counter drugs than with prescribed medication.

    d. all of the above are true.

7. The over-the-counter addicts

    a. are usually teenagers.

    b. often don't recognize they have a problem.

    c. usually die from the addiction because they can't stop.

    d. will usually become prescription or illegal drug addicts.

8. You can infer from the article that

    a. people can rarely recognize the side effects of these drugs.

    b. some people have personalities that lead to these addictive behaviors.

    c. we can safely use over-the-counter drugs if we follow the instructions.

    d. the drug companies are legally responsible for the problem.

Short Answer

9. Why should you read the labels on OTC medications?

    _____

    _____

10. Give an example of abuse of an OTC drug.

    _____

    _____

Essay

Discuss at least five over-the-counter drugs that can have dangerous side effects. Explain how to break a dependency on them.

_____

_____

_____

_____

_____

_____

_____

_____

VOCABULARY IN CONTEXT

Write the best word from this list in the blank in each sentence below.

Part A

exert   cold turkey   psychic   aftermath   abruptly

agitation   binging   touted   chronic   plague

1. Experts often say that _____ television viewing is harmful to the mental development of children.

2. Migraine headaches _____ millions of people.

3. The car stopped _____ when the driver saw the young child running into the street.

4. In the _____ of an earthquake, it is important to have previously stored food, water, and medical supplies.

5. Wearing garlic around the neck was once _____ as a way to ward off evil spirits.

6. Constant _____ on your favorite foods might indicate an eating disorder.

7. Many alcoholics find that rather than cutting down on their drinking, the only

    way they can stop is by quitting _____ .

8. Some people develop such a _____ dependence on television
    soap operas that they must watch them every day.

9. In some ways friends _____ a more powerful influence on
    teenagers than parents do.

10. Worries can keep us in such a state of _____ that it is difficult to
    sleep.

Part B

withdrawal   pharmacologists   bulimia   generic   habitual

degenerates   tolerance   substance   die-hard   stimulants

11. Most people's hearing _____ as they become older.

12. Teenagers are often criticized for their _____ talking on the
    telephone.

13. After years of use, most people build up a _____ to coffee,
    cigarettes, or even prescribed medications, requiring a greater amount to
    achieve the same effect.

14. Because the nicotine in cigarettes causes people to become addicted, heavy

    smokers who try to stop smoking experience _____ symptoms.

15. _____ abusers can come from all age groups and economic
    backgrounds.

16. Many college students use _____ such as No-Doz so that they
    can study late into the night.

17. A _____ Republican will never vote for a Democratic candidate.

18. _____ are only now finding out about the damaging effects of
    secondhand smoke on nonsmokers' lungs.

19. _____ is a serious eating disorder more commonly suffered by
    teenage girls than other people.

20. _____ aspirin can be bought at a drug store for less money than the name-brand equivalent.

VOCABULARY REVIEW

Word Memory

1. Word Associations: In the space next to each of the following words from the reading, write a familiar word that can help you remember the new one.

a. generic _____

b. habitual _____

c. aftermath _____

d. pharmacologist _____

2. Word Parts: On the line after each word part below, write in the number of its definition. Use the dictionary if you need help. The definitions may be used more than once.

a. *chron*	= _____	*ic*	= _____	**1.**	drug
				2.	time
b. *psych*	= _____	*ic*	= _____	**3.**	one who
				4.	from
c. *gener*	= _____	*ic*	= _____	**5.**	origin, race
				6.	to become
d. *de*	= _____	*gener* = _____		**7.**	mind
ate	= _____			**8.**	having to do with
e. *pharmaco* = _____		*log*	= _____	**9.**	science
ist	= _____				

3. Make flash cards. Find ten words from any of your classes that you are having trouble remembering. On the front of the card write the word and its pronunciation. On the back, write the definition in your own words and use the word in a sentence. Test yourself by looking at the front of the card and trying to restate the definition and a sentence. Refer to sample flash cards on page 11.

Analogies

Write the word from the following list that best completes each analogy.

degenerate   **abruptly**   **chronic**   **psychic**   **agitated**

1. plague : torment : : _____ : mental

2. tout : praise : : _____ : suddenly

3. binging : starving : : _____ : calm

4. stimulant : depressant : : _____ : improve

5. tolerance : resistance : : _____ : habitual

9

Improving Test-Taking Strategies

Vocabulary Preview

format (fôr′mat): general arrangement or plan

cognitive (käg′nə tiv): having to do with thinking, knowing, remembering

adage (ad′ij): an old saying

empirical (em pir′i kəl): based on practical experience rather than theory

explicit (eks plis′it): clearly stated; leaving nothing implied

implausible (im plô′zə bəl): not likely to be true

generalization (jen′ər əl i zā′shən): a general, unspeciic idea, statement, etc.

vigilant (vij′ə lənt): watchful; alert

assertion (ə sʉr′shən): positive statement; declaration

concise (kən sīs′): brief and to the point; short and clear

cat, āte, fäther; pen, ēvil; if, kīte; nō, ôr, fōōd, book; boil, house; up, turn; chief, shell; thick, *the*; zh, treasure; ŋ, sing; ə for *a* in *about*; ' as in *able* (ā′b'l)

Step I: Preread

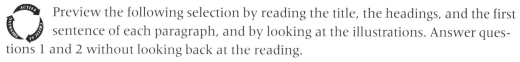 Preview the following selection by reading the title, the headings, and the first sentence of each paragraph, and by looking at the illustrations. Answer questions 1 and 2 without looking back at the reading.

1. What is the subject?

2. What is the main idea?

3. Look at Figures 1 and 2 and read the captions.

   a. What is the subject of Figure 1?

b. What is the main idea of Figure 1?

_____

c. What is the subject of Figure 2?

_____

d. What is the main idea of Figure 2?

_____

e. What inference can you make from Figures 1 and 2?

_____

4. Take a moment to think about test-taking strategies. Think about what you know, what you don't know, and what you might find out from reading the selection. Make up three questions.

a. _____

b. _____

c. _____

Step 2: Read

Read the selection without underlining.

Write your starting time here: _____

Improving Test-Taking Strategies

Wayne Weiten

L ET'S FACE IT—SOME STUDENTS ARE better than others at taking tests. *Testwiseness* is the ability to use the characteristics and format of a cognitive test to maximize one's score. Students clearly vary in testwiseness, and such variations are reflected in performance on exams. Testwiseness is not a substitute for knowledge of the subject matter. However, skill in taking tests can help you show what you know when it is critical to do so.

A number of myths exist about the best way to take tests. For instance, it is widely believed that students shouldn't go back and change their answers to multiple-choice questions. Benjamin, Cavell, and Shallenberger (1984) found this to be the dominant belief among college faculty as well as students (see Figure 1). However, the old adage that "your first hunch is your best hunch on tests" has been shown to be wrong. Empirical studies clearly and consistently indicate that, over the long run, changing answers pays off. Benjamin and his colleagues reviewed 20 studies on this issue; their findings are presented in Figure 2. As you can see, answer changes that go from a wrong answer to a right answer outnumber changes that go from a right answer to a wrong one by a sizable margin. The popular belief that answer changing is harmful is probably attributable to painful memories of right-to-wrong changes. In any case, you can see how it pays to be familiar with sound test-taking strategies.

General Tips

- If efficient time use appears crucial, set up a mental schedule for progressing through the test. Make a mental note to check whether you're one-third finished when a third of your time is gone.

- Don't waste time pondering difficult-to-answer questions excessively. If you have no idea at all, just guess and go on. If you need to devote a good deal of time to the question, skip it and mark it so you can return to it later if time permits.

- Adopt the appropriate level of sophistication for the test. Don't read things into questions. Sometimes students make things more complex than they were intended to be. Often, simple-looking questions are just what they appear to be.

- Unless it is explicitly forbidden, don't hesitate to ask the examiner to clarify a question when necessary. Many examiners will graciously provide a great deal of useful information.

FIGURE 1 Beliefs about the effects of answer changing on tests. Benjamin et al. asked 58 college faculty whether changing answers on tests is a good idea. Like most students, the majority of the faculty felt that answer changing usually hurts a student's test score, even though the evidence contradicts this belief (see Figure 2).

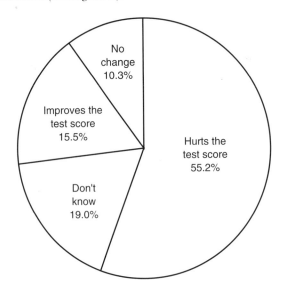

- If you complete all of the questions and still have some time remaining, review the test. Make sure that you have recorded your answers correctly. If you were unsure of some answers, go back and reconsider them.

Tips for Multiple-Choice Exams

Sound test-taking strategies are especially important with multiple-choice (and true-false) questions. These types of questions often include clues that may help you converge on the correct answer. You may be able to improve your performance on such tests by considering the following advice:

- As you read the stem of each multiple-choice question, anticipate the answer if you can, before looking at the options. If the answer you anticipated is among the options, it is likely to be the correct one.

- Always read each question completely. Continue reading even if you find your anticipated answer among the options. There may be a more complete option farther down the list.

- Learn how to quickly eliminate options that are highly implausible. Many questions have only two plausible options, accompanied by "throwaway" options for filler. You should work at spotting these implausible options so that you can quickly discard them and narrow your task.

Figure 2 Actual effects of changing answers on multiple-choice tests. When the data from all the relevant studies are combined, they indicate that answer changing on tests generally does not reduce students' test scores. It is interesting to note the contrast between beliefs about answer changing (see Figure 1) and the actual results of this practice.

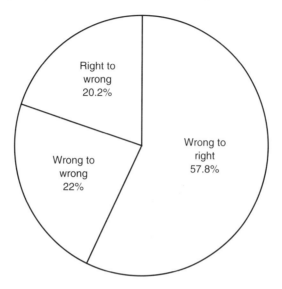

- Be alert to the fact that information relevant to one question is sometimes given away in another test item.

- On items that have "all of the above" as an option, if you know that just two of the options are correct, you should choose "all of the above." If you are confident that one of the options is incorrect, you should eliminate this option and "all of the above" and choose from the remaining options.

- Options that represent broad, sweeping generalizations tend to be incorrect. You should be vigilant for words such as *always, never, necessarily, only, must, completely, totally,* and so forth that create those improbable assertions.

- In contrast, options that represent carefully qualified statements tend to be correct. Words such as *often, sometimes, perhaps, may,* and *generally* tend to show up in these well-qualified statements.

Tips for Essay Exams

There is little research on testwiseness as it applies to essay exams. This is because there are relatively few clues to take advantage of in the essay format. Nonetheless, various books offer tips based on expert advice, including the following:

- Time is usually a crucial factor on essay tests. Therefore, you should begin by looking over the questions and making time allocations on the basis of (1) your knowledge, (2) the time required to answer each question, and (3) the points available for answering each question. Usually it's a good idea to answer the questions that you know best first.

- Many students fail to appreciate the importance of good organization in their essay responses. If your instructor can't follow where you are going with your answers, you won't get many points. Test essays are often poorly organized because students feel pressured for time and plunge into answering questions without any planning. It's a good idea to spend a minute getting organized first. Also, many examiners appreciate it if you make your organization quite explicit by using headings or by numbering the points you're making.

- In writing essays, the trick is to be concise while being complete. You should always try to get right to the point, and you should never pad your answer. Many examiners get cross when they have to wade through excess padding to track down the crucial ideas they're looking for. However, you should avoid writing in such a "shorthand" manner that you leave things ambiguous.

- In many courses you'll learn a great deal of jargon or technical terminology. Demonstrate your learning by using this technical vocabulary in your essay answers.

1000 words

Write your ending time here: _____

Subtract your starting time: _____

Total time: _____

Check the Rate Chart in the back of the book to find out how many words per minute you have read and then record your score on the Progress Chart.

Step 3: Analyze What You Read

Make Graphic Organizers

Fill in the following outline:

Improving Test-Taking Strategies

I. General tips

    A. _____

    B. _____

    C. _____

    D. _____

    E. _____

II. Tips for multiple-choice exams

    A. _____

    B. _____

    C. _____

    D. _____

          _____

    E. _____

          _____

    F. _____

    G. _____

III. Tips for essay exams

    A. _____

          _____

    B. _____

    C. _____

    D. _____

Use the outline to fill in the idea map below. Write the title in the circle. Write the Roman numeral headings in the rectangles. Write the capital letter headings in the triangles.

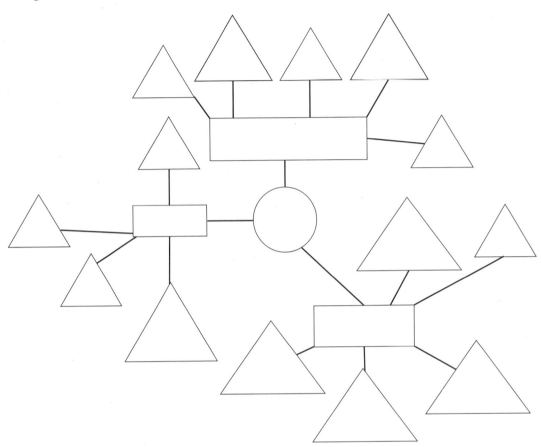

Step 4: Remember What's Important

 Test yourself or have someone test you on the outline until you think you can remember it.

Step 5: Make Use of What You Read

 When you are ready, complete the Comprehension Check. Do not look back at the reading or the outline.

Step 6: Evaluate Your Active Critical Thinking Skills

 After your test has been graded, answer the questions on the chart on page 465.

COMPREHENSION CHECK

True-False

Mark T or F.

_____ **1.** Students shouldn't go back and change their answers.

_____ **2.** Your essay answers will be better if you write using a graphic organizer.

_____ **3.** You should look over a test as a first step so that you can make time allocations.

_____ **4.** On a multiple-choice question, you should eliminate incorrect options first.

_____ **5.** The author implies that, unless there is a penalty for guessing, you should not leave any questions unanswered.

Multiple Choice

Circle the letter before the best answer to each of the following questions.

6. One tip that objective and essay tests have in common is

   a. use technical vocabulary.

   b. eliminate implausible options.

   c. organize your answers.

   d. budget your time.

7. You can infer that

   a. very few things are always true or always false.

   b. your first hunch on a test is your best hunch.

   c. you should be on the lookout for "trick" questions.

   d. all of the above are true.

8. You can infer that

   a. testwise people still have to study.

   b. testwiseness can be learned.

   c. students who are testwise get better grades than those who are not.

   d. all of the above are true.

Short Answer

9. Give a definition of testwiseness.

   _____

10. How should you allocate your time during a test?

   _____

   _____

Essay

1. List some tips for taking multiple-choice tests.

2. List some tips for taking essay tests.

_____

_____

_____

_____

_____

_____

_____

_____

_____

_____

_____

_____

_____

_____

_____

_____

_____

VOCABULARY IN CONTEXT

Write the best word from this list in the blank in each sentence below.

format   cognitive   adage   empirical   explicit

implausible   generalization   vigilant   assertions   concise

1. "A penny saved is a penny earned" is an _____ .

2. "Asians are good in math" is a _____ that is only sometimes true.

3. Instructors appreciate written work that is _____ , so they don't have to spend time wading through meaningless or repetitive words in order to find the point.

4. If you want people to be able to follow your directions, you should be
   very _____ ; leave nothing open to interpretation.

5. The traditional _____ of a newspaper article is the "inverted pyramid"; the most important information is at the top, and the details are underneath.

6. Jurors have to weigh the evidence that points to guilt against the defendant's
   _____ of innocence.

7. Some people find it _____ that anyone other than O. J. Simpson had a motive to kill his ex-wife.

8. Being a good parent has _____ as well as emotional aspects; while you have to love your kids, you also have to know something about child rearing.

9. "Neighborhood watch" programs require that neighbors be
   _____ and report anything that looks suspicious.

10. We have only _____ evidence about some medicines; we know they work for some ailments, but we don't know why.

VOCABULARY REVIEW

Dictionary: Confused Words

Here are dictionary entries for three pairs of words that are commonly confused. Fill in the blanks with the correct word from the pair that precedes each group of sentences.

af•fect[1] (ə fekt′; *for* n. 2, af′ekt′) *vt.* [ME *af-fecten* < L *affectare*, to strive after < *affec-tus*, pp. of *afficere*, to influence, attack < *ad-*, to + *facere*, DO[1]] **1.** to have an effect on; influence; produce a change in [bright light *affects* the eyes] **2.** to move or stir the emotions of [his death *affected* us deeply] – *n.* **1.** [Obs.] a disposition or tendency **2.** [Ger *affekt* < L *affectus*, state of mind or body: see the *v.*] *Psychol.* a) an emotion or feeling attached to an idea, object, etc. b) in general, emotion or emotional response –**af•fect′able** *adj.* SYN. –**affect** implies the producing of an effect strong enough to evoke a reac-tion; to **influence** is to affect in such a way as to produce a change in action, thought, nature, or behavior [to *influ-ence* legislation]; **impress** is used of that which produces a deep or lasting effect on the mind; **touch** and the stronger **move**, as considered here, are both ap-plied to the arousing of emotion, sym-pathy, etc., but **move** also denotes an influencing so as to effect a change; **sway** emphasizes an influencing in-tended to turn a person from a given course [threats will not *sway* us]

ef•fect (e fekt′, i-; *often* ē-, ə-) *n.* [ME < OFr (& L) < L *effectus*, orig., pp. of *efficere*, to bring to pass, accomplish < *ex-*, out + *facere*, DO[1]] **1.** anything brought about by a cause or agent; result **2.** the power or ability to bring about results; efficacy [a law of little *effect*] **3.** influence or ac-tion on something [the drug had a ca-thartic *effect*] **4.** general meaning; purport [he spoke to this *effect*] **5.** a) the impression produced on the mind of the observer or hearer, as by artistic design or manner of speaking, acting, etc. [to do something just for *effect*] b) some-thing, as a design, aspect of nature, etc., that produces a particular impression [striking cloud *effects*] c) a scientific phe-nomenon [the Doppler *effect*] **6.** the condition or fact of being operative or in force [the law goes into *effect* today] **7.** [*pl.*] belongings; property [household *effects*] – *vt.* to bring about; produce as a result; cause; accomplish [to *effect* a compromise] –**give effect to** to put into practice; make operative –**in effect 1.** in result; actually; in fact **2.** in essence; virtually **3.** in operation; in force –**take effect** to begin to produce results; be-come operative –**to the effect** with the purport or meaning –**ef•fect′er** *n.*

1. The film had a powerful _____ on its viewers.

2. Her _____ seemed strange; she laughed when most people would have cried.

3. Some say that garlic has an antibiotic _____ .

4. Career and family decisions that we make as young adults can

_____ the rest of our lives.

5. It will take about thirty minutes until the drug takes _____ .

prin·ci·pal (prin′sə pəl) *adj.* [OFr < L *principalis* < *princeps:* see PRINCE] **1.** first in rank, authority, importance, degree, etc. **2.** that is or has to do with PRINCIPAL (*n.* 3) – *n.* **1.** a principal person or thing; specif., *a*) a chief; head *b*) a governing or presiding officer, specif. of a school *c*) a main actor or performer *d*) either of the combatants in a duel **2.** *a*) any of the main end rafters of a roof, supporting the purlins *b*) a roof truss **3.** *Finance a*) the amount of a debt, investment, etc. minus the interest, or on which interest is computed *b*) the face value of a stock or bond *c*) the main body of an estate, etc., as distinguished from income **4.** *Law a*) a person who employs another to act as his agent *b*) the person primarily responsible for an obligation *c*) a person who commits a crime or is present as an abettor to it (cf. ACCESSORY) **5.** *Music a*) any of the principal open stops of an organ *b*) the soloist in a concert *c*) the first player of any section of orchestral instruments except the first violins *d*) the subject of a fugue (opposed to ANSWER) –*SYN.* CHIEF –**prin′ci·pally** *adv.* –**prin′ci·pal·ship′** *n.*

prin·ci·ple (prin′sə pəl) *n.* [ME, altered < MFr *principe* < *principium:* see prec.] **1.** the ultimate source, origin, or cause of something **2.** a natural or original tendency, faculty, or endowment **3.** a fundamental truth, law, doctrine, or motivating force, upon which others are based [moral *principles*] **4.** *a*) a rule of conduct, esp. of right conduct *b*) such rules collectively *c*) adherence to them; integrity, uprightness [a man of *principle*] **5.** an essential element, constituent, or quality, esp. one that produces a specific effect [the active *principle* of a medicine] **6.** *a*) the scientific law that explains a natural action [the *principle* of cell division] *b*) the method of a thing's operation [the *principle* of a gasoline engine is internal combustion] –**in principle** theoretically or in essence –**on principle** because of or according to a principle

1. When you have extra money you can use it to reduce your mortgage

_____ .

2. Even though I would have profited by the deal, I rejected it

on _____ .

3. The most basic moral _____ is to treat other people the way you would want to be treated.

4. When you sell a house, you are the _____ , and the real estate broker is your agent.

5. A high school _____ is an administrator.

phase (fāz) *n.* [ModL. *phasis* < Gr. *phasis* < *phainesthai,* to appear, akin to *phainein:* see FANTASY] **1.** any of the recurring stages of variation in the illumination and apparent shape of the moon or a planet **2.** any of the stages or forms in any series or cycle of changes, as in development **3.** any of the ways in which something may be observed, considered, or presented; aspect; side; part [a problem with many *phases*] **4.** *Chem.* a solid, liquid, or gaseous homogeneous form existing as a distinct part in a heterogeneous system [ice is a *phase* of H_2O] **5.** *Physics* the fractional part of a cycle through which a periodic wave, as of light, sound, etc., has advanced at any instant, measured from an arbitrary starting point or assumed moment of starting **6.** *Zool.* any of the characteristic variations in color of the skin, fur, plumage, etc. of an animal, according to season, age, etc. –*vt.* **phased, phas'ing 1.** to plan, introduce, carry out, etc. in phases, or stages (often with *in, into,* etc.) **2.** to put in phase –*vi.* to move by phases –**in** (or **out of**) **phase** in (or not in) a state of exactly parallel movements, oscillations, etc.; in (or not in) synchronization –☆ **phase out** to bring or come to an end, or withdraw from use, by stages –**pha•sic** (fā'zik) *adj.* *SYN.* –**phase** applies to any of the ways in which something may be observed, considered, or presented, and often refers to a stage in development in a cycle of changes, etc. [the *phases* of the moon]

faze (fāz) *vt.* **fazed, faz'ing** [var. of FEEZE] to disturb; disconcert –*SYN.* EMBARRASS

1. I hope my daughter's selfish behavior is just a _____ she's going through.

2. The larval _____ is part of the development of a butterfly.

3. She was able to be a nonconformist because the disapproval of other people didn't _____ her.

4. The waxing crescent is one _____ of the moon; the others are first quarter, waxing gibbous, full moon, waning gibbous, last quarter, and waning crescent.

5. Because teenagers are so self-conscious, the slightest criticism can

    _____ them.

Pronunciation Practice

Following are 10 words from Reading 11 in Unit III. Match each word with the correct pronunciation. Write the letter before each word in the space before the pronunciation. Use your dictionary if you need help.

_____ **1.** sut'l

_____ **2.** dis kresh'ən ər'ē

_____ **3.** ən sə fis'tə kā tid

_____ **4.** tur'mə nāt

_____ **5.** di sēt'fəl

_____ **6.** səb vur'siv

_____ **7.** ə kyoom'yə lāt

_____ **8.** un wer'ē

_____ **9.** ô'dē ō fīl

_____ **10.** frô'jə lənt

a. unwary
b. accumulate
c. subversive
d. discretionary
e. unsophisticated
f. deceitful
g. fraudulent
h. subtle
i. terminate
j. audiophile

cat, āte, fäther; pen, ēvil; if, kīte; nō, ôr, food, book; boil, house; up, turn; chief, shell; thick, *the*; zh, treasure; ŋ, sing; ə for *a* in *about*; ' as in *able* (ā'b'l)

10

Improving Coping and Stress Management

Vocabulary Preview

rational (ra′shən əl): based on reasoning

catastrophic (kat′ə strä′fik): having to do with disaster, calamity, or great misfortune

sequence (sē′kwəns): the following of one thing after another in order

premise (prem′is): a previous statement that serves as the basis for a conclusion

pessimism (pes′ə miz′əm): the tendency to expect the worst outcome in any situation

recede (ri sēd′): to go or move back

discharge (dis chärj′): to release

strategy (strat′ə jē): plan of action

cardiologist (kär dē äl′ə jist): a doctor who specializes in the heart

vulnerability (vul′nər ə bil′ə tē): the state of being open to injury or disease

cat, āte, fäther; pen, ēvil; if, kīte; nō, ôr, food, book; boil, house; up, turn; chief, shell; thick, *the*; zh, treasure; ŋ, sing; ə for *a* in *about*; ′ as in *able* (a′b′l)

Step 1: Preread

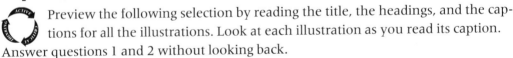
Preview the following selection by reading the title, the headings, and the captions for all the illustrations. Look at each illustration as you read its caption. Answer questions 1 and 2 without looking back.

1. What is the subject?

_____

2. What is the main idea?

_____

3. Look at Table 1.

    a. What is the subject?

   b. What is the main idea?

   c. Which coping strategy seems to be the healthiest?

   d. Which seems the unhealthiest?

4. Look at Figure 1.

   a. What is the subject?

   b. What is the main idea?

5. Look at Figure 2.

   a. What is the subject?

   b. What is the main idea?

6. Look at Figure 3.

   a. What is the subject?

   b. What is the main idea?

7. Look at Figure 4.

    a. What is the subject?

    _____

    b. What is the main idea?

    _____

8. Take a moment to think about stress. Think about what you know, what you don't know, and what you might find out from reading the selection. Make up three questions.

    a. _____

    b. _____

    c. _____

Step 2: Read

Read the selection without underlining.

Write your starting time here: _____

Improving Coping and Stress Management

Wayne Weiten

COURSES AND BOOKS ON STRESS MANAGEMENT have multiplied at a furious pace in the last ten years. The experts seem to agree that the key to managing stress does *not* lie in avoiding it. Stress is inevitable in modern life. Although researchers have tended to focus on the negative effects of stress, studies have shown that stress can also lead to personal growth and self-improvement. Thus, most stress-management programs encourage people to confront stress rather than try to avoid it. These programs train people in action-oriented, rational, reality-based *constructive coping.*

People cope with stress in different ways. Some researchers have sorted people's coping tactics into fourteen categories, which are listed in Table 1. They compared each person's coping strategies with personality factors, such as self-esteem and anxiety. They found that some coping patterns were associated with high self-esteem and low anxiety. In other words, some coping patterns are healthier than others. We will examine several constructive coping tactics, beginning with Albert Ellis's ideas.

Reappraisal: Ellis's Rational Thinking

Albert Ellis is a well-known psychologist. He believes that people can change their emotional reactions to stress by changing how they view stressful events. This idea is the basis for his widely used system of therapy called *rational-emotive therapy.* In this approach the psychologist works to change the client's patterns of thinking in order to change emotions and behavior.

According to Ellis, you feel the way you think. He argues that negative emotional reactions are caused by negative self-talk, which he calls *catastrophic thinking.* Catastrophic thinking means that you evaluate stress in ways that exaggerate your problems. Ellis uses a simple A-B-C sequence to explain his ideas (see Figure 1).

A: *Activating Event.* The A in Ellis's system stands for the activating event that produces the stress. The activating event may be any stressful situation. Examples might include an automobile accident, a canceled date, a delay waiting in line at the bank, or a failure to get a promotion at work.

B: *Belief System.* B stands for your belief about the event. According to Ellis, people often view minor setbacks as disasters. Thus, they engage in catastrophic thinking: "This is awful! I can't stand it! Things never turn out right for me! I'll never get promoted!"

C: *Consequence.* C stands for the consequences of your negative thinking. When you view stressful events as more negative than they are, you have emotional distress. Thus, people feel angry, outraged, anxious, panic-stricken, disgusted, or depressed.

Table 1
Types of Coping Strategies

Coping Strategy	Example	Correlation with Self-Esteem	Correlation with Anxiety
Active coping	I take additional action to try to get rid of the problem.	.27*	−.25*
Planning	I try to come up with a strategy about what to do.	.22*	−.15
Suppression of competing activities	I put aside other activities in order to concentrate on this.	.07	−.10
Restraint coping	I force myself to wait for the right time to do something.	−.03	−.19*
Seeking social support for instrumental reasons	I ask people who have had similar experiences what they did.	.12	.01
Seeking social support for emotional reasons	I talk to someone about how I feel.	.06	.14
Positive reinterpretation and growth	I look for something good in what is happening.	.16*	−.25*
Acceptance	I learn to live with it.	.12	−.15
Turning to religion	I seek God's help.	−.06	.11
Focus on and venting of emotions	I get upset and let my emotions out.	−.01	.36*
Denial	I refuse to believe that it has happened.	−.28*	.35*
Behavioral disengagement	I give up the attempt to get what I want.	−.31*	.37*
Mental disengagement	I turn to work or other substitute activities to take my mind off things.	−.08	.21*
Alcohol-drug disengagement	I drink alcohol or take drugs in order to think about it less.	−.11	.11

*Statistically significant.

Figure 1 Albert Ellis's A-B-C model of emotional reactions. Although most people are prone to attribute their negative emotional reactions directly to events, Ellis argues that people *feel* the way they *think*.

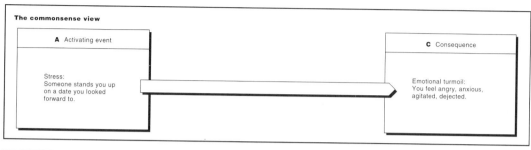

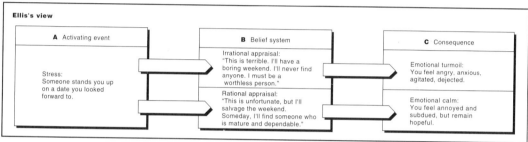

Ellis says that most people don't understand the importance of phase B in this three-stage sequence. They think that the activating event (A) causes the emotional turmoil (C). Ellis maintains that A does *not* cause C. One's emotional distress is actually caused by the catastrophic thinking.

According to Ellis, people often make mountains out of molehills. For instance, imagine that someone stands you up on a date. You might think, "This is terrible. I'm going to have another rotten, boring weekend. People always mistreat me. I'm never going to find anyone to fall in love with. I must be a crummy, worthless person." Ellis would argue that such thoughts are irrational. He would point out that it is not logical to think that, just because you were stood up, (1) you must have a lousy weekend, (2) you will never fall in love, and (3) you are a worthless person.

Ellis argues that much stress comes from irrational beliefs. He says that if you examine your catastrophic thinking, you'll find that your reasoning is based on an illogical premise, such as "I must have approval from everyone" or "I must do well at everything." These unconscious beliefs cause catastrophic thinking and emotional stress. Irrational beliefs that are especially common are described in Figure 2.

How can you reduce your unnecessary stress? Ellis says that you must learn (1) how to recognize catastrophic thinking and (2) how to counteract the irrational beliefs that cause it. You must learn how to spot unrealistic pessimism and wild exaggeration in

Figure 2 Irrational assumptions that can cause and sustain emotional disturbance. Assumptions such as these are often held unconsciously, and one may have to work at detecting them before one can change to a more positive way of thinking.

	Irrational assumption	Rational alternative
1	I must be loved or approved by everyone for everything I do.	It's best to concentrate on my own self-respect, on winning approval for practical purposes, and on loving rather than being loved.
2	I must be thoroughly competent, adequate, and achieving in order to be worthwhile.	I'm an imperfect creature who has limitations and fallibilities like anyone else—and that's okay.
3	It's horrible when things aren't going the way I'd like them to be.	I can try to change or control the things that disturb me—or temporarily accept conditions I can't change.
4	There isn't much I can do about my sorrows and disturbances, because unhappiness comes from what happens to you.	I *feel* how I *think*. Unhappiness comes mostly from how I look at things.
5	If something is dangerous or fearsome, I'm right to be terribly upset about it and to dwell on the possibility of its occurring.	I can frankly face what I fear and either render it nondangerous or accept the inevitable.
6	It's easier to avoid facing difficulties and responsibilities than to face them.	The "easy way out" is invariably the much harder alternative in the long run.
7	I'm dependent on others and need someone stronger than I am to rely on.	It's better to take the risk of relying on myself and thinking and acting independently.
8	There's always a precise and perfect solution to human problems, and it's catastrophic not to find it.	The world is full of probability and chance, and I can enjoy life even though there isn't always an ideal solution to a problem.
9	The world—especially other people—should be fair, and justice (or mercy) must triumph.	I can work toward seeking fair behavior, realizing that there are few absolutes in life.
10	I must not question the beliefs held by society or respected authorities.	It's better to evaluate beliefs for myself—on their own merits, not on who happens to hold them.

your thinking. Examine your self-talk closely. Ask yourself why you're getting upset. Force yourself to put your concerns into words, silently or out loud. Look for key words that often show up in catastrophic thinking, such as *should, ought, never,* and *must.*

Counteracting your irrational beliefs means examining your entire reasoning process. Try to root out the beliefs that lead to stressful conclusions. Once the premises are found, their irrationality may be quite obvious. If your beliefs seem reasonable, ask yourself whether your conclusions follow logically. Try to replace your catastrophic thinking with lower-key, more rational analyses. These strategies should help you redefine stressful situations in ways that are less threatening. Strangely enough, another way to make stressful situations less threatening is to turn to humor.

Humor as a Stress Reducer

A few years ago, the Chicago area experienced its worst flooding in about a century. Thousands of people saw their homes wrecked when two rivers spilled over their banks. As the waters receded, the flood victims returning to their homes were subjected to the inevitable TV interviews. A remarkable number of victims, surrounded by the ruins of their homes, *joked* about their misfortune. When the going gets tough, it may pay to laugh about it.

Researchers believe that finding something funny in a stressful situation makes the situation less threatening. Laughter can also serve to discharge pent-up emotions. These two functions of humor may make joking about life's problems a useful coping strategy. Apparently a good sense of humor reduces stress.

Releasing Pent-Up Emotions

No matter how hard you try to reduce stress, there will still be times you can't. When this happens, you should try to release the feelings. The reason is that the physical symptoms that accompany emotions can become problematic. For example, one study of high school students found that those who held in their anger tended to have higher blood pressure. Sometimes you can reduce your physical symptoms by *expressing* your emotions. The key, of course is to express your emotions in a mature and socially acceptable manner. This is particularly important when the emotion is anger.

"Talking it out" can be valuable in dealing with stress. Research indicates that talking or writing about traumatic events can be helpful. For example, in one study of college students, half were asked to write three essays about their problems in adjusting to college. The other half wrote three essays about other topics. Those who wrote about their personal problems enjoyed better health in the following months than the other group did. Thus, if you can find a good listener, you may be able to discharge emotions by talking about your fears, misgivings, and suspicions.

Learning to Relax

Relaxation is a stress-management technique that can soothe the emotions and reduce physical symptoms. One study even suggests that relaxation training may improve the immune response.

Herbert Benson is a Harvard Medical School cardiologist who studied the effects of meditation. According to Benson, the religious aspects of meditation do not account for its beneficial effects. He believes that what is beneficial is the relaxation that occurs. He devised a procedure called the *relaxation response*. Benson studied several relaxation techniques and concluded that there are four important factors.

1. *A quiet environment.* It's easiest to relax when there are few distractions. After you are experienced with the relaxation response, you may be able to practice it on a crowded bus. At first, however, you should practice in a quiet, calm place.

2. *A mental device.* To shift attention inward and keep it there, you need to focus attention on something. It could be a sound or a word that you keep repeating.

3. *A passive attitude.* It's important not to get upset when your attention wanders. You must understand that distractions are inevitable. When your mind wanders, *calmly* bring it back to your mental device.

4. *A comfortable position.* If you are uncomfortable, your mind will wander. Simply sitting up straight usually works. Lying down usually causes you to fall asleep.

Benson's simple relaxation procedure is described in Figure 3. For full benefit, it should be practiced every day.

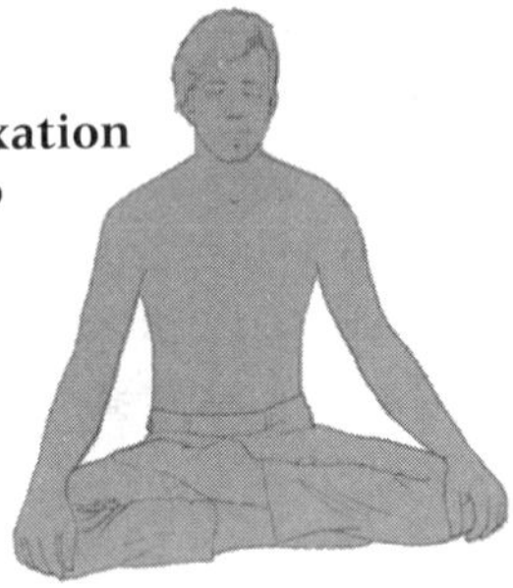

**Figure 3
Benson's relaxation
procedure.** To
benefit from
the procedure,
you should
practice it
daily.

1 Sit quietly in a comfortable position.

2 Close your eyes.

3 Deeply relax all your muscles, beginning at your feet and progressing up to your face. Keep them relaxed.

4   Breathe through your nose. Become aware of your breathing. As you breathe out, say the word "one" silently to yourself. For example, breathe in . . . out, "one"; in . . . out, "one"; and so forth. Breathe easily and naturally.

5   Continue for 10 to 20 minutes. You may open your eyes to check the time, but do not use an alarm. When you finish, sit quietly for several minutes, at first with your eyes closed and later with your eyes opened. Do not stand up for a few minutes.

6   Do not worry about whether you are successful in achieving a deep level of relaxation. Maintain a passive attitude and permit relaxation to occur at its own pace. When distracting thoughts occur, try to ignore them by not dwelling on them, and return to repeating "one." With practice, the response should come with little effort. Practice the technique once or twice daily but not within two hours after any meal, since digestive processes seem to interfere with the elicitation of the relaxation response.

Minimizing Physiological Vulnerability

Your body is involved in your response to stress, and the wear and tear of stress can damage your health. Therefore, it's important to keep your body in good shape. You should eat a balanced diet, get enough sleep, and exercise moderately. It's also a good idea to learn how to control overeating and the use of tobacco, alcohol, and other drugs. Doing these things will not prevent stress, but not doing them may make you vulnerable to stress-related diseases.

Even a moderate amount of exercise—such as taking a brisk, half-hour walk each day—can reduce your risk of disease (see Figure 4). Exercise can also improve your mood and your ability to deal with stress. For example, one study found that regular exercise led to a decline in depression and anxiety in a study of older adults (ages 50–65).

Starting an exercise program is hard for many people. Exercise takes time, and if you're out of shape it may be painful and discouraging. Here are some recommendations:

1. Select an activity that you enjoy.

2. Gradually increase your activity.

3. Exercise regularly but don't overdo.

4. Reward yourself for your efforts.

If you choose a competitive sport, such as basketball or tennis, don't fall into the competition trap. If you become too involved with winning, you'll put pressure on yourself and *add* to the stress in your life.

Figure 4 Physical fitness and mortality. Blair and colleagues studied death rates among men and women who exhibited low, medium, or high fitness. As you can see, fitness was associated with lower mortality rates in both sexes.

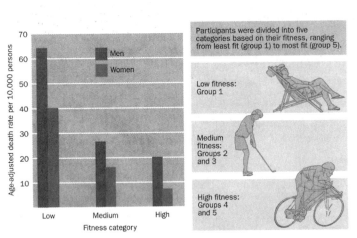

1600 words

Write your ending time here: _____

Subtract your starting time: _____

Total time: _____

Check the rate chart in the back of the book to find out how many words per minute you have read and then record your score on the Progress Chart.

Step 3: Analyze What You Read

 Make Graphic Organizers

Fill in the following concept map:

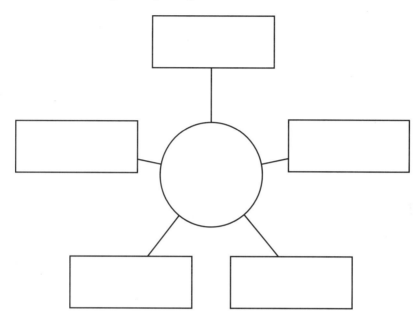

Step 4: Remember What's Important

 Test yourself or have someone test you on the concept map until you think you can remember it.

Step 5: Make Use of What You Read

 When you are ready, complete the Comprehension Check. Do not look back at the reading or the outline.

Step 6: Evaluate Your Active Critical Thinking Skills

 After your test has been graded, answer the questions on the chart on p. 465.

COMPREHENSION CHECK

True-False

Mark T or F.

_____ **1.** Constructive coping means learning to avoid stress.

_____ **2.** According to Ellis, an activating event causes emotional turmoil.

_____ **3.** The author implies that the best way to deal with stress is to always express your emotions.

_____ **4.** The relaxation response involves using a mental device.

_____ **5.** One function of humor is to discharge pent-up emotions.

Multiple Choice

Circle the letter before the best answer to each of the following questions.

6. Rational-emotive therapy involves

   a. releasing pent-up emotions.

   b. discharging feelings through humor.

   c. changing irrational beliefs.

   d. learning the relaxation response.

7. The reason the author gives for releasing pent-up emotions is that

   a. emotions are accompanied by physical symptoms.

   b. your personal relationships are improved by talking.

   c. self-esteem is increased by getting emotional support.

   d. all of the above are true.

8. The relaxation response is based on

   a. exercise.

   b. religion.

   c. discharging emotions.

   d. meditation.

Short Answer

9. For what is Albert Ellis mentioned in this reading?

    _____

10. For what is the Harvard Medical School cardiologist mentioned?

    _____

    _____

Essay

Describe the methods of stress management that were discussed in the reading.

_____

_____

_____

_____

_____

_____

_____

_____

_____

_____

_____

_____

VOCABULARY IN CONTEXT

Write the best word from this list in the blank in each sentence below.

rational   catastrophic   sequence   premise   pessimist
recede   discharge   strategy   cardiologist   vulnerability

1. One aspect of getting along with people is learning to _____ your feelings in ways that others will accept.

2. The _____ I use to get moving in the morning is to take a shower as soon as I wake up.

3. If you feel pain in your chest, you should see a _____ .

4. _____ behavior means behaving in ways that will help you achieve your goals.

5. A _____ sees the glass as half empty instead of half full.

6. In middle age many men find their hairlines starting to _____ .

7. Names in the telephone directory are in alphabetical _____ .

8. Getting a chill is supposed to increase _____ to colds and flu.

9. The conclusion that students who failed the test didn't study is based on the _____ that the test covered the assigned material.

10. Attacking your employer can have _____ results.

VOCABULARY REVIEW

Dictionary: Confused Words

The following ten pairs of words are often confused. Fill in the blanks with the correct word from the pair that precedes each group of sentences.

com•ple•ment (käm′plə mənt; *for v.*, -ment′) *n.* [ME < L *complementum*, that which fills up or completes < *complere:* see COMPLETE] **1.** that which completes or brings to perfection **2.** the amount or number needed to fill or complete **3.** a complete set; entirety **4.** something added to complete a whole; either of two parts that complete each other **5.** *Gram.* a word or group of words that, with the verb, completes the meaning and syntactic structure of the predicate (Ex.: *foreman* in "make him foreman," *paid* in "he expects to get paid") **6.** *Immunology* any of a group of proteins in the blood plasma that act with specific antibodies to destroy corresponding antigens, as bacteria or foreign proteins **7.** *Math. a)* the number of degrees that must be added to a given angle or arc to make it equal 90 degrees *b)* the subset which must be added to any even subset to yield the original set **8.** *Music* the difference between a given interval and the complete octave **9.** *Naut.* all of a ship's personnel, including the officers, required to operate a ship –*vt.* to make complete; be a complement to

com•pli•ment (käm′plə mənt; *for v.*, -ment′) *n.* [Fr < It *complimento* < Sp *cumplimiento* < *cumplir*, to fill up < VL **complire*, for L *complere*, to COMPLETE] **1.** a formal act or expression of courtesy or respect **2.** something said in admiration, praise, or flattery **3.** courteous greetings; respects *[send with our *compliments]* **4.** [Now Chiefly Dial.] a gift given for services; tip –*vt.* **1.** to pay a compliment to; congratulate **2.** to present something to (a person) as an act of politeness or respect

1. John and Martha _____ each other; her personality is outgoing and emotional, while his is quiet and thoughtful.

2. Most people feel good when you give them a _____ .

al•lu•sion (ə lōō′zhən, a-) *n.* [LL *allusio*, a playing with < *allusus*, pp. of *alludere:* see ALLUDE] **1.** the act of alluding **2.** an indirect reference; casual mention

il•lu•sion (i lōō′zhən) *n.* [ME *illusioun* < OFr *illusion* < L *illusio*, a mocking (in LL(Ec), deceit, illusion) < *illusus*, pp. of *illudere*, to mock, play with < *in-*, on + *ludere*, to play: see LUDICROUS] **1.** a false idea or conception; belief or opinion not in accord with the facts **2.** an unreal, deceptive, or misleading appearance or image [a large mirror giving the *illusion* of space in a small room] **3.** *a*) a false perception, conception, or interpretation of what one sees, where one is, etc. *b*) the misleading image resulting in such a false impression **4.** HALLUCINATION **5.** a delicate, gauzy silk tulle used for veils, etc. –*SYN.* DELUSION –**il•lu′sion•al** or **il•lu′sion•ar′y** *adj.*
il•lu•sion•ism (-iz′əm) *n.* the use of illusions in art –**il•lu′sion•is′tic** *adj.*

1. A mirage is an optical _____ .

2. The character in the play made an _____ to Shakespeare.

loath (lōth, lō*th*) *adj.* [ME *loth* < OE *lath*, hostile, hateful, akin to Ger *leid*, sorrow (orig. *adj.*) < IE base **leit-*, to detest, abhor > Gr *aleitēs*, sinner] unwilling, reluctant: usually followed by an infinitive [to be *loath* to depart] –*SYN.* RELUCTANT –**nothing loath** not reluctant(ly); willing(ly) –**loath′ness** *n.*

loathe (lō*th*) *vt.* **loathed, loath′ing** [ME *lothen* < OE *lathian*, to be hateful < base of *lath*: see prec.] to feel intense dislike, disgust, or hatred for; abhor, detest –*SYN.* HATE –**loath′er** *n.*

1. I am _____ to get injections.

2. I _____ spiders.

cite (sīt) *vt.* **cit'ed, cit'ing** [ME *citen* < OFr *citer*, to summon < L *citare*, to arouse, summon < *ciere*, to put into motion, rouse < IE base **kei-* > Gr *kinein*, to move, OE *hatan*, to command] **1.** to summon to appear before a court of law **2.** to quote (a passage, book, speech, writer, etc.) **3.** to refer to or mention as by way of example, proof, or precedent ☆**4.** to mention in a CITATION (sense 5) **5.** [Archaic] to stir to action; arouse –*n* [Colloq.] CITATION (sense 3) –**cit'able** or **cite'able** *adj.*

site (sīt) *n.* [ME < L *situs*, position, situation < pp. of *sinere*, to put down, permit, allow < IE base **sei-*, to cast out, let fall: see SIDE] **1.** a piece of land considered from the standpoint of its use for some specified purpose /a good *site* for a town/ **2.** the place where something is, was, or is to be; location or scene /the *site* of a battle/ –*vt.* **sit'ed, sit'ing** to locate or position on a site

1. If you break a traffic law, the police may _____ you.

2. The usual _____ for a fortified castle was at the top of a hill.

elic•it (ē lis'it, i-) *vt.* [< L *elicitus*, pp. or *elicere*, to draw out < *e-*, out + *lacere*, to entice, akin to *laqueus:* see LACE] **1.** to draw forth; evoke /to *elicit* an angry reply/ **2.** to cause to be revealed /to *elicit* facts/ –SYN. EXTRACT –**elic'it•able** *adj.* –**elic'i•ta'tion** *n.* –**elic'i•tor** *n.*

il•lic•it (il lis'it, i lis'-) *adj.* [Fr *illicite* < L *illicitus*, not allowed: see IN-² & LICIT] not allowed by law, custom, rule, etc.; unlawful; improper; prohibited; unauthorized –**il•lic'it•ly** *adv.* –**il•lic'it•ness** *n.*

1. The teacher tried to _____ the students' opinions.

2. Cocaine is an _____ drug.

aes•thet•ic (es thet'ik) *adj.* [Gr *aisthētikos*, sensitive < *aisthanesthai*, to perceive < IE base **awis-* > L *audire*, to hear] **1.** of or in relation to aesthetics **2.** of beauty **3.** sensitive to art and beauty; showing good taste; artistic Also **aes•thet'i•cal** –*n.* an aesthetic theory or viewpoint

as•cet•ic (ə set'ic) *adj.* [Gr(Ec) *askētikos*, austere < Gr, laborious, exercised < *askein*, to exercise, train (for athletic competition)] of or characteristic of ascetics or asceticism; self-denying; austere Also **as•cet'i•cal** –*n.* [< Gr *awkētēs*, monk, hermit] **1.** a person who leads a life of contemplation and rigorous self-denial for religious purposes **2.** anyone who lives with strict self-discipline and without the usual pleasures and comforts –SYN. SEVERE –**as•cet'i•cal•ly** *adv.*

1. A yogi who lives in a cave is an _____ .

2. Most people agree that Rembrandt's paintings have great _____ value.

em·i·nent (em'ə nənt) *adj.* [ME < L *emi-nens:* see EMINENCE] **1.** rising above other things or places; high; lofty **2.** projecting; prominent; protruding **3.** standing high by comparison with others, as in rank or achievement; renowned; exalted; distinguished **4.** outstanding; remarkable; noteworthy [*a man of eminent courage*] –*SYN.* FAMOUS –**em'i·nent·ly** *adv.*

im·mi·nent (im'ə nənt) *adj.* [L *imminens,* prp. of *imminere,* to project over, threaten < *in-,* on + *minere,* to project: see MENACE] likely to happen without delay; impending; threatening: said of danger, evil, misfortune –**im'mi·nent·ly** *adv.*

1. Sigmund Freud was an _____ psychologist.

2. The next election is _____ .

flaunt (flônt) *vi.* [15th & 16th c., prob. < dial. *flant,* to strut coquettishly, akin to Norw *flanta* < ON *flana,* run back and forth < IE **plano-* < base **pla-,* broad, flat, spread out > Gr *planos,* wandering] **1.** to make a gaudy, ostentatious, conspicuous, impudent, or defiant display **2.** to flutter or wave freely –*vt.* **1.** to show off proudly, defiantly, or impudently [to *flaunt* one's guilt] **2.** FLOUT: usage objected to by many –*n.* [Archaic] the act of flaunting –*SYN.* SHOW –**flaunt'ingly** *adv.*

flout (flout) *vt.* [prob. special use of ME *flouten,* to play the flute, hence, whistle (at)] to mock or scoff at; show scorn or contempt for –*vi.* to be scornful; show contempt; jeer; scoff –*n.* a scornful or contemptuous action or speech; mockery; scoffing; insult –**flout'er** *n.* –**flout'-ing·ly** *adv.*

1. Actresses and models are often asked to _____ their sex appeal.

2. Old-style beatniks and hippies were people who liked to _____ conventional values.

hoard (hōrd) *n.* [ME *hord* < OE, akin to Ger *hort*, Goth *huzd* < IE **keus-* < base **(s)keu-*, to cover, conceal > HIDE[1], Gr *skylos*, animal's skin] a supply stored up and hidden or kept in reserve *–vi.* to get and store away money, goods, etc. *–vt.* to accumulate and hide or keep in reserve *–***hoard'er** *n.* *–***hoard'ing** *n.*

horde (hōrd) *n.* [Fr < Ger, earlier *horda* < Pol < Turk *ordū*, a camp < Tat *urdu*, a camp, lit., something erected < *urmak*, to pitch (a camp)] **1.** a nomadic tribe or clan of Mongols **2.** any wandering tribe or group **3.** a large, moving crowd or throng; swarm *–vt.* **hord'ed, hord'ing** to form or gather in a horde *–SYN.* CROWD[1]

1. A whole _____ of customers showed up at the garage sale.

2. Misers like to _____ their wealth.

li·able (lī'ə bəl; *often, esp. for 3*, lī'bəl) *adj.* [prob. via Anglo-Fr < OFr *lier*, to bind < L *ligare*, to bind (see LIGATURE) + -ABLE] **1.** legally bound or obligated, as to make good any loss or damage that occurs in a transaction; responsible **2.** likely to have, suffer from, etc.; exposed to or subject to [*liable* to heart attacks] **3.** subject to the possibility of; likely (*to* do, have, get, etc. something unpleasant or unwanted) [*liable* to cause hard feelings] *–SYN.* LIKELY

li·bel (lī'bəl) *n.* [ME, little book < OFr < L *libellus*, little book, writing, lampoon, dim. of *liber*, a book: see LIBRARY] **1.** any false and malicious written or printed statement, or any sign, picture, or effigy, tending to expose a person to public ridicule, hatred, or contempt or to injure a person's reputation in any way **2.** the act of publishing or displaying publicly such a thing **3.** anything that gives an unflattering or damaging picture of the subject with which it is dealing **4.** in ecclesiastical law and formerly in maritime law, a written statement containing the plaintiff's grievances; initial pleading *–vt.* **-beled** or **-belled, -bel·ing** or **-bel·ling 1.** to publish or make a libel against **2.** to give an unflattering or damaging picture of **3.** to bring suit against by presenting a LIBEL (*n.* 4)

1. If you start false rumors about someone, you can be sued for

   _____ .

2. If you don't turn in assignments, you are _____ to fail the class.

Pronunciation

Following are ten words from Reading 11 in Unit III. Match each word with the correct pronunciation. Write the letter before each word in the space before the pronunciation.

_____ **1.** in dīt′id

_____ **2.** in sid′ē əs

_____ **3.** ploi

_____ **4.** pyoo′nə tiv

_____ **5.** void′id

_____ **6.** pʉr′pə trāt′id

_____ **7.** trô′ma′tik

_____ **8.** trumpt up′

_____ **9.** dē fek′tiv

_____ **10.** kän′sə lā′shən prīz

a. ploy
b. consolation prize
c. insidious
d. perpetrated
e. traumatic
f. voided
g. trumped up
h. indicted
i. defective
j. punitive

cat, āte, fäther; pen, ēvil; if, kīte; nō, ôr, food, book; boil, house; up, turn; chief, shell; thick, _the_; zh, treasure; ŋ, sing; ə for _a_ in _about_; ' as in _able_ (a′b′l)

UNIT III

Using ACT for Study

Good students use a study system. A study system does three things. First, it helps you figure out what will be on a test so that you know what to study. Second, it gives you a way to study that leads to success. Third, it takes as little time as possible. The six-step ACT system accomplishes all three purposes.

STEP 1: PREREAD

As you remember from Unit II, prereading increases your comprehension in two ways. First, it sets up mental categories to increase comprehension. In psychology, these categories are called *advance organizers*. Second, the process of activating your background knowledge and generating questions sets the stage for active rather than passive reading.

Prereading Textbooks

When you first buy your books, take five or ten minutes to preview each one. First, look at the front matter: author, title, date of publication, table of contents, preface, foreword, or introduction. Second, look at the back matter: is there a glossary, appendix, index, bibliography? Then flip through the book, noting its organization. Are there chapter objectives or outlines, chapter summaries, review questions at the ends of the chapters? Are there clear headings? Are there many illustrations? This preview lets you know what is in the book and how it is organized. It also lets you know whether there are any study aids.

Prereading Chapters

When a chapter is assigned, take a few minutes to preview it before reading. Read the chapter title, the outline if there is one, and all the headings and subheadings. If there are illustrations, read the caption of each one and try to figure out the main idea by looking at the illustration. Read the summary or review questions at the end of the chapter, if they are included. This preview will give you an overview of all the main ideas in the chapter, and it will increase your comprehension, memory, and speed.

Next, take a moment to activate your mind. Think about what you know and don't know about the topic. Make up some questions that you think might be answered by the reading.

STEP 2: READ

If the chapter is long, break it into logical sections. Use the headings as guides to the sections. Take the first section and read *with your pencil down*. Do not underline or highlight at this point. Just try to understand what you are reading and find answers to your questions. There are several things you can do if you find material you don't understand. First, mark what you don't understand. Then look for an explanation. You can ask your instructor in class or during his or her office hours. You can ask other students. You can also find books, tapes, or computer programs that cover the same subject using different explanations and/or different examples. Sometimes, especially in math, the problem isn't really that you don't understand it. It's that you just need more practice. So, for example, if you have problems with percentages, find an extra textbook or workbook that you can use to get the practice you need. The same goes for grammar or any other subject that requires practice. One way or another, do what you need to make sure you understand the material.

STEP 3: ANALYZE WHAT YOU READ—CREATE A STUDY GUIDE

First, find out whatever you can about the test. You can ask the instructor which chapters and lectures will be covered, how much time you will have, and the number and types of questions. There are four different types of test questions: objective, essay, application, and problem solving. The study guide you create will depend on the type. You can also ask other students who have taken the class about the tests. If you can obtain copies of old tests, so much the better.

Second, you must predict the questions. This may sound hard to do, but it really isn't. Put yourself in the instructor's place. What you (the instructor) really want to do is find out who learned the material and who didn't so you can assign grades. You hope the students do well on the test, because that means you did a good job teaching them. Therefore, most instructors will test the students on the most important material and skip what is less important.

Review both the text and the lecture notes. Pay attention to the topics your instructor stressed in class. Let's say the test will cover five chapters and will have fifty objective items (true-false, multiple choice, matching, and or completion/short answer). The test will probably cover the fifty most obvious items. If you pick the seventy most obvious items to memorize, you will probably get an A. If the test will have five essay questions, and you pick the ten most obvious ones to memorize, you should score very well.

Study Guide for Objective Tests

Underline   Let's say you have just finished reading the first section of a chapter as described in Step 2. Look it over, thinking about what is likely to be on the test and which of those things you might have trouble remembering. Underline or highlight *only those things*. Do not underline too much. The purpose of underlining is quick review for tests. If you underline too much, you will defeat your purpose.

Make Marginal Notes   In the margin, next to each idea you have underlined, write a note that you can use to test your memory. Don't write a summary. Write something you can use as a question. Another way of thinking about it is to consider the marginal note as the subject and the underlining as the main idea. Look at this example:

It is convenient to distinguish three main types of insomnia.   *3 types of*
People with onset insomnia have trouble falling asleep. Those   *insomnia*
with termination insomnia awaken early and cannot get back to
sleep. Those with maintenance insomnia awaken frequently
during the night, though they get back to sleep each time. (From
James Kalat, *Introduction to Psychology,* 3rd Ed. Brooks/Cole, 1993,
p. 193.)

Notice that the marginal note doesn't give a definition. It only lets you test your memory.

Flash Cards   Instead of, or in addition to, marking in your book, you can use flash cards. On the front of the flash card, write what you *would* have put in the margin (the subject). On the back write what you would have underlined (the main idea). Here is an example:

Front	Back
3 types *of insomnia*	1. *Onset insomnia* 2. *Termination insomnia* 3. *Maintenance insomnia*

Flash cards can easily be carried in a pocket or purse. One secret of successful study is to use small bits of time instead of waiting until you have a few hours free. For example, while you are eating lunch alone, standing in line, or riding the bus, you could be memorizing your flash cards. Look at the topic on the front, and test yourself to see if you remember what's on the back. If you get your memorization done in advance, you won't have much to worry about just before the exam.

Study Guide for Essay Tests

Essay questions are broader and more general than most objective questions. Therefore, you will have to look for important ideas rather than details when you predict the questions.

After you have predicted the questions, you have to put the answers in a form that can be memorized. This means making up pictures, or *graphic organizers*. A graphic organizer can be an outline, a study map, a chart, a time line, or whatever other visual format you can think of. They are just like the ones you already used in Unit II. You can put them on flash cards or paper, depending on the amount of room you need. Put the subject on the front and the graphic organizer on the back. If your graphic organizers are small enough to carry with you, you can use them like flash cards to take advantage of small bits of time you would otherwise waste.

Study Guide for Problem-Solving or Application Exams

Problem-solving tests often occur in mathematics and science courses. Application tests occur when you have to *use* what you've learned, as in foreign languages or music. In either case, try to predict the types of problems or performance that will be tested. Then make a plan to make sure you get enough practice to reach the level of mastery you need. For example, if you know the test will cover decimals, schedule enough time to practice decimals until you feel confident. If the test requires swimming the backstroke, schedule the number of practice sessions you will need.

Some tests require more than one type of preparation. For example, a Spanish test might require memorization of flash cards for vocabulary and grammar. It might also require application; it could test your reading or listening comprehension or your speaking ability in Spanish. Many classes have both objective and essay questions on tests. Also, some objective questions can test application or problem-solving ability. Here are some examples:

True or false: The product of 2 and 2 is 4. **(True)**

Multiple choice:
   Which of the following is a complete sentence?

   a.   Hurry up!

   b.   Having a good day.

   c.   Jimmy and his brother.

   d.   All of the above are complete sentences. **(The answer is a.)**

Learning Style

During your years in school, you probably liked some subjects better than others. The ones you liked were probably easier for you. Part of the reason is your learning style. For example, some people understand the logic of mathematics and science. Others enjoy the creativity of literature or art. Some people find it easy to memorize facts, but they hate to write essays. Others enjoy expressing themselves in words, but they hate to memorize. Some learn best from reading; they understand things better when they see them. Others learn best from lectures and discussions; they learn better from hearing.

Just as you have a learning style, each of your instructors also has a teaching style. Some prepare well-organized lectures and assignments. Others come to class without notes and teach through informal discussion. Some give tests that focus on memorizing facts. Others give tests that require you to analyze information and draw conclusions.

You will probably have little trouble when your learning style matches your instructor's teaching style. You are more likely to have problems when there is a mismatch. One of the best things you can do in that case is join a study group with people whose learning styles are more like the instructor's. For example, let's say you are studying for a history exam that will require analysis, and you have trouble with analysis. Try to find other students who can help you predict questions. Then you can make your graphic organizers and memorize.

STEP 4: REMEMBER WHAT'S IMPORTANT

In this step you memorize what is on your study guides for essay and objective tests, or you practice what is on your study guides for problem-solving and application tests.

Remembering

Some students try to memorize by reading the underlining over and over, hoping something will stick. A better way to memorize is by self-testing. Test yourself the first time immediately after Step 3. If you cannot remember the material at this point, you probably won't remember it for a test.

If your study guide consists of underlining and marginal notes, cover the page and use the marginal notes to test your memory of what you have underlined. Pay attention to any points you miss. Keep self-testing until you remember everything.

If you are using flash cards, test yourself on the subject written on the front of the card. Put the cards away as you memorize them, so you don't keep retesting on those you already know. Try to have no more than ten to twenty cards to work on at one time. The night before the exam you should have just a few that still need reviewing. Review them before going to bed, get a good night's sleep, and review them again just before the test.

If you have broken the chapter into sections for Steps 2, 3, and 4, repeat the steps for each section until you reach the end of the chapter.

When you have finished a chapter, retest yourself on the marginal notes or flash cards for the whole chapter. Concentrate on what is most difficult, and keep testing until you reach mastery. If you are using graphic organizers, self-test the same way you would with flash cards. If you need to, you can draw each graphic organizer from memory and make sure it matches the original. If there are any study questions at the end of the chapter, answer them. Check your answers by looking back at the chapter. Review again about one week later and then as often as needed until the test. The more difficult the chapter, the more frequent the review should be. That way you won't have to cram for the test.

Practicing

If your study guide contains a plan or schedule for practicing for application or problem-solving tests, follow the study guide. Keep practicing until you reach mastery.

STEP 5: MAKE USE OF WHAT YOU READ—TAKE THE TEST

The following suggestions are good for taking all types of tests:

1. Arrive at the test on time. Bring pencils, blue books, calculator, or whatever you need.

2. Look the test over and then look at the clock. Make a schedule that will give you the most points. For example, if you have to answer fifty multiple choice questions in fifty minutes, make sure that after twenty-five minutes have gone by, you are somewhere near the twenty-fifth question. If there is an essay worth fifty points and fifty objective questions worth one point each, make sure you spend approximately half your time on the essay. Allow enough time to review the test before you turn it in.

3. Answer the easy questions first. Mark those you don't know and come back to them later. Unless there is a penalty for guessing, don't leave anything blank. If there is a penalty, find out what it is and figure out mathematically when you should guess. For example, let's say there are five multiple choices and 25 percent is deducted for each wrong answer (as on the SAT test). If you have absolutely no idea which choice is right, you have a 20 percent (one-fifth) chance of being right by making a wild guess. However, 25 percent (one-fourth of a point) is deducted if you're wrong. In that case, don't guess. If, however, you can eliminate one of the choices that you are sure is wrong, then you have a 25 percent chance of being right by guessing among the remaining four. Your reward for being right is equal to your penalty for

being wrong. If you can eliminate two choices, then your odds increase to 33 percent (one-third). In that case, you should definitely guess.

Essay Tests

In addition to the skills described above, there are some special skills you need for essay tests.

1. *Follow the directions.* The topics you memorized by using your graphic organizers will be turned into test questions by your instructor. You will have to direct your answers in such a way that they answer what is asked. The following words are often used in the directions for essay tests. Review them carefully and be sure you know what they mean so you can do exactly what they say when you take a test:

    List = make a list

    Compare = show similarities

    Contrast = show differences

    Discuss = give an overview

    Outline = make an outline

    Enumerate = list with numbers

    Trace = describe in order

    Summarize = write the major ideas in a few words

    Diagram = draw an illustration

    Criticize = say what's wrong with it

    Evaluate = give good and bad points

2. *Organize.* Before writing an essay, draw the outline, map, or other graphic organizer from your study guide. Write the essay from your graphic organizer, and use an introduction, conclusion, and signal words (*first, most important, finally*). If your essay is disorganized, the instructor will think you don't know the answer. If you really don't know the answer, write anything that comes to mind in the hopes that you will pick up a few points.

Application and Problem-Solving Tests

Follow the general directions given earlier. As with essay tests, if you don't know an answer or have not mastered a skill, and if credit is given for partial mastery, do whatever you can in the hopes of picking up a few points.

STEP 6: EVALUATE YOUR ACT SKILLS— ANALYZE TEST RESULTS

When you get your test back, first make sure you understand your mistakes. Then analyze your test-taking skills. Answering the following questions will help you do better next time.

- Did you find out enough about the test? For example, did you study the right chapters, did you prepare for the right number and types of questions (essay, objective, problem-solving)? If not, ask more questions next time.

- Did you predict the right questions? If there were any questions you didn't expect, go back to the book and find out why you didn't anticipate them.

- Did you use good test-taking skills? Did you arrive on time with the right materials? Did you organize your time so you were able to answer all the questions and check them over before turning in the test?

- Did you remember the material you studied? If not, make better use of marginal notes, flash cards, and graphic organizers for self-testing.

- If there were essay questions, did you follow directions and organize your answers before beginning to write?

- If there were problem-solving or application questions, did you practice enough?

At first the ACT system might seem uncomfortable because it is new, but keep trying. By the end of this unit, you will find that your time and effort have been well spent.

11

Some Businesses Take Advantage of the Unwary

Vocabulary Preview

unwary (un wer'ē): not cautious; unwatchful

accumulate (ə kyo͞om'yə lāt'): to pile up or collect

subversive (səb vʉr'siv): tending or seeking to overthrow or destroy

discretionary (dis kresh'ən er'ē): left to or regulated by one's own discretion or judgment

unsophisticated (ən sə fis'tə kā'tid): lacking in experience; unworldly

deceitful (di sēt'fəl): apt to lie or cheat; dishonest

fraudulent (frô'jə lənt): based on or using a trickery or falsehood

subtle (sut''l): crafty; not obvious

terminate (tʉr'mə nāt'): to put an end to; stop

audiophile (ô'dē ō fīl'): a devotee of high-fidelity sound reproduction, as on record players

ploy (ploi): an action intended to outwit someone; trick

consolation prize (kän sə lā'shən prīz): a prize given to a contestant who does well but who does not win

insidious (in sid'ē əs): secretly harmful; deceptive; sly

perpetrated (pʉr'pə trāt'id): did (something evil or criminal)

traumatic (trô' ma tik): shocking; producing substantial and lasting damage

voided (void'id): made ineffective or useless

trumped-up (trumpt up'): devised by trickery; false

indicted (in dīt'id): charged with a crime

defective (dē fek'tiv): faulty

punitive (pyo͞o'nə tiv): inflicting or concerned with punishment

cat, āte, fäther; pen, ēvil; if, kīte; nō, ôr, fo͞od, book; boil, house; up, tʉrn; chief, shell; thick, *the*; zh, treasure; ŋ, sing; ə for *a* in *about*; ' as in *able* (ā'b'l)

Step 1: Preread

 Preview the following selection by reading the title, the headings, and subheadings. Answer the following questions without looking back at the reading.

1. What is the subject?

   _____

2. What is the main idea?

   _____

   _____

3. Take a moment to think about deceptive business practices. Think about what you know, what you don't know, and what you might find out from reading the selection. Make up three questions:

   a. _____

   b. _____

   c. _____

Step 2: Read

 Read the selection without underlining. Ignore the notes written in the margin.

   Write your starting time here: _____

Some Businesses Take Advantage of the Unwary

J. Norman Swaton

Business is an essential part of the American economy. Greed, apparently, is also an inescapable part of human nature. This unfortunate combination can work against you in your efforts to accumulate investment capital just as much as inflation does.

There's nothing subversive about business going after discretionary funds. In fact, it's healthy and makes for progress in many ways. You, as consumer, are supposed to learn to play the game and exercise your free will to buy only those things that fit into your life plan. That part's simple enough. What muddies the picture are the countless companies that prey on the lonely, insecure, and immature (or at least unsophisticated). Their advertising effectively promises to fulfill needs and desires that can in no way be met through use of the product involved. The dishonesty of such practices is probably somewhat a matter of definition. If the fantasy of satisfaction brings temporary pleasure at relatively little expense, there's probably no reason to mount a case against it. Women are going to spend money for *some* kind of pantyhose and whether it's the kind Joe Namath wears or just some unknown model is really a matter of little concern. Similarly, the clothing budget isn't affected too much if the dress shirts bought this month are the kind women on TV can't resist tearing from your body or plain old Sears page 395.

Actually, the last two statements are minor lies, but they serve here to make the point that some common business practices are less harmful than others. Puffery (flattering publicity or extravagant recommendation, according to the dictionary) is one thing. It has become an expected part of the marketing approach. But beyond this are still more deceitful and fraudulent practices that take billions of dollars out of the economy each year by taking advantage of unsophisticated people who believe the world is as honest as they are. We're going to look at some of the most common of these here because some of them might be unfamiliar to you. Knowing about them can make a considerable difference in how soon you reach your financial goals.

Reason to know about business practices

SOME COMMON DECEPTIONS TO WATCH FOR

The following are practices that usually can't be prosecuted under the law but that can take your dollars in sneaky, underhanded ways.

7 deceptions that aren't illegal

Bait and Switch Ads

These will probably be with us forever. "Singer Portable Sewing Machine—$29.95!" says the little ad in the classifieds or display section of the paper. The price is so great you run right down. If you call ahead, you'll be told they only have a few left so you'd better hurry because they can't hold them at that price. When you get there, of course, it's a rebuilt machine with no guarantee. The salesperson either won't even bring it out to show you or puts it down so much you're ashamed you asked about it. What they do have, for a little more money, is the Dynamite Superfine free-arm machine that zigs, zags, and butters your toast.

Vacuum cleaners, refrigerators, television sets, freezers, meat, carpeting, even eyeglasses are sold this way. And the stores aren't always fly-by-night operations, either. Some of the most prestigious names in the department store field resort to the tactic. Some of the switches are so subtle you believe you did it yourself and actually feel pretty smart about it. The harm is that you are tricked into overspending—even if you receive value, which is usually not the case. Your budget is messed up for some time to come. Remember that whatever you spend in excess of what you hoped to spend comes right out of your investment capital and sets your plan back a corresponding length of time. If a merchant or salesperson you've invited to your home tries it on you, you're well advised to terminate the interview immediately and shop elsewhere.

False List Prices

This technique, which allows unjustified advertising claims of great discounts, is a common way of business in some lines. The hi-fi industry in the fifties became so addicted to this practice that national merchandising companies included the false list prices in their catalogs. The discounted "audiophile net" price was in fact the list price. It was virtually impossible to find any store that sold for either the false list or truly discounted prices. Competition and consumer education eventually eliminated this particular practice. Today examples of the phony list price are usually confined to individual brands and stores, although from time to time the "sticker price" on new automobiles becomes meaningless. Your best defense against this practice is careful shopping and comparison of prices at several dealers.

Phony Contest Awards

These may start out as a phone call advising you that your name has been selected as a contestant to receive a free this or that if you can answer two questions. The questions, of course, would make Groucho Marx blush. All you have to do to claim your free encyclopedia set is sign up for the reader service and the annual yearbooks. Cost? Strangely, about the same as the cost of the set with the other stuff thrown in. The same ploy works as a variation on the bait and switch: you receive a letter advising you you have won second prize or consolation prize in a contest you may or may not remember having entered (at a recent home show or county fair, for example). Your certificate is worth half or two-thirds the cost of a moderately priced sewing machine. When you try to buy it, you find there is no guarantee. So you have to buy a service policy, or a cabinet, or instructions in sewing technique, all of which come free with the higher-priced, better-quality machine that zigs, zags, and butters toast.

Free Gifts

These often never appear. The gifts "have to be mailed out from our regional headquarters" or some such excuse when the salesperson arrives at your home. Whether the consumer buys or not, the free gift never quite makes it. But the family budget has been unnecessarily strained, or at least exposed to the probability of strain, through a deceptive advertising practice.

Phony Sales

This is a variation on the theme of false list prices because much, if not all, of the merchandise on sale is brought in for the event. Well-established department stores still do this. They often mix lower-priced merchandise with some legitimately marked-down goods. It's distressing to find that the sale price you paid for something is really more than its normal retail price, but it happens every day in stores all over the country. Refinements and variations include such practices as advertising a sale price on a 17-inch television set and showing a picture of a deluxe 25-inch. Another is the "going out for business" sale. The merchant will claim mere cuteness if brought to task for this deceitful substitution of words. More subtle still is the use of price comparisons such as "$20 value" in the obvious hope that the reader will take it to mean "$20 regular price," which, of course, it isn't.

Wholesale to the Public

This claim is by definition impossible. Wholesale is to retailers and retail is to the public. Still, millions of Americans daily buy from such stores in the belief they are saving money. Only when the price of an item is well established can such a claim be put to the test. Usually it fails. Usually the item can be bought from normal channels as cheaply and often with service that isn't available through the "wholesaler." A variation of this practice is the way some major manufacturers make a well-established product line of quality, and a very similar-appearing product line (often with a confusingly similar name) for sale in discount department stores. Luggage, typewriter, and sporting goods manufacturers are particularly guilty of this near-conspiracy. Consumers are led to believe they are getting a discount when in fact the product is sold for at least normal retail prices, considering the lowered quality.

Easy Credit

This one is usually accompanied by an advertisement to the effect that the seller of some item carries his own credit. You can qualify even if you're new in town, been bankrupt, and so on. It can be the most insidious victimization of all. It's always of most appeal to those who can least afford it, and the price is *high*.

SOME PRACTICES TO BE WARY OF

4 frauds

Up to now we've been talking about sharp practices that manage to stay within the law. There are also countless full-blown frauds that are perpetrated on people every day. These are more traumatic in their impact on a financial program because they usually involve larger amounts of money—often the entire savings of a family. More often than not the service or merchandise bought is worthless if it exists at all.

Unordered Merchandise

This is one of the cheapest of the scams and probably remains so because very few people are about to lay out more than a few dollars to cover a "COD" delivery for an absent neighbor. (When the neighbor comes home, of course, it turns out that nobody ordered anything in the first place and the box is probably empty in the second place.) A variation is the delivery of actual merchandise which wasn't ordered but then becomes the subject of repeated billings and threats of court action if payment isn't made as demanded. The law is on your side in most cases, but be sure to check with a lawyer if you're in doubt.

Vanity Publications

These can be relatively inexpensive if all you have to buy is a single copy of the book in which your biography is included as an outstanding biology student of the year, state PTA president, or retail hardware clerk of the week. An entirely different story is the $5,000 it may cost to get your book of poems "published" (quotes because *publication* implies intended sale and the vanity press industry intends to print only a few copies to stroke the frustrated ego of the author). Legitimate publishers never charge an author cash for publishing a work they intend to sell for a profit. Certain minor costs may by contract be charged to a royalty account, but the author never has to put up front money.

Auto Repair

Repair frauds are particularly effective in areas of mystery, such as automatic transmissions. Thousands of cases have been documented where a $3 or $4 part is installed in an automatic transmission in half an hour, and the customer charged $300 for his own repainted transmission as a "rebuilt." Guarantees are frequently voided by trumped-up situations which either never happened or are as totally unrelated as the wrong kind of gasoline being used. One of the world's largest retailers was recently indicted by a Los Angeles County grand jury for practices in some of its auto shops that included making unneeded repairs and charging for parts not installed. Fan belts are sometimes slashed by service station attendants and then pointed out as defective. One classic case in Los Angeles involved a woman who left her Mercedes in a dealer's repair shop for a new battery and got it back weeks later with a $1,900 bill for work unauthorized by her. At this writing, the courts have just settled a $90,000 award in her favor (including punitive damages intended as a warning to the repair industry). But an appeal has been filed by the dealer. The amount of time and money this cost the owner of the car (even though the attorney took the case on a percentage of award basis) is hard to measure. She lost her apartment, car, and job in the process. Also, presumably, her taste for expensive European motor cars; she now drives a Nissan.

Anyone who has a competent mechanic who can be trusted should count this fact among the prime blessings of life.

Mail Order Frauds

These come in all sizes. At the cheap end are such scams as chain letters, which only take small amounts of money and large amounts of hope from the victim. "Send your dollar to the name at the top of the list. Add your name to the bottom of the list. Make ten copies of this letter and mail them to friends. In two weeks your name will be at the top of the list and thousands of people will be mailing their dollar to you." So the song goes, often laced with stories of tragedy befalling those who dared "break the chain." Mathematically, of course, the chain breaks itself in a few days, but neither that nor the illegality of the letters stops them.

At the other end are land sales that can cost thousands of dollars for property that ends up being on the side of a cliff, under a swamp, or two miles from the nearest water faucet.

A variation of mail order racketeering is the industry that advertises opportunities for wealth through running a mail order business from your home. "You can make millions as I have," is the typical approach. All you have to do is buy your merchandise from the self-professed wizard, and he'll share with you the secrets that made it all happen. Along the way you find out that you'll also need a catalog. That's another two or three thousand, plus a mailing list, which he'll rent to you at a price, and a postage bill you wouldn't believe. Before long it becomes apparent that the way he made his million in mail order was from suckers like yourself.

Similar cons involving earthworms, chinchillas, rabbits, potted palms, stuffed dates, and unstuffed envelopes have been around forever. The one thing they all have in common is that you must buy something before you can start in business and watch the profits roll in. The problem is that the market always seems to be a little soft when your crop is ready to harvest. The contract you thought you had for the buy back of the initial investment is a little tougher than you realized.

AVOIDING THE CON

3 rules for avoiding scams

The list of frauds and deceits is almost endless. Every year local police publicize them in newspapers to warn people of the possibility of being taken. Every year people who didn't get the word are taken anyway. It's impossible to learn all the varieties of scam, because new ones are made up every day. However, you can and should try to remember a few basic commonsense principles that will let you recognize that you are being hustled, even if you don't yet know just how. For example, these three rules can save you a lot of trouble and lost time in your progress toward financial goals.

1. *Never be forced into a hasty decision.* A salesperson who tries to convince you you have to decide right now or miss out is almost certainly a hustler. If it's good tonight, it'll be good in the morning. Sleep on it and see how it looks in the daylight. If he says he can't wait, you can be sure that you should.

2. *Don't believe you're getting a special deal.* Unless, of course, you know the seller personally (sometimes not even then!). If the deal is because you've somehow been singled out to star in an advertising campaign, get the person's license number if you can and call the police. Chances are excellent he or she is trying to pick your pockets.

3. *Don't buy something expensive to save money.* There's an old story about a weary housewife who decided to pass on the freezer full of beef because ". . . we're already paying for our foreign car with what we save on gasoline, our television with what we save on movies, our washer-dryer with what we save on laundry bills, and our sewing machine with what we save on clothes. We really can't afford to save any more right now." Unless actual experience shows that you'll really save money every month—and that means your cost *including the payment* will be less—you may be saving money in the long run but perishing in the short run. Any salesperson who doesn't see it that way is not your friend, no matter what it says on his business card.

2700 words

Write your ending time here: _____

Subtract your starting time: _____

Total time: _____

Check the Rate Chart in the back of the book to find out how many words per minute you have read, and then record your score on the Progress Chart.

Step 3: Analyze What You Read—Create a Study Guide

Objective Questions

Go back to the reading and think about what would likely be on a test. Then think about whether or not you will remember it. <u>Underline or highlight only (1) what you believe will be on a test and (2) what you don't think you will remember.</u> Since this is your first selection for study reading, we have written the marginal self-test notes for you. You can use the notes as a guide to what should be underlined. Remember that the notes are like the subject and the underlining is like the main idea. If you prefer, you may write the self-test note on the front of a flash card and write what you would have underlined (change it into your own words) on the back.

Essay/Application Questions

PREDICT ESSAY QUESTIONS   There are two topics in this reading important enough for an essay question. Write them here:

1. _____

2. _____

MAKE GRAPHIC ORGANIZERS

1. Fill in the following outline:

Some Businesses Take Advantage of the Unwary

Main idea: _____

_____

   I. _____

      A. _____

      B. _____

      C. _____

      D. _____

      E. _____

      F. _____

      G. _____

  II. _____

      A. _____

      B. _____

      C. _____

      D. _____

III. _____

    A. _____

    B. _____

    C. _____

2. Convert your outline into an idea map. Use a separate sheet of paper.

3. For each of the 11 business practices, write a definition or example.

Practice	Definition or Example
1.	
2.	
3.	
4.	
5.	
6.	
7.	
8.	
9.	
10.	
11.	

Skill Development: Summarizing

Summarizing and most other types of writing are easy if you have a graphic organizer. Writing is much harder if you don't. For this reading you have four graphic organizers. The first one consists of the underlining and notes in the margin of the article. The second one is the outline. The third one is the idea map. The fourth one is the chart. Here is how to summarize using each of them.

1. To summarize using the underlining and marginal notes: First, write the main idea in a complete sentence. Then turn each marginal note into a complete sentence. Use words that let the reader recognize your organization. For example, you might say, "There are *seven* common deceptive business practices that aren't illegal. First, . . . second, . . . etc."

2. To summarize using the outline: First, write the main idea in a complete sentence. Next, make each heading in the outline into a complete sentence. Use paragraph form, not outline form. Use signal or transition words that show your organization.

3. To summarize using the idea map: First, write the main idea in a complete sentence. Then, using paragraph form, convert each rectangle and the triangles that go with it into sentences. Use signal or transition words

4. You can use the chart in the same way.

Now write a summary of Reading 11. Use a separate piece of paper.

Step 4: Remember What's Important

 Use the marginal self-test notes or the flash cards and the graphic organizers to memorize the material.

To use the marginal self-test notes, cover the page with your hand, look at the note, and see if you can give the answer. Remove your hand and check your answer. If it is not correct, do it again until it is correct.

To use flash cards, look at the topic on the front and try to give the answer. Check the answer on the back. If it is not correct, keep self-testing until you can remember it.

You can use the first graphic organizer (outline) by trying to rewrite it from memory. Check your answer and do it again until it is correct. You can use the second graphic organizer (chart) by covering up the right side (definitions or examples) with your hand and testing yourself.

If it's easier or more fun for you to have someone else test you, that's fine. Remember to keep testing until you think you can remember everything for the Comprehension Check.

Step 5: Make Use of What You Read.

 When you are ready, complete the Comprehension Check. Do not look back at the reading or the study guides.

Step 6: Evaluate Your Active Critical Thinking Skills

After your test has been graded, use the checklist on p. 465 to evaluate your skills.

COMPREHENSION CHECK

Short Answer

Give three rules for avoiding a scam.

1. _____

2. _____

3. _____

Multiple Choice

Circle the letter before the best answer to each question below.

4. Puffery is

   a. flattering publicity.

   b. legal cheating.

   c. an illegal business practice.

   d. avoided by advertisers.

5. Bait and switch ads

   a. try to get you to buy shoddy merchandise.

   b. try to get you to buy merchandise that is more expensive than the merchandise that was advertised.

   c. are used only by fly-by-night operations.

   d. lie about the price of merchandise.

6. "Wholesale to the public" deceptions are

   a. not really dishonest.

   b. always easy to check out.

   c. illegal.

   d. legal.

7. If you have been "baited-and-switched" but the merchandise still looks like a good buy, you should

   a. grab it.

   b. refuse it and call the police.

   c. give the store a bad check for it.

   d. go home and think about it.

8. In general, consumers should

   a. be trusting.

   b. be suspicious.

   c. be deceptive.

   d. retain a lawyer.

9. Which of the following practices is illegal?

   a. false list prices

   b. phony contest awards

   c. free gifts

   d. unordered merchandise

10. If you are offered an appliance for $200 that the store calls "a $500 value," you should

   a. check the price in other stores.

   b. buy it.

   c. refuse to do business with this store.

   d. report the store to a consumer protection agency.

Essay

List and give examples of deceptive business practices. Use a separate piece of paper.

VOCABULARY IN CONTEXT

Write the best word from the list in the blank in each sentence below.

Part A

unwary   accumulate   unsophisticated   deceitful   terminate

ploy   consolation prize   traumatic   trumped-up   punitive

1. Being in a serious car accident is a very _____ experience.

2. When people don't pay their bills as they receive them, bills tend to

    _____ .

3. The manager of the convenience store used the _____ of telling
    the thief he had pushed a button to call the police.

4. During economic recessions, businesses are forced to _____ the
    employment of many workers.

5. Most young children are _____ enough to believe tall tales.

6. Being forced to sit in the corner wearing a dunce cap is now considered too

    _____ a practice to use in public schools.

7. A _____ friend who betrays your trust can hurt you more than
    an obvious enemy.

8. It is wrong for a police officer to arrest someone on _____
    charges.

9. _____ visitors to big cities like New York might get mugged
    walking down dark alleys.

10. Only one person could win the grand prize for best Halloween costume, but all

    the contestants got a _____ .

Part B

subversive   discretionary   perpetrated   subtle   audiophiles

fraudulent   void   insidious   indicted   defective

11. People of Japanese descent were put in camps during World War II because the

    U.S. government was afraid of _____ activity such as spying.

12. Going on a cruise uses a greater amount of _____ funds than visiting relatives.

13. John Dillinger _____ so many criminal acts during the 1920s that the FBI declared him Public Enemy Number 1.

14. In the Old West phony doctors sold worthless "medicine" by making

    _____ claims of miraculous cures.

15. _____ were very pleased when CDs replaced records because of the superior quality of the sound.

16. If you want to be sure nobody tries to cash your blank check, you should write

    " _____ " across it.

17. When you want an expensive gift, a _____ approach may be better than asking for it directly.

18. Most appliances come with a guarantee against _____ parts.

19. Notorious 1920s gangster Al Capone was finally _____ and sent to jail for income tax evasion.

20. Skilled con artists are very _____ ; their victims trust them until it's too late.

12

Music Formats

Vocabulary Preview

innovative (in′ə vā′tiv): new; changed, inventive

counterculture (koun′tər kul′chər): the culture of those whose lifestyle is opposed to the prevailing culture

spectrum (spek′trəm): continuous range or entire extent

genre (zhän′rə): kind or type

syndicated (sin′də kāt′id): organized for a purpose

demented (dē ment′id): insane; mad

contended (kən tend′id): argued; asserted

irrepressible (ir′i pres′ə b'l): unstoppable; unrestrainable

buoyed (boid): lifted up

permutation (pʉr′myo͞o tā′shən): transformation; rearrangement

discern (di sʉrn′): recognize clearly; perceive

esoteric (es′ə ter′ik): meant for or understood by only a chosen few

capitalize (kap′ət′l īz): use to one's advantage (with *on*)

predominantly (pri däm′ə nənt lē): largely; most frequently

alienating (āl′yən āt′iŋ): making unfriendly; causing a feeling of not belonging

raucous (rô′kəs): loud and rowdy

patter (pat′ər): the glib, rapid speech of sales people, deejays, etc.

ethic (eth′nik): having to do with cultural or racial groups

subsidized (sub′sə dīzd): granted or given money for support

incessant (in ces′ənt): never stopping; constant

cat, āte, fäther; pen, ēvil; if, kīte; nō, ôr, fo͞od, book; boil, house; up, tʉrn; chief, shell; thick, *the*; zh, treasure; ŋ, sing; ə for *a* in *about*; ' as in *able* (a′b'l)

Step I: Preread

Preview the following selection by reading the title, the headings, and the illustration. Answer questions 1 and 2 without looking back at the reading.

1. What is the subject? _____

2. What is the main idea? _____

3. Look at the cartoon.

    a. What is the subject? _____

    b. What is the main idea? _____

    _____

4. Take a moment to think about radio music. Think about what you know, what you don't know, and what you might find out from reading the selection. Make up three questions:

    a. _____

    b. _____

    c. _____

Step 2: Read

 Read the selection without underlining. Ignore the lines in the margin.

Write your starting time here: _____

Music Formats

Edward Jay Whetmore

ALTHOUGH NO TWO RADIO STATIONS ARE exactly alike, a number of basic formulas exist. These formulas, or *formats,* involve a specific blend of certain types of music and talk. The format is designed to attract a large, desirable audience to the station. Radio formats are not permanent things. They are constantly being adjusted as management perception of audience needs evolves.

Commercial radio is often ignorant of the cutting edge of musical trends. It always takes some time for new styles to catch on with the mass audience. When they do, you can be sure some innovative radio programmers somewhere will find a way to fit them into current programming.

Disco music was quite popular in the mid-1970s, but it took several years before disco formats began to appear. By the time "all-disco" radio had gotten under way, the disco craze had cooled. A similar cycle occurred with the coming of rap music in the 1980s. NWA and 2 Live Crew may generate large retail sales, but their music is rarely heard on commercial radio.

Another example involved punk and new-wave music. Punk pioneers like the Sex Pistols and the Ramones were played little, if at all, by established rock stations in the mid- and late 1970s. Today, former counterculture groups like Metallica enjoy mainstream airplay and MTV exposure. But the darker sounds of heavy-metal groups such as Megadeath, Slayer, and Prong are largely excluded from mainstream rock formats.

Occasionally a commercial station will follow the lead of a college station. KUSF-FM, the station licensed to the University of San Francisco, offered punk and new-wave music in the late 1970s. By 1982 a new-wave format had emerged along with a large and loyal audience. Finally the city's commercial KQAK adopted a similar format. Soon several other commercial rock stations began adding more new music to their playlists. However, KQAK ultimately failed, as did many commercial "new music" format stations across the country during this period. There were simply not enough new-music fans to sustain the format.

1. _____
   _____
   _____

2. _____
   _____
   _____

3. _____
   _____
   _____
   _____

The basic formats of radio cover a wide spectrum of listener needs and tastes. Some, like classical, are tried and true and have been around since the beginning of broadcasting. Others, like new age, are relatively recent and experimental. In each case,

4. ———————

———————

———————

the goal is to get and hold as many listeners as possible, particularly those with desirable audience characteristics. With that in mind, here are the formats reflecting the radio trends of the 1990s.

CHR: Contemporary Hit Radio

5. ———————

———————

———————

Hot hits, CHR, Top 40—by any name this jukebox method of radio programming has seen its ups and downs over the years. Credit for the creation of the format is generally given to Todd Storz, who convinced his father to purchase Omaha's ailing KOWH in 1949. While sitting in a restaurant one afternoon he observed the patrons putting money into a jukebox to listen to the same songs over and over. "Why can't radio be like a jukebox?" he asked himself. At that moment "Top 40" radio was born. Success came swiftly and soon young Storz was running a string of Top 40 stations all over the Midwest.

Top 40 reigned supreme on the airwaves from the mid-1950s until album-oriented rock found success in the early 1970s. It appeared that Top 40 would die with the decrease in AM listeners in the 1970s, but a new, less cluttered version appeared on FM in the early 1980s. Dubbed CHR or hot hits, this "new" format became the rage on the FM dial. By the mid-1980s it was enjoying healthy ratings in New York (WPLJ), Los Angeles (KIIS), Chicago (WLS), and many other markets.

The top 40 genre spawned some giants. Bill Drake's success came in the early 1960s with KHJ, a Los Angeles Top 40 station. While sitting by his pool at Malibu Beach, he picked the songs that were to be played on his station. His method was simple: Play only the very top singles, and play them more often than anyone else.

Another giant is Casey Kasem, who helped form Watermark Productions to begin his syndicated "American Top 40" in 1970. Kasem got his hits from the number one authority in the industry, *Billboard* magazine. Every week he "counted 'em down in order" for millions of listeners in hundreds of cities from New York to Newberg, Oregon. Kasem's show was also heard in Europe and Asia. His trademark was airing little-known facts about stars, along with his final advice to listeners each week: "Keep your feet on the ground, and keep reaching for the stars."

Kasem parted company with "AT40" in a contract dispute in 1988 and was replaced by Shadoe Stevens. The show survived, but before long there was some new, yet familiar competition. Today "Casey's Top 40" reaches some 8 million listeners world-wide. It is the premiere countdown show in an industry that *Newsweek* estimates generates about $50 million in annual ad revenues. There are other countdown shows of course, from country to Hispanic to R&B. Even trivia buff Dr. Demento offers a countdown of the week's "most demented tunes." Neverthe-less, there remains only one Casey Kasem "counting 'em down in order" for his loyal listeners around the world.

Album-Oriented Rock

Album-oriented rock began in the late 1960s when it became evident that a growing number of rock enthusiasts were tired of the limitations of Top 40. Rebellious deejays contended that the more innovative rock music was not getting on the air because songs were often too long or too controversial to fit on tight Top 40 playlists.

6. _____
_____
_____

The founding father of AOR is generally acknowledged to be Tom "Big Daddy" Donahue. He was a dissatisfied Top 40 deejay who left a successful job at San Francisco's KYA to start a new kind of radio, first at that city's KMPX-FM and later at KSAN-FM. Donahue and his irrepressible (some would say irresponsi-ble) deejays would play anything that struck their fancy, and that was a lot. In the early days, it was not unusual to hear a 15-minute "home tape" of the Grateful Dead sandwiched between a sitar piece by Ravi Shankar and a song by the Jefferson Airplane about the virtues of an illegal drug. Because the music and the deejays' comments often centered on counterculture themes, the format was initially called "underground radio."

At first, most underground stations struggled for listeners, advertising dollars, and respectability. What's more, many sta-tions were found on the then less-popular FM dial. Corporate owners responded by bringing in more conservative program directors, they fired radical deejays and instituted mainstream-oriented playlists. The result was called "progressive" radio for a time, and its popularity was buoyed by the rise of FM. Progressive radio eventually evolved into album-oriented rock in the 1970s.

Many AOR stations still feature heavy-duty rock, but as the counterculture generation aged, its music tastes mellowed. Elton John seems right at home in most of today's AOR stations. Yet listeners can also hear everything from Stevie Wonder to Def Leppard and Neil Young to U2.

7. _____

"Mellow rock" began making inroads in the mid-1970s. Sometimes called "easy rock," mellow-rock stations feature music from the softer side of the rock spectrum. It features such artists as the Beatles, Elton John, Lionel Richie, Dan Fogelberg, James Taylor, and Phil Collins.

8. _____

"Classic rock" is yet another version of AOR. Highly popular with the baby-boomer crowd, this AOR variant features the 60s-oriented sounds of the Beatles, the Rolling Stones, and Jimi Hendrix, blended with more current boomer favorites like Bob Seger, U2, and Tom Petty. Whatever the permutation, AOR remains rock's most popular musical format.

New Music/Modern Rock

9. _____

A recent and innovative rock format is *new music,* or *modern rock,* generally found on FM. The distinctions between these and AOR stations are sometimes difficult to discern. However, the emergence of punk, new-wave, and new-music songs in the late 1970s and early 1980s generated a tremendous interest in and enthusiasm for rock that had not been seen since the 1960s. A few stations, mostly in major markets, responded to this interest by featuring what they called "new music" exclusively.

Currently, KROQ in Los Angeles plays modern rock exclusively. Labeling its format "rock of the 90s," the rock station features only what it considers the most innovative of contemporary songs. The playlist includes mainstream acts like U2 and Billy Idol, as well as more esoteric music by such acts as R.E.M., Morrissy, and Depeche Mode.

Noting the connection between experimental music of the 1980s and the more innovative music of the 1960s by groups like the Doors and the Jimi Hendrix Experience, Lee Abrams, a renowned radio consultant, created his "Superstars II" format. Currently syndicated around the country, this format capitalizes on both modern rock trends and the desirability of reaching the older listeners who identify with the 1960s. If a station in your market has a daily feature known as the "Psychedelic Supper," you can bet it is an Abrams-programmed station.

Urban Contemporary

In the early 1980s, the term *urban contemporary* became commonplace in many markets around the country. The format is often found on CHR-type stations on the AM dial that program a large amount of dance music and upbeat hits to appeal to the black and inner-city audience. Often this audience is heavily populated with teens and young adults.

10. _____
_____
_____

Many urban contemporary formats evolved from the soul or R&B stations of the 1960s, which appealed predominantly to the black audience, though they were often owned and listened to by nonblacks. San Francisco's KSOL was so successful with urban contemporary that it was, for a time, the city's top-rated music station. There are numerous examples in the Midwest and East Coast as well. Acts such as Hammer, Boyz II Men, and Ice-T currently dominate their playlists.

"Urbancontemp" has been a boon to many AM stations in their ongoing battle with FM competition. It is credited with helping the AM band survive. But success breeds imitation in radio. In markets where the format succeeded it was not too long before one or more FM stations adopted it. As with all music formats, listeners tend to prefer FM over AM because it offers stereo and clearer, static-free reception.

Middle of the Road

MOR radio began as "chicken rock" in the 1950s. Stations afraid of playing the hard-driving sounds of upstarts like Elvis Presley would lean toward the softer love ballads of then-contemporary artists and blend them with songs by the standard crooners like Bing Crosby and Frank Sinatra. As MOR evolved, the idea was to get some young listeners without alienating the older crowd who found the more raucous rock tunes unacceptable. Unlike Top 40 deejays, MOR personalities feature a continual patter

11. _____
_____
_____

between songs in an effort to entertain the audience with their words as well as the music.

Adult Contemporary

12. _____
_____
_____

Adult contemporary is a blend of MOR and AOR programming. In the 1970s, MOR programmers found their audience growing older and thus less desirable to many advertisers. They spiced up their playlist with soft-rock songs, particularly those that had been popular in the late 1960s and early 1970s, in an attempt to reach the 18- to 34-year-old audience. Most major markets have several stations that call themselves adult contemporary.

Country

13. _____
_____
_____

Country stations employ what is probably America's most commercially successful radio format. Though rock, with all of its permutations, is the most popular format, it is the numerous country stations that tend to be most profitable. More than 50 percent of all popular-music radio stations play some country music. Every major metropolitan market has at least one country station. The format is common in the rural western states. In the Deep South, it competes with Top 40 and AOR for the highest ratings.

For years it was easy to separate country music from Top 40. The recent country influence on rock groups has made the distinction less clear. In addition, many country singers have found success on the Top 40 charts. The result has been an introduction to country music for many listeners. Several stations now follow a "pop-corn" formula, alternating rock and country hits, hoping to attract listeners from both camps. Country-music artists like Garth Brooks enjoy huge record sales that rival those of Michael Jackson and Guns n' Roses.

Beautiful Music

14. _____
_____
_____

Originally called "easy listening" or "good music" by its fans, beautiful music is one of today's most popular radio formats. The music of such artists as Henry Mancini and Mantovani forms the basis for this format. More adventurous beautiful-music stations may occasionally program a soft vocal track by the Carpenters or Neil Diamond. This trend has become more noticeable of late, because beautiful music, like MOR, appeals to an audience that is growing older.

The secret of the success of beautiful music lies in the nature of radio itself. Often, radio is something we listen to while we're doing something else. It provides a kind of backdrop or sound track for our daily activities. Beautiful-music programming is perfectly suited to this background function.

Beautiful-music fans see their stations as an oasis amid the "noise" of the other outlets. The announcers display little emotion or personality. They simply and softly announce the songs. News and commercials (when possible) are done in the same soft-spoken way. The idea is never to violate the listener's trust by starting to sound like "those other stations." Beautiful-music formats are usually automated or prerecorded, with the computer selecting programming elements according to a formula (three instrumentals, one vocal, two commercials, and so on).

The competition among beautiful-music stations is fiercer than the name might suggest. Although fans are as devoted to their format as are any radio listeners, they also tend to be less tolerant of commercials. Typically, a new beautiful-music station will enter a market with few sponsors. As the ratings grow, so does the number of commercials. Soon, listeners are tuning elsewhere.

The more conservative strains of beautiful music are often piped into dentists' and doctors' offices. Sometimes these offices pay to receive a closed-circuit broadcast of such music, such as the one called Muzak. The Muzak format is the easy listeners' dream—no commercials, no disc jockey, no interruptions, just music. Critics contend that Muzak isn't music at all, but simply a pleasant, mindless noise.

Jazz

In a few urban markets, the jazz format still receives a comfortable chunk of the ratings. Jazz stations were once quite popular, but enthusiasm dwindled in the 1960s. Those fans that remained were hard-core, however. They went to great lengths to find a station that offered what they wanted. Now there is some indication that young people are becoming interested in jazz again.

15. _____

_____

_____

Pop performers like Joni Mitchell and Sting are combining traditional and experimental jazz sounds with rock.

New Age

16. _____
_____
_____

New age is radio's newest format, featuring light jazz and classical-like instrumentals from labels such as Windham Hill and ECM. Artists like George Benson, Michael Franks, Pat Metheny, and Kitaro are new-age favorites. Critics often refer to this format as "Muzak for yuppies." The much-sought-after 18–39 young urban professionals do indeed form the core of its audience. New-age stations such as Los Angeles' KTWV—"The Wave" have not enjoyed overpowering ratings to date. But the desirable demographics of those listeners they do attract have helped them keep their heads above water while they attempt to build a larger audience.

Ethnic

17. _____
_____
_____

Ethnic stations are so labeled because their programming tends to be targeted largely to one ethnic group. Many offer programs in foreign languages. Of these, the Spanish-speaking stations are most numerous, particularly in New York City and the Sunbelt areas.

Because ethnic programming tends to appeal to a small, specialized audience, its impact is often overlooked. Yet it is important to recognize the cultural contributions made by various ethnic formats over the years. For many Americans, native-language programming and music formats offer a lifeline. Often ethnic programming can be found on noncommercial outlets, because the smaller audience cannot always support a commercial station.

Classical

18. _____
_____
_____

The commercial classical station, once a firmly established format, is now virtually extinct. About 20 full-time commercial classical stations remain today, down from more than 50 in 1965. Classical music may be alive and well, but teaming it with the financial realities of commercial radio seems an impossible task. Often classical stations are subsidized by listeners or survive because a wealthy owner writes off station losses at tax time.

Classical fans now find themselves drawn primarily to the noncommercial stations. Many of them broadcast from colleges and can be found between 88 and 92 on the FM dial. Many non-commercial National Public Radio (NPR) stations offer classical music along with other fine-arts and information programming.

Big Band

One solution for some struggling AM stations has been to switch to a nostalgia–big band format. Big band was most popular during the 1940s. Hence the format appeals to older groups. These listeners generally support news and talk stations and would not otherwise listen to music radio.

19. _____
_____
_____

Music Radio Today

You've now been briefed on the basic music formats that make up radio today. Many stations offer a combination of two or more formats. Thus it is difficult to know exactly where CHR ends and urban contemporary begins or what the differences are between more progressive AOR formats and those that feature modern rock. Even stations that do admit to following an established format have program directors who claim that their sound is "one-of-a-kind" in order to convince advertisers that they are buying something unique.

Yet the truth is that most stations stay within the boundaries of established formats. These confines, initially set up in the 1950s and refined for decades, have spelled success for many stations: Although station programmers always think that they should be allowed to experiment, station owners are usually more concerned with the bottom line. If the station is making money, let's keep it the way it is. If it's not, *then* we can talk about change.

20. _____
_____
_____

According to *Broadcasting* magazine, more commercial music stations report losses than profits each year, but those figures can be misleading. Owners often pay excessive salaries to themselves or their top executives to avoid heavy profit taxes at the end of the year. Actually, as soon as a station is a real moneyloser, it will change formats, go up for sale, or both.

Despite incessant competition from MTV and numerous other audio and video sources, music radio continues to be a vital force in the music industry. From the big-band sounds of "Make-Believe Ballroom" to the big blare of Metallica it remains the cornerstone of commercial radio.

3250 words

Write your ending time here: _____

Subtract your starting time: _____

Total time: _____

Check the Rate Chart in the back of the book to find out how many words per minute you have read, and then record your score on the Progress Chart.

Step 3: Analyze What You Read—Create a Study Guide

Objective Questions

Go back to the reading and underline or highlight what you think will be asked on a test. Then fill in the missing marginal notes to test your memory of what you have underlined. To make this easier, the self-test notes are written in random order here. Write each note on its correct lines in the reading. If you prefer, you may write the self-test note on the front of a flash card and what you would have underlined on the back.

Beautiful music	Classical
Definition of format	AOR history
Classic rock	Commercial radio and musical trends
Big band	Music radio today
CHR history	Goal of formats
New music/modern rock	Role of college stations
Urban contemporary	Country
Middle of the road	Ethnic
New age	Adult contemporary
Jazz	Mellow rock

Essay/Application Questions

PREDICT ESSAY QUESTIONS   What is the most likely topic for an essay question?

_____

MAKE GRAPHIC ORGANIZERS   Fill in the following idea map:

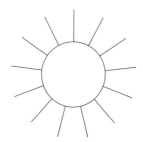

Skill Development: Summarizing

Use your graphic organizer to summarize this article. Take each heading from the idea map and turn it into one or more sentences (say something about each heading). Use paragraph form and write on a separate piece of paper.

Step 4: Remember What's Important

 Use the marginal notes or the flash cards and the graphic organizer for self-testing. Keep testing until you know the material.

Step 5: Make Use of What You Read

 When you are ready, complete the Comprehension Check. Do not look back at the reading or the study guide.

Step 6: Evaluate Your Active Critical Thinking Skills.

 After your test has been graded, use the checklist on p. 465 to evaluate your skills.

COMPREHENSION CHECK

Multiple Choice

Circle the letter before the best answer to each of the following questions.

1. The most commercially successful format is
    a. urban contemporary.
    b. adult contemporary.
    c. country and western.
    d. new age.

2. Muzak is a type of
    a. beautiful music.
    b. jazz.
    c. ethnic music.
    d. classical music.

3. Commercial radio stations make money by
    a. attracting donations.
    b. attracting sponsors.
    c. receiving payoffs from record companies.
    d. selling records and tapes.

4. Radio stations vary their formats to
    a. keep in the forefront of musical trends.
    b. attract the largest audience they can.
    c. provide the highest quality music.
    d. appear noncommercial.

5. Compared with commercial stations, college stations usually play
    a. newer music.
    b. more news.
    c. more oldies.
    d. all of the above.

Short Answer

6. What name does the reading use to refer to the jukebox or "Top 40" method of programming?

    _____

7. "Mellow rock" and "classic rock" are subtypes of which genre?

    _____

8. To what type of audience does "urban contemporary" music tend to appeal?

    _____

9. Which type of music began in the 1950s as "chicken rock"?

    _____

10. Which of the types of music discussed in the reading would most likely be heard in a dentist's office?

    _____

Essay

Describe at least ten types of radio music formats.

_____

_____

_____

_____

_____

_____

_____

_____

_____

_____

_____

_____

_____

VOCABULARY IN CONTEXT

Write the best word from this list in the blank in each sentence below.

Part A

innovative	**spectrum**	**genres**	**syndicated**	**demented**
contended	**irrepressible**	**discern**	**predominantly**	**raucous**

1. Because humans have an _____ urge to breathe, a child holding his breath may turn blue and pass out, but he cannot die.

2. To be a successful inventor you must have _____ ideas.

3. From the facts she had gathered, the private investigator was able to

   _____ that certain individuals could not have been involved in the crime.

4. Elementary school students are often _____ when there is a substitute teacher.

5. In his trial for murder his lawyer _____ that he was innocent.

6. Different literary _____ include essays, poems, novels, and plays.

7. The most popular TV shows are usually _____ and aired across the nation.

8. The membership of the NAACP is _____ African American.

9. Comedians will often wear clothing and hairdos that make them look

   _____ .

10. Politicians will appear to stand for nothing at all when they try to please the

    entire _____ of voters.

Part B

counterculture   buoyed   permutations   esoteric   capitalizes

alienating   patter   ethnic   subsidize   incessant

11. Employers cannot legally discriminate based on one's _____
    background.

12. Some words are so _____ they can be found only in an
    unabridged dictionary.

13. The hippie movement in the late 1960s was an example of a

    _____ .

14. When an individual invests money and makes a profit, she

    _____ on her investment.

15. Fund raisers are often held because groups need money to _____
    their programs.

16. When the coffee shop started raising prices, the owners found they were

    _____ their regular customers.

17. The stock market was _____ by the poor performance of the
    bond market.

18. Deejays talking about the music and the musicians they play is a type of

    _____ .

19. Those who live next to the ocean or next to a major highway have to get used

    to _____ noise.

20. Potatoes in all their _____ are an important food in both North
    and South America.

13

Shared Characteristics of Life

Vocabulary Preview

analogy (ə nal′ə jē): similarity in some respects between things otherwise dissimilar

secretion (sə krē′shən): the release of a substance from a gland

hormone (hôr′mōn): a substance formed in some organ of the body and carried by a body fluid to another organ or tissue, where it has a specific effect

sabotage (sab′ə täzh): to cause deliberate destruction or damage

impaired (im perd′): damaged; weakened

cat, āte, fäther; pen, ēvil; if, kīte; nō, ôr, fo͞od, book; boil, house; up, turn; chief, shell; thick, _the_; zh, treasure; ŋ, sing; ə for _a_ in _about_; ′ as in _able_ (a′b′l)

Step 1: Preread

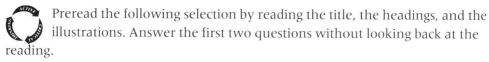

Preread the following selection by reading the title, the headings, and the illustrations. Answer the first two questions without looking back at the reading.

1. What is the subject?

2. What is the main idea?

3. Look at Figure 1.

   a. What is the subject?

   b. What is the main idea?

4. Look at Figure 2.

   a. What is the subject?

   _____

   b. What is the main idea?

   _____

   _____

5. Look at Figure 3.

   a. What is the subject?

   _____

   b. What is the main idea?

   _____

   _____

   _____

   _____

6. Take a moment to think about shared characteristics of life. Think about what you know about the subject, what you don't know, and what you might find out from reading this selection. Make up three questions.

   a. _____

   b. _____

   c. _____

Step 2: Read

 Read the selection without underlining. Ignore the lines in the margin.

   Write your starting time here: _____

Shared Characteristics of Life

CECIE STARR

Energy, DNA, and Life

PICTURE A FROG ON A ROCK, BUSILY croaking. Without even thinking about it, you know the frog is alive and the rock is not. At a much deeper level, however, the difference between them blurs. They and all other things are composed of the same particles (protons, electrons, and neutrons). The particles are organized as atoms, according to the same physical laws. At the heart of those laws is something called **energy**—a capacity to make things happen, to do work. Energetic interactions bind atom to atom in predictable patterns. These patterns give rise to the structured bits of matter we call molecules. Energetic interactions among molecules hold a rock together—and they hold a frog together.

It takes a special molecule called deoxyribonucleic acid, or **DNA,** to set living things apart from the nonliving world. No chunk of granite or quartz has it. DNA molecules contain instructions for assembling each new organism from "lifeless" molecules that contain carbon, hydrogen, and a few other kinds of substances. By analogy, think of what you can do with a little effort and just two kinds of ceramic tiles in a crafts kit. By following the kit's directions, you can glue the tiles together to form organized patterns (Figure 1). Similarly, life emerges from lifeless matter with DNA "directions," some raw materials, and inputs of energy.

1. _____
   _____
   _____

Levels of Biological Organizations

Look carefully at Figure 2, which outlines the levels of organization in nature. The properties of life emerge at the level of cells. A **cell** is an organized unit that can survive and reproduce on its own, given DNA instructions and sources of energy and raw materials. In other words, the cell is the basic *living* unit.

2. _____
   _____
   _____

That definition obviously fits an organism that is a single, free-living cell, such as an amoeba. Does it fit a **multicelled organism,** which has specialized cells organized into tissues and organs? Yes. You might find this a strange answer. After all, your own cells could never live all by themselves in nature. They

3. _____
   _____
   _____

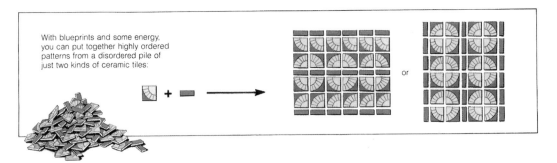

With blueprints and some energy, you can put together highly ordered patterns from a disordered pile of just two kinds of ceramic tiles:

or

Figure 1 Emergence of organized patterns from disorganized beginnings. Two ceramic tile patterns are shown here. (Can you visualize other possible patterns using the same two kinds of tiles?) Similarly, the organization characteristic of life emerges from simple pools of building blocks, given energy sources and specific DNA "blueprints."

must be bathed by fluids inside your body. Yet even human cells can be isolated and kept alive under controlled laboratory conditions. Researchers around the world routinely maintain human cells for use in cancer studies and other experiments.

4. _____

Referring again to Figure 2, we find a more inclusive level of organization, called the **population**. This is a group of single-celled or multicelled organisms of the same kind in a given area. A group of emperor penguins at their breeding grounds in Antarctica is an example. Next is the **community,** which includes all populations of all species (penguins, whales, seals, fishes, and so on) living in the same area. The next level, the **ecosystem,** includes the community and its physical and chemical environment. The most inclusive level of organization is the **biosphere**. The word refers to all regions of the earth's waters, crust, and atmosphere in which organisms live.

5. _____

6. _____

Metabolism: Life-Sustaining Energy Transfers

7. _____

You never, ever will find a rock engaged in metabolic activities. Only living cells can do this. **Metabolism** refers to the cell's capacity to (1) extract and convert energy from its surroundings and (2) use energy and so maintain itself, grow, and reproduce. Simply put, metabolism means *energy transfers* within cells.

8. _____

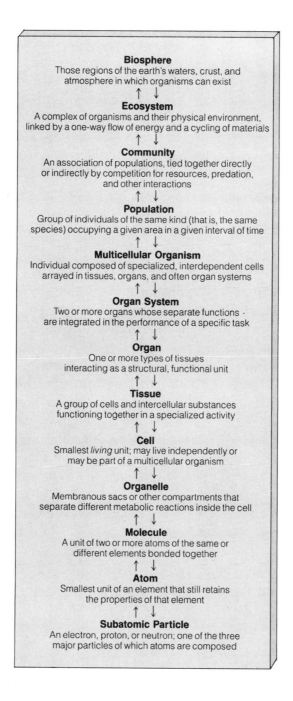

Figure 2 Levels of organization in nature. Cells represent the level at which the properties of life emerge.

9. _____

_____

_____

       Think of a rice plant. Many of its cells engage in **photosynthesis**. In the first stage of this process, cells trap sunlight energy, then convert it to another form of energy. In the second stage, cells use the chemical energy to build sugars, starch, and other substances. As part of the process of photosynthesis, molecules

10. _____

_____

_____

of **ATP,** an "energy carrier," are put together. ATP transfers energy to other molecules that function as metabolic workers (enzymes), building blocks, or energy reserves.

       In rice plants, some of the stored energy becomes concentrated in starchy seeds—rice grains. Energy reserves in countless trillions of rice grains provide energy for billions of rice-eating humans around the world.

Interdependency Among Organisms

With few exceptions, a flow of energy from the sun maintains the great pattern of organization in nature. Plants and some other photosynthetic organisms are the entry point for this flow.

11. _____

_____

_____

They are food **producers** for the world of life. Animals are **consumers**. Directly or indirectly, they feed on energy stored in plant parts. Thus zebras tap directly into the stored energy when they nibble on grass. Lions tap into it indirectly when they chomp on zebras. Bacteria and fungi are **decomposers**. When they feed on tissues or remains of other organisms, they break down sugars and other biological molecules to simple raw materials—which can be cycled back to producers.

       And so we have interdependency among organisms based on a one-way flow of energy *through* them and recycling of materials *among* them (Figure 3).

       Such interactions among organisms influence populations, communities, and ecosystems. They even influence the global environment. Understand the extent of the interactions and you will gain insight into amplification of the greenhouse effect, acid rain, and many other modern-day problems.

Sensing and Responding to Change

It is often said that only organisms "respond" to the environment. Yet a rock also "responds" to the environment, as when it yields to gravity and tumbles downhill or changes shape slowly under the battering of wind, rain, or tides. The real difference is

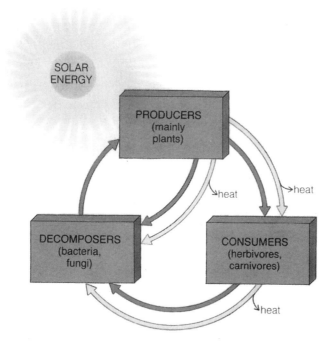

Figure 3 Energy flow and the cycling of materials in the biosphere. Humans are consumers and are inextricably linked with both producers and decomposers.

this: *Organisms have the cellular means to sense changes in the environment and make controlled responses to them.* They do so with the help of **receptors**. Receptors are molecules and structures that can detect specific information about the environment. When cells receive signals from receptors, they adjust their activities in ways that bring about an appropriate response.

Your body, for example, can withstand only so much heat or cold. It must rid itself of harmful substances. Certain foods must be available, in certain amounts. Yet temperatures shift, harmful substances may be encountered, and food is sometimes plentiful or scarce.

Think about what happens after you eat and simple sugar molecules enter your bloodstream. Blood is part of the body's "internal environment" (the other part is the tissue fluid bathing your cells). When the sugar level in blood rises, liver cells step up their secretion of insulin. Most cells in your body have receptors for insulin, a hormone that prods the cells into taking up sugar

12. _____
   _____
   _____

13. _____
   _____
   _____

molecules. With so many cells taking up sugar, the blood sugar level returns to normal.

Suppose you skip breakfast, then lunch, and the blood sugar level falls. Now a different hormone prods liver cells to dig into their stores of energy-rich molecules. These molecules are broken down to simple sugars, which are released into the bloodstream—and again the blood sugar level returns to normal.

Usually the internal environment of a multicelled organism is kept fairly constant. When conditions in the internal environment are being maintained within tolerable limits, we call this a state of **homeostasis**.

14. _____

Reproduction

We humans tend to think we enter the world rather abruptly and leave it the same way. Yet we and all other organisms are more than this. *We are part of an immense, ongoing journey that began billions of years ago.* Think of the first cell produced when a human sperm penetrates an egg. The cell would not even exist if the sperm and egg had not formed earlier, according to DNA instructions passed down through countless generations. With those time-tested instructions, a new human body develops in ways that will prepare it, ultimately, for helping to produce individuals of the next generation. With **reproduction**—that is, the production of offspring—life's journey continues.

15. _____

Or think of a moth. Do you simply picture a winged insect? What of the tiny fertilized egg deposited on a branch by a female moth? The egg contains the instructions necessary to become an adult. By those instructions, the egg develops into a caterpillar, a larval stage adapted for rapid feeding and growth. The caterpillar eats and grows until an internal "alarm clock" goes off. Then its body enters a so-called pupal stage of development, which involves wholesale remodeling. Some cells die, others multiply and become organized in different patterns. In time an adult moth emerges. It has organs that contain eggs or sperm. Its wings are brightly colored and flutter at a frequency appropriate for attracting a mate. In short the adult stage is adapted for reproduction.

None of these stages is "the insect." The insect is a series of organized stages from one fertilized egg to the next. Each stage is vital for the ultimate production of new moths. The instructions for each stage were written into moth DNA long before each moment of reproduction—and so the ancient moth story continues.

Mutation: Source of Variations in Heritable Traits

Reproduction involves **inheritance**. The word means that parents transmit DNA instructions for duplicating their traits, such as body form, to offspring.

DNA has two striking qualities. Its instructions assure that offspring will resemble parents—and they also permit *variations* in the details of traits. For example, having five fingers on each hand is a human trait. Yet some humans are born with six fingers on each hand instead of five! Variations in traits arise through **mutations,** which are heritable changes in the structure or number of DNA molecules.

16. _____
_____
_____

Many mutations are harmful. A change in even a bit of DNA may be enough to sabotage the steps necessary to produce a vital trait. In *hemophilia A,* for example, a tiny mutation leads to an impaired ability to clot blood. Bleeding continues for an abnormally long time after even a small cut or bruise.

Yet some mutations are harmless, even beneficial, under prevailing conditions. A classic example is a mutation in light-colored moths that leads to dark-colored offspring. Moths fly by night and rest during the day, when birds that eat them are active. What happens when a light moth rests on a light-colored tree trunk? Birds simply don't see it. Suppose, as a result of heavy industry, light trunks in a forested region become soot covered—and dark. The dark moths are less conspicuous, so they have a better chance of living long enough to reproduce. Under sooty conditions, the mutated form of the trait is more adaptive.

An **adaptive trait** simply is one that helps an organism survive and reproduce under a given set of environmental conditions.

17. _____
_____
_____

1700 words

Write your ending time here: _____

Subtract your starting time: _____

Total time: _____

Check the Rate Chart in the back of the book to find out how many words per minute you have read, and then record your score on the Progress Chart.

Step 3: Analyze What You Read—Create a Study Guide

Objective Questions

Go back to the article and underline or highlight what you think will be asked on a test. Then fill in the missing marginal notes to test your memory of what you have underlined. We have provided the lines for the notes, but you will have to figure out the topics to write on the lines. If you prefer, you may write the self-test note on the front of a flash card and what you would have underlined on the back.

Essay/Application Questions

PREDICT ESSAY QUESTIONS   What are the two most likely topics for essay questions?

1. _____

2. _____

MAKE GRAPHIC ORGANIZERS

1. Fill in the following idea map for the six shared characteristics of life.

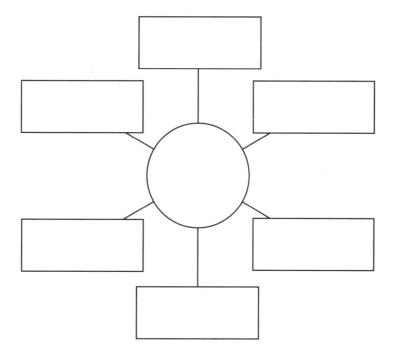

2. Make an idea map showing the 13 levels of organization in nature. Use a separate piece of paper.

Skill Development: Mnemonic Devices

When you have lists of material to memorize, it helps to use *mnemonic devices,* or memory tricks. To memorize the six shared characteristics of life you can use the first letter of each item on the idea map to make up a nonsense sentence that's easy to remember, such as *Don's Mother Irene Serves Red Meat.* To make it easier to remember the 13 levels of organization in nature, you could group them as follows:

1. Living and nonliving: SAM (Subatomic particle, Atom, Molecule)
2. Living organisms: OCTOOM (Organelle, Cell, Tissue, Organ, Organ system, Multicellular organism)
3. Groups of organisms: PCEB (Population, Community, Ecosystem, Biosphere)

For practice, make up a nonsense sentence to remember the order of the planets from the sun outwards (*Mercury, Venus, Earth, Mars, Jupiter, Saturn, Uranus, Neptune, Pluto*).

1. _____

2. Now group the following shopping list into four categories: hamburger, lettuce, hamburger buns, ketchup, tomatoes, mustard, onions, muffins, bacon

a. _____

b. _____

c. _____

d. _____

Skill Development: Summarizing

Use your graphic organizer to summarize this reading. First write the main idea. Then take each heading from the outline and make it into one or more sentences (say something about each heading). Use paragraph form.

Step 4: Remember What's Important

 Use the marginal notes or flash cards, the graphic organizers, and mnemonic devices for self-testing. Keep testing until you know the material.

Step 5: Make Use of What You Read

 When you are ready, complete the Comprehension Check. Do not look back at the reading or the study guide.

Step 6: Evaluate Your Active Critical Thinking Skills

 After your test has been graded, use the checklist on p. 465 to evaluate your skills.

COMPREHENSION CHECK

Multiple Choice

Circle the letter before the best answer to each question below.

1. Living and nonliving things both have

    a. molecules.

    b. cells.

    c. tissues.

    d. organs.

2. Only living things have

    a. molecules.

    b. atoms.

    c. particles.

    d. DNA.

3. A population is a group of

    a. cells.

    b. molecules.

    c. organs.

    d. organisms.

4. Living things can be categorized as

    a. molecules or mutations.

    b. metabolic or homeostatic.

    c. populations, communities, or biosystems.

    d. producers, consumers, or decomposers.

5. A group of lions, zebras, and rhinos living in the African plains comprises

    a. a population.

    b. a community.

    c. an ecosystem.

    d. a biosphere.

6. The advantage of mutation is that it

    a. weeds out the weaker organisms.

    b. is a creative energy.

    c. may lead to better adaptations.

    d. prevents defective organisms from reproducing.

7. Animals that require a great deal of energy to live must have a high rate of

    a. homeostasis.

    b. metabolism.

    c. reproduction.

    d. all of the above.

8. Photosynthesis is accomplished mainly by

    a. atoms.

    b. cells.

    c. plants.

    d. animals.

Fill-ins

Fill in the following blanks.

9. A _____ is an organized unit that can survive and reproduce on

    its own, given _____ instructions and sources of energy and raw
    materials.

Essays

1. What are the characteristics that are shared by all living things?
2. List the levels of organization in nature.

_____

_____

_____

_____   _____

_____   _____

_____   _____

_____   _____

_____   _____

_____   _____

_____

VOCABULARY IN CONTEXT

Write the best word from this list in the blank in each sentence below.

analogy   **secretion**   **hormone**   **sabotage**   **impaired**

1. The _____ of perspiration is the function of our body's sweat glands.

2. Estrogen is a female _____ .

3. You can make an _____ between bees in a hive and human workers in a factory.

4. The word _____ came from French factory workers' practice of breaking machinery by throwing their wooden shoes (*sabots*) into it during labor disputes.

5. Older people often suffer from _____ hearing and vision.

14

Interpersonal Attraction: Liking and Loving

Vocabulary Preview

dynamics (dī nam′iks): the various forces operating in a field

social psychologist (sō′shəl sī käl′ə jist): one who studies individuals in relation to other people

encompass (en kum′pəs): include

proximity (präks im′ə tē): nearness

reciprocity (res ə präs′ə tē): mutual action or exchange

spatial (spā′shəl): happening or existing in space

arbitrary (ar′bə trer′ē): chance

rationale (rash′ə nal′): reasons

correlated (kôr′ə lāt′id): compared to show the relation between two things

assess (ə ses′): evaluate

variable (ver′ē ə bəl): a quantity that may change

subsequent (sub′si kwənt): following in time, place, or order

replicate (rep′lə kāt): repeat or duplicate

enhance (en hans′): improve

hypothesis (hī päth′ə sis): an unproved theory used as a basis for further investigation

illicit (il lis′it): unlawful or improper

self-concept (self kän′sept): the image one has of oneself

repulsion (ri pul′shən): strong dislike

disdain (dis dān′): scorn

ingratiation (in grā′shē ā′shən): bringing oneself into another′s favor or good graces by conscious effort

cat, āte, fäther; pen, ēvil; if, kīte; nō, ôr, fōod, book; boil, house; up, turn; chief, shell; thick, *the*; zh, treasure; ŋ, sing; ə for *a* in *about*; ′ as in *able* (a′b′l)

Step 1: Preread

 Preread the following selection by reading the title, the headings, and the illustration. Answer the first two questions without looking back at the reading.

1. What is the subject?

   _____

2. What is the main idea?

   _____

3. Look at the illustration.

   a. What is the subject?

   _____

   b. What is the main idea?

   _____

   _____

4. Take a moment to think about interpersonal attraction. Think about what you know about it, what you don't know, and what you might find out from reading the selection. Make up three questions.

   a. _____

   b. _____

   c. _____

Step 2: Read

 Read the selection without underlining.

   Write your starting time here: _____

Interpersonal Attraction: Liking and Loving

WAYNE WEITEN

"I JUST DON'T KNOW WHAT SHE SEES IN HIM. She could do so much better for herself. I suppose he's a nice guy, but they're just not right for each other." You've probably heard similar remarks on many occasions. These comments illustrate people's interest in analyzing the dynamics of attraction. **Interpersonal attraction refers to positive feelings toward another.** Social psychologists use this term broadly to encompass a variety of experiences, including liking, friendship, admiration, lust, and love.

Key Factors in Attraction

Many factors influence who is attracted to whom. Here we'll discuss factors that promote the development of liking, friendship, and love. Although these are different types of attraction, the interpersonal dynamics at work in each are surprisingly similar. Each is influenced by proximity, physical attractiveness, similarity, and reciprocity.

Proximity Effects

It would be difficult for you to develop a friendship with someone you never met. It happens occasionally (among pen pals or users of on-line computer services, for instance). But attraction usually depends on people being in the same place at the same time. Proximity is a major factor in attraction. **Proximity refers to geographic, residential, and other forms of spatial closeness** (classroom seating, office arrangements, and so forth). Generally, people become acquainted with, and attracted to, people who live, work, shop, and play nearby. The importance of spatial factors in living arrangements was apparent in a classic study of friendship patterns among married graduate students living in university housing projects. The closer people's doors were, the more likely they were to become friends.

Proximity effects may seem self-evident, but it's sobering to realize that your friendships and love interests are shaped by arbitrary office desk arrangements, dormitory floor assignments, and traffic patterns in apartment complexes. In spite of the increasing geographic mobility in modern society, people still tend to marry someone who grew up nearby.

Physical Attractiveness

People often say that "beauty is only skin deep." But the empirical evidence suggests that most people don't really believe it. The importance of physical attractiveness was demonstrated in a study of first-year college students. Their dates for a dance were supposedly selected by a computer. Actually, the couples had been paired randomly, but the computer cover story provided a good rationale for asking students to rate their desire to go out with their dates again. These ratings were then correlated with their dates' physical attractiveness (assessed by impartial judges). A host of personality, interest, and background variables were also studied.

For both sexes, a partner's good looks was the *only* variable that predicted subjects' desire to go out with their date again. Subsequent studies have replicated the prominence of physical attractiveness in the initial stage of dating. They have also shown that it continues to influence the course of commitment as dating relationships evolve.

In the realm of romance, being physically attractive appears to be more important for females than males. This gender gap was apparent in a recent study of the tactics people use in pursuing romantic relationships. David Buss asked 208 newlywed individuals to describe the things they did when they first met their spouse, and during the remainder of their courtship, to make themselves more appealing to their partner. Buss found that men were more likely than women to emphasize their material resources. They flashed lots of money, bought nice gifts, showed off expensive possessions, and bragged about their importance at work (see Figure 1). In contrast, women were more likely than men to work at enhancing their appearance. They dieted, wore stylish clothes, tried new hairstyles, and got a tan. As the data in Figure 1 show, *both sexes* strived to enhance their physical attractiveness, but women relied on these tactics more.

Figure 1 Similarities and differences between the sexes in tactics of attraction. David Buss asked newlywed subjects to rate how often they had used 23 tactics of attraction to make themselves more appealing to their partner. The tactics used by one sex significantly more often than the other are listed in the first two sections of the figure. Although there were significant differences between the sexes, there were also many similarities. The 11 tactics used most frequently by each sex (those above the median) are highlighted, showing considerable overlap between males and females in the tactics they use most. (Note: Higher means in the data reflect higher frequency of use, but the numbers do not indicate frequency per day or week.)

Tactics of attraction	Mean frequency (N = 102)	Mean frequency (N = 106)
Tactics used significantly more by males	*Men*	*Women*
Display resources	0.67	0.44
Brag about resources	0.73	0.60
Display sophistication	1.18	0.88
Display strength	0.96	0.44
Display athleticism	1.18	0.94
Show off	0.70	0.47
Tactics used significantly more by females	*Men*	*Women*
Wear makeup	0.02	1.63
Keep clean and groomed	2.27	2.44
Alter appearance—general	0.39	1.27
Wear stylish clothes	1.22	2.00
Act coy	0.54	0.73
Wear jewelry	0.25	2.21
Wear sexy clothes	0.68	0.91
Tactics for which no significant sex differences were found	*Men*	*Women*
Act provocative	0.77	0.90
Flirt	2.13	2.09
Keep hair groomed	2.20	2.31
Increase social exposure	0.89	0.90
Act nice	1.77	1.86
Display humor	2.42	2.28
Act promiscuous	0.30	0.21
Act submissive	1.24	1.11
Dissemble (feign agreement)	1.26	1.09
Touch	2.26	2.16

Although people prefer physically attractive partners in romantic relationships, they may consider their own level of attractiveness in pursuing dates. The *matching hypothesis* **proposes that males and females of approximately equal physical attractiveness are likely to select each other as partners.** The matching hypothesis is supported by evidence that married couples tend to be very similar in level of physical attractiveness. However, there's some debate about whether people match up by their own choice. Some theorists believe that people mostly pursue high attractiveness in partners. Their matching may be the result of social forces beyond their control, such as rejection by more attractive others.

Most of the studies of physical beauty and attraction have focused on dating relationships. Only a few have looked at friendship formation. However, the studies of friendship suggest that people prefer attractiveness in their opposite-sex friends as well as their dates. Researchers have also found evidence for matching effects in same-sex friendships. Interestingly, this same-sex matching appears to occur among male friends but not among female friends.

Similarity Effects

Is it true that "birds of a feather flock together," or do "opposites attract"? Research provides far more support for the former than the latter. Married and dating couples tend to be similar in age, race, religion, social class, personality, education, intelligence, physical attractiveness, and attitudes. In married couples, personality similarity appears to be associated with greater marital happiness. Similarity is also seen among friends. For instance, adolescent friends are more similar than nonfriends in educational goals and performance, political and religious activities, illicit drug use, and self-concept. Adult friends also tend to be relatively similar in terms of income, education, occupational status, ethnicity, and religion.

The most obvious explanation for these correlations is that similarity causes attraction. Laboratory experiments on *attitude similarity,* conducted by Donn Byrne and his colleagues, suggest that similarity does cause liking. In these studies, subjects who have previously provided information on their own attitudes are led to believe that they'll be meeting a stranger. They're given information about the stranger's views that has been manipulated to show various degrees of similarity to their own views. As attitude similarity increases, subjects' ratings of the likability of the stranger increase. This evidence supports the notion that similarity promotes attraction. But it's also consistent with a somewhat different explanation proposed by Rosenbaum.

Rosenbaum has marshaled evidence suggesting that similarity effects occur in attraction not because similarity fosters liking but because *dissimilarity* leads to *dislike* of others. In one study of his "repulsion hypothesis," Rosenbaum found that Democrats did not rate other Democrats (similar others) higher than controls as much as they rated Republicans (dissimilar others) lower than controls. Rosenbaum acknowledges that similarity sometimes causes liking. But he maintains that *dissimilarity causes disdain* more frequently. Thus, there is reason to believe that liking is influenced by *both* similarity and dissimilarity in attitudes.

Reciprocity Effects

In his book *How to Win Friends and Influence People,* Dale Carnegie (1936) suggested that people can gain others' liking by showering them with praise and flattery. However, we've all heard that "flattery will get you nowhere." Which advice is right? The evidence suggests that flattery will get you somewhere, with some people, some of the time.

In interpersonal attraction, *reciprocity* **involves liking those who show that they like you**. In general, it appears that liking breeds liking and loving promotes loving. However, this principle must be qualified carefully. People realize that others sometimes try to butter them up. *Ingratiation* **is a conscious effort to cultivate others' liking by complimenting them, agreeing with them, and doing them favors**. If affection appears to be part of an ingratiation strategy, it's not likely to be reciprocated.

Studies of proximity, physical attractiveness, similarity, and reciprocity shed some light on the formation and evolution of friendships and romantic relationships but tell us very little about the mystery of love.

1300 words

Write your ending time here: _____

Subtract your starting time: _____

Total time: _____

Check the Rate Chart in the back of the book to find out how many words per minute you have read, and then record your score on the Progress Chart.

Step 3: Analyze What You Read—Create a Study Guide

Objective Questions

Go back to the reading and underline or highlight what you think will be on the test. For each idea that you underline, write a note in the margin that you can use to test yourself on the idea. If you prefer, you may write the self-test note on the front of a flash card and what you would have underlined on the back.

Essay/Application Questions

PREDICT ESSAY QUESTIONS   What is the most likely topic for an essay question?

MAKE GRAPHIC ORGANIZERS   Fill in the blanks in the following idea map.

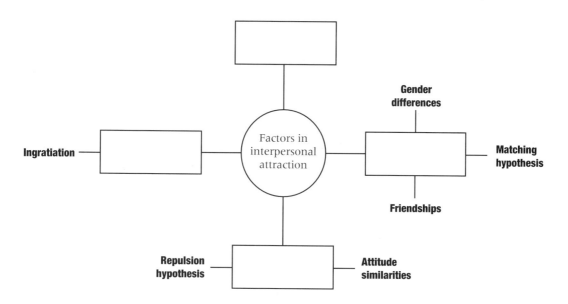

Skill Development: Memory   Make up a nonsense phrase or sentence in which each word begins with the first letter of one of the four factors in interpersonal attraction.

SKILL DEVELOPMENT: SUMMARIZING

Use your graphic organizer to summarize this article. First write the main idea. Then take each heading from the idea map and make it into one or more sentences (say something about each heading). Use paragraph form, and use a separate piece of paper.

Step 4: Remember What's Important

 Use the marginal notes or flash cards and the graphic organizer for self-testing. Keep testing until you know the material.

Step 5: Make Use of What You Read

 When you are ready, complete the Comprehension Check. Do not look back at the reading or the study guide.

Step 6: Evaluate Your Active Critical Thinking Skills

 After your test has been graded, use the checklist on p. 465 to evaluate your skills.

COMPREHENSION CHECK

True-False

Mark T or F.

_____ **1.** Using ingratiation is a good way to get people to like you.

_____ **2.** Opposites attract.

_____ **3.** Most people believe that "Beauty is only skin deep."

_____ **4.** The similarity effect is caused by either the attraction of like to like or the repulsion between like and unlike, or both.

Multiple Choice

Circle the letter before the best answer to each question below.

5. The matching hypothesis says that we prefer others who

    a. are similar to us in personality.

    b. live or work near us.

    c. like us.

    d. are about as attractive as we are.

6. Similarity is associated with

    a. greater marital happiness.

    b. adolescent friendships.

    c. adult friendships.

    d. all of the above.

7. The repulsion hypothesis says that people dislike those who

    a. are less attractive.

    b. are different.

    c. don't like us.

    d. don't live or work near us.

8. You can infer from the reciprocity effect that

   a. friendly, caring people get more love.

   b. people who are "hard to get" get more love.

   c. high achievers get more love.

   d. beautiful people get more love.

Short Answer

9. What are some gender differences in the tactics people use to pursue romantic relationships?

   _____

10. What is the difference between showing that you like someone and using ingratiation as a strategy?

    _____

    _____

    _____

Essay

Discuss the key factors in interpersonal attraction.

VOCABULARY IN CONTEXT

Write the best word from this list in the blank in each sentence below.

Part A

dynamics   social psychologist   encompass   proximity

reciprocity   spatial   arbitrary   rationale   correlated   assess

1. When you work in close _____ to a good-looking person of the opposite sex, an attraction is likely to develop.

2. A _____ might study how people react to peer pressure.

3. "You scratch my back and I'll scratch yours" is an example of

   _____ .

4. The choice of a career should be made carefully; it should not be based on

   something _____ like having a brother-in-law who knows somebody in the business.

5. The biological sciences _____ botany and zoology.

6. Career counselors use tests to _____ their clients' personality factors, interests, values, and abilities.

7. Studies show that cigarette smoking is _____ with lung cancer.

8. Psychologists try to explain the personality _____ that cause deviant behavior like child abuse and spousal abuse.

9. Architects and decorators often use models to illustrate the

   _____ relationships between design elements.

10. Parents should try to explain the _____ behind the rules they set so that children will understand their thinking.

Part B

variable	subsequent	replicate	enhance	hypothesis
illicit	self-concept	repulsion	disdain	ingratiation

11. In studies of stress and heart disease, one _____ is whether or not a heart attack has occurred.

12. If your research was done with a particular age group, the way to find out whether you would get the same results with another age group is to

   _____ the study with the new group.

13. Most people react to slugs with _____ .

14. People's levels of ambition are related to their _____ ; they tend to get the kinds of jobs they think they deserve.

15. If a person is very good looking but has a bad personality, you tend to like him a lot at first, and then you like him less with each _____ contact.

16. Courtship behaviors like bringing flowers or candy are attempts at

    _____ .

17. Marijuana and cocaine are _____ drugs.

18. Usually additional education will _____ one's socioeconomic status.

19. Scientists cannot presume that something is true; they must test each

    _____ to find out how often and under what circumstances it works.

20. After the politician was convicted of taking bribes, the voters looked on him

    with _____ .

15

History of Calculating Devices

Vocabulary Preview

denomination (di näm′ə na′shən): a unit of specified value

eccentric (ik sen′trik): unconventional; odd; out of the ordinary

grandiose (gran′dē ōs′): impressive; grand

ratchets (rach′its): toothed wheels or bars whose teeth slope in one direction so as to catch and hold a pawl, which thus prevents backward movement

ballistics (bə lis′tiks): the science of dealing with the motion and impact of projectiles

cat, āte, fäther; pen, ēvil; if, kīte; nō, ôr, fo͞od, book; boil, house; up, turn; chief, shell; thick, *the*; zh, treasure; ŋ, sing; ə for *a* in *about*; ' as in *able* (a′b'l)

Step 1: Preread

Preview the following selection by reading the title, the headings, and the illustrations. Answer the following questions without looking back at the reading.

1. What is the subject? _____

2. What is the main idea? _____

_____

3. Think about what you know about computers, what you don't know, and what you might find out from reading the selection. Make up three questions.

    a. _____

    b. _____

    c. _____

Step 2: Read

Read the selection without underlining.

Write your starting time here: _____

History of Calculating Devices

KARL J. SMITH

O NE OF THE BIGGEST SURPRISES OF OUR time has been the impact of the personal computer on everyone's life. Few people foresaw that computers would jump the boundaries of scientific and engineering communities and create a revolution in our way of life in the last half of the 20th century. No one expected to see a computer sitting on a desk, much less on desks in every type of business, large and small, and even in our homes. Today no one is ready to face the world without some knowledge of computers. What has created this change in our lives is not only the advances in technology that have made computers small and affordable. It is also the tremendous imagination shown in developing ways to use them.

In this section we will consider the historical achievements leading to the easy availability of calculators and computers.

First Calculating Tool: Finger Calculating

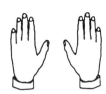

The first "device" for arithmetic computations is finger counting. It has the advantages of low cost and instant availability. You are familiar with addition and subtraction on your fingers, but here is a method for multiplication by 9. Place both hands as shown in the margin. To multiply 4 × 9, simply bend the fourth finger from the left as shown:

The answer is read as 36, the bent finger serving to distinguish between the first and second digits in the answer. What about 36 × 9? Separate the third and fourth fingers from the left (as shown in the margin), since 36 has 3 tens. Next, bend the sixth finger from the left, since 36 has 6 units. Now the answer can be read directly from the fingers:

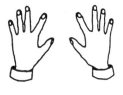

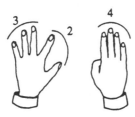

Aristophanes devised a complicated finger-calculating system in about 500 B.C., but it was very difficult to learn. Figure 1 shows an illustration from a manual published about two thousand years later, in 1520.

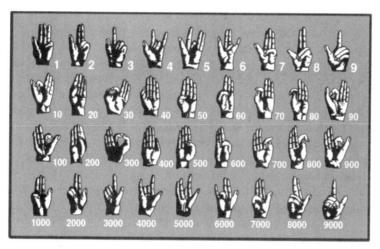

Figure 1 Finger calculation was important in the Middle Ages.

Other Early Calculating Devices

Numbers can be represented by stones, slip knots, or beads on a string. These devices evolved into the abacus, as shown in Figure 2. Abaci (plural of abacus) were used thousands of years ago, and

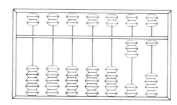

Figure 2 Abacus: The number shown is 31.

Figure 3 Napier's rods (1617).

are still used today. In the hands of an expert, they even rival calculators for speed in performing certain calculations. An abacus consists of rods that contain sliding beads. There are four or five in the lower section, and two in the upper that equal one in the lower section of the next higher denomination. The abacus is useful today for teaching mathematics to youngsters. One can actually see the "carry" in addition and the "borrowing" in subtraction.

In 1624, John Napier invented a device similar to a multiplication table with movable parts, as shown in Figure 3. These rods are known as **Napier's rods** or **Napier's bones.**

A device used for many years was a **slide rule** (see Figure 4), which was also invented by Napier. The answers given by a slide rule are only visual approximations. They do not have the precision that is often required.

Figure 4 Slide rule.

Mechanical Calculators

The 17th century saw the beginnings of calculating machines. When Pascal was 19, he began to develop a machine to add long columns of figures. He built several versions, and since all proved to be unreliable, he considered this project a failure. But the machine introduced basic principles that are used in modern calculators.

The next advance in mechanical calculators came from Germany in about 1672, when the great mathematician Gottfried Leibniz studied Pascal's calculators, improved them, and drew up plans for a mechanical calculator. In 1695 a machine was finally built, but this calculator also proved to be unreliable.

In the 19th century, an eccentric Englishman, Charles Babbage, developed plans for a grandiose calculating machine. It was called a "difference engine," and had thousands of gears, ratchets, and counters.

Four years later, in 1826, even though Babbage had still not built his difference engine, he began an even more elaborate project—the building of what he called an "analytic engine." This machine was capable of an accuracy to 20 decimal places. However it, too, could not be built because the technical knowledge to build it was not far enough advanced. Much later, IBM built both the difference and analytic engines based on Babbage's design. They used modern technology, and they work perfectly.

Hand-Held Calculators

In the past few years pocket calculators have been one of the fastest growing items in the United States. There are probably two reasons for this increase in popularity. Most people (including mathematicians!) don't like to do arithmetic, and a good calculator is very inexpensive.

First Computers

The devices discussed thus far in this section would all be classi-fied as calculators. With some of the new programmable calcula-tors, the distinction between a calculator and a computer is less well defined than it was in the past. Stimulated by the need to make ballistics calculations and to break secret codes during World War II, researchers made great advances in calculating machines. During the late 1930s and early 1940s John Vincent Atanasoff, a physics professor at Iowa State University, and his graduate student Clifford E. Berry built an electronic digital com-puter. However, the first working electronic computers were invented by J. Presper Eckert and John W. Mauchly at the University of Pennsylvania. All computers now in use derive from the original work they did between 1942 and 1946. They built the first fully electronic digital computer called ENIAC (*Electronic Numerical Integrator and Calculator*). The ENIAC filled a space 30 × 50 feet, weighed 30 tons, had 18,000 vacuum tubes, and cost $487,000 to build. It used enough electricity to operate three 150-kilowatt radio stations.

There is some controversy over who actually invented the first computer. In the early 1970s there was a lengthy court case over a patent dispute between Sperry Rand (who had acquired the ENIAC patent) and Honeywell, who represented those who originally worked on the ENIAC project. The judge in that case ruled that "between 1937 and 1942, Atanasoff . . . developed and built an automatic electronic digital computer for solving large systems of linear equations. . . . Eckert and Mauchly did not themselves invent the automatic electronic digital computer, but instead derived that subject matter from one Dr. John Vincent Atanasoff." Others who believe that a court of law is not the place for deciding questions about the history of science give Eckert and Mauchly the honor of inventing the first computer. In 1980, the Association for Computing Machinery honored them as founders of the computer industry.

The UNIVAC I, built in 1951 by the builders of the ENIAC, became the first commercially available computer. It could han-dle alphabetic data as well as numeric data. The invention of the transistor in 1947 and solid-state devices in the 1950s provided the technology for smaller, faster, more reliable machines.

Present-Day Computers

In 1958, Seymour Cray developed the first **supercomputer,** a computer that can handle at least 10 million instructions per second. It is used in major scientific research and military defense installations.

Throughout the 1960 and early 1970s, computers continued to become faster and more powerful; they became a part of the business world. The "user" often never saw the machines. A **job** would be submitted to be "batch processed" by someone trained to run the computer. The notion of "time sharing" developed. The computer could handle more than one job, apparently simultaneously, by switching quickly from one job to another. Using a computer at this time was often frustrating. An incomplete job would be returned because of an error and the user would have to resubmit the job. It often took days to complete the project.

The large computers, known as *mainframes,* were followed by the **minicomputers.** They took up less than 3 cubic feet of space and no longer required a controlled atmosphere. These were still used by many people at the same time, though often directly through the use of terminals.

In 1976, Steven Jobs and Stephen Wozniak built the Apple. It was the first personal computer to be commercially successful. This computer proved extremely popular. Small businesses could afford to purchase these machines. With a printer attached they took up only about twice the space of a typewriter. Technology "buffs" could purchase their own computers. This computer was designed so that innovations that would improve or enlarge the scope of performance of the machine could be added with relatively little difficulty. Owners could open up their machines and install new devices. This increased contact between the user and the machine produced an atmosphere of tremendous creativity and innovation. In many cases, individual owners brought their own machines to work. They introduced their superiors to the potential usefulness of the personal computer.

In the fast-moving technology of the computer world, the invention of language to describe it changes as fast as teenage slang. Today there are battery-powered **laptops,** which are more powerful than the huge ENIAC. In 1989 a pocket computer was introduced. The most recent trend has been to link together several personal computers so that they can share software and

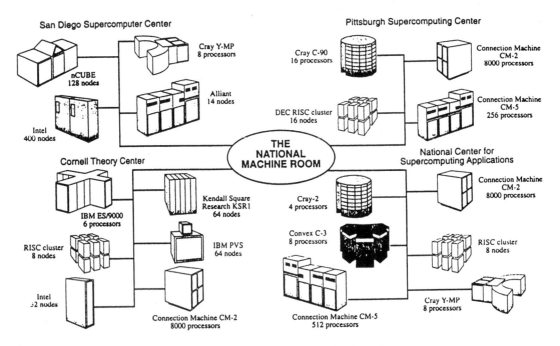

Figure 5 An example of a high-speed network linking four supercomputers.

different users can easily access the same documents. These are called **LANs,** or local area networks. The most comprehensive high-speed network is known as *The National Machine Room.* It links together the high-performance computers at the four National Science Foundation supercomputer centers. Figure 5 shows the network in 1993.

What does the future hold? Any prediction that could be made would most likely become outdated before you read this page. Instead of a prediction, we invite you to visit a computer store.

1600 words

Write your ending time here: _____

Subtract your starting time: _____

Total time: _____

Check the Rate Chart in the back of the book to find out how many words per minute you have read, and then record your score on the Progress Chart.

Step 3: Analyze What You Read—Create a Study Guide

Objective Questions

Go back to the reading and underline what you think might be on a test. Make marginal self-test notes to remember what you have underlined. If you prefer, you may write each self-test note on a flash card and paraphrase the underlining on the back.

Essay/Application Questions

PREDICT ESSAY QUESTIONS   There is only one likely topic for an essay question. Write it here.

_____

MAKE GRAPHIC ORGANIZERS

1. Following is a time line. Fill in the blanks with what happened next to each date.

500 B.C.   _____

Thousands of years ago   _____

17th century   _____

                                _____

                                _____

19th century   _____

Late 1930s–early 1940s   _____

1942–1946   _____

1951   _____

1958	_____
1976	_____
	_____
1989	_____
Most recent trend	_____

Skill Development: Summarizing

Use your underlining and marginal notes and your graphic organizers to summarize this reading.

_____

_____

_____

_____

_____

_____

_____

_____

_____

_____

_____

_____

_____

_____

Step 4: Remember What's Important

 Use the marginal notes or flash cards and the graphic organizers for self-testing. Use mnemonic devices as needed. Keep testing until you know the material.

Step 5: Make Use of What You Read

 When you are ready, complete the Comprehension Check. Do not look back at the reading or the study guide.

Step 6: Evaluate Your Active Critical Thinking Skills

 After your test has been graded, use the checklist on p. 465 to evaluate your skills.

COMPREHENSION CHECK

Multiple Choice

Circle the letter before the best answer to each of the following questions.

1. Computers have become consistently
    a. smaller.
    b. faster.
    c. cheaper.
    d. all of the above.

2. The first electronic digital computers used
    a. vacuum tubes.
    b. transistors.
    c. batteries.
    d. silicon chips.

3. The first successful personal computer was the
    a. IBM.
    b. Apple.
    c. Atari.
    d. Commodore.

4. Software includes
    a. the physical parts (mechanical, magnetic, electronic) of a computer.
    b. computer programs.
    c. peripherals.
    d. all of the above.

5. The first computer was the
    a. slide rule.
    b. abacus.
    c. ENIAC.
    d. analytic engine.

6. People unfamiliar with computers will
   a. not understand modern culture.
   b. not be able to support themselves.
   c. have to go into the liberal arts.
   d. do all of the above.

7. The history of computers suggests that creative geniuses regularly
   a. make a lot of money.
   b. experience failure.
   c. become famous during their lifetimes.
   d. die in poverty.

8. The author seems to find the future of computers
   a. frightening.
   b. exciting.
   c. depressing.
   d. boring.

Short Answer

What are two calculating devices used before 1600?

9. _____

10. _____

Essay

Trace the history of calculating devices from 500 B.C. to the present. Write your answer on a separate piece of paper.

VOCABULARY IN CONTEXT

Write the best word from the following list in the blank in each sentence below.

denominations   eccentric   grandiose   ratchet   ballistic

1. The construction of each ancient Egyptian pyramid was a _____
    project, considering the difficulties of transporting massive blocks of stone before
    the invention of the wheel.

2. U.S. coins come in only six _____ : silver dollar, half dollar,
    quarter, dime, nickel, and penny.

3. _____ tests can prove which gun shot a particular bullet.

4. A strap that goes around a refrigerator when it is being moved on a dolly has a

    _____ so that it can be tightened and won't slip.

5. It is said that most great geniuses are _____ ; they get so occupied
    with thinking about their ideas that they forget trivial items like changing their
    socks or getting haircuts.

16

Choosing an Occupation or Career

Vocabulary Preview

idealized (ī dē′ə līzd′): perfect or seen as perfect

attained (ə tānd′): gained; accomplished; achieved

socioeconomic (sō′sē ō ek′ə näm′ik): involving both social and economic factors

envision (en vizh′ən): to imagine something not yet in existence

aptitude (ap′tə tŏŏd): a natural tendency, ability, or talent

cat, āte, fäther; pen, ēvil; if, kīte; nō, ôr, fōōd, book; boil, house; up, turn; chief, shell; thick, *the*; zh, treasure; ŋ, sing; ə for *a* in *about*; ' as in *able* (a′b′l)

Step 1: Preread

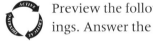 Preview the following selection by reading the title, the headings, and subheadings. Answer the following questions without looking back at the reading.

1. What is the subject? _____

2. What is the main idea? _____

   _____

3. Think about what you know about career planning, what you don't know, and what you might find out from reading the selection. Make up three questions.

   a. _____

   b. _____

   c. _____

Step 2: Read

 Read the selection without underlining.

   Write your starting time here: _____

Choosing an Occupation or Career

GERALD COREY

WHAT DO YOU EXPECT FROM WORK? WHAT factors do you stress in selecting a career or an occupation? In working with college students, we find that many of them haven't really thought seriously about why they are choosing a given vocation. For some, parental pressure or encouragement is the major reason for their choice. Others have idealized views of what it would be like to be a lawyer, engineer, or doctor. Many of these people haven't looked at what they value the most and whether these values can be attained in their chosen vocation. John Holland's theory of career decision making is based on the assumption that career choices are an expression of personality: "The choice of an occupation is an expressive act that reflects the person's motivation, knowledge, personality, and ability. Occupations represent a way of life, an environment rather than a set of isolated work functions or skills."

Being Active in Career Planning

One of the major factors that might prevent you from becoming active in planning for a career is the temptation to put off doing what needs to be done to *choose* your work. If you merely "fall into" a job, you will probably be disappointed with the outcome.

A reviewer of this book called our attention to predictions that typical workers will make five to seven occupational changes in their life. Thus, it could well be a mistake to think about selecting *one* occupation that will last a lifetime. Instead, it may be more fruitful to think about choosing a general type of work or a broad field of endeavor that appeals to you. You can consider your present job or field of study as a means of gaining experience and opening doors to new possibilities, and you can focus on what *you* want to learn from this experience. It can be liberating to realize that your decisions about work can be part of a developmental process and that your jobs can change as you change.

The Dangers of Choosing an Occupation Too Soon

So much emphasis is placed on what you will do "for a living" that there is a real danger of feeling compelled to choose an occupation or a career before you're really ready to do so. In our society there is pressure from an early age to grow up. The encouragement to identify with some occupation begins in childhood with the often-heard question "What are you going to be when you grow up?" (Part of the implication of this question is that we're not grown up until we've decided to *be* something.) If freshman year in high school isn't too early to start worrying about acceptance to college, then no grade is too early to start worrying about acceptance to the right high school! Carney and Wells write that society expects young people to identify their values, choose a vocation and a lifestyle, and then settle down. The implication is that once young people make the "right decision," they should be set for life. Yet deciding on a career is not that simple.

One of the dangers in focusing on a particular occupation too soon is that students' interest patterns are often not sufficiently reliable or stable in high school or, sometimes, even the college years to predict job success and satisfaction. Furthermore, the typical student does not have enough self-knowledge or knowledge of educational offerings and vocational opportunities to make realistic decisions. The pressure to make premature vocational decisions often results in choosing an occupation in which one does not have the interests and abilities required for success.

Factors in Vocational Decision Making

Making vocational choices is a process spanning a considerable period rather than an isolated event. Researchers in career development have found that most people go through a series of stages in choosing the occupation or, more typically, occupations that they will follow. . . . Various factors emerge or become influential during each phase of development. The following factors have been shown to be important in determining a person's occupational decision-making process: self-concept, interests, abilities, values, occupational attitudes, socioeconomic level, parental influence, ethnic identity, gender, and physical, mental, emotional, and social handicaps. In choosing your vocation (or evaluating the choices you've made previously), you may want to consider which factors really mean the most to you. Let's consider some of these factors, keeping in mind that vocational choice is a process, not an event.

Self-Concept

Some writers in career development contend that a vocational choice is an attempt to fulfill one's self-concept. People with a poor self-concept, for example, are not likely to envision themselves in a meaningful or important job. They are likely to keep their aspirations low, and thus their achievements will probably be low. They may select and remain in a job that they do not enjoy or derive satisfaction from, based on their conviction that such a job is all they are worthy of. In this regard choosing a vocation can be thought of as a public declaration of the kind of person we see ourselves as being.

Occupational Attitudes

Research indicates that the higher the educational requirements for an occupation, the higher its status, or prestige. We develop our attitudes toward the status of occupations by learning from the people in our environment. Typical first-graders are not aware of the differential status of occupations, yet in a few years these children begin to rank occupations in a manner similar to that of adults. Some research has shown that positive attitudes toward most occupations are common among first-graders but that these preferences narrow steadily with each year of school. As students advance to higher grades, they reject more and more occupations as unacceptable. Unfortunately, they rule out some of the very jobs from which they may have to choose if they are to find employment as adults. It is difficult for people to feel positively about themselves if they have to accept an occupation they perceive as low in status.

Abilities

Ability or aptitude has received as much attention as any of the factors deemed significant in the career decision-making process, and it is probably used more often than any other factor. *Ability* refers to your competence in an activity; *aptitude* is your ability to learn. There are both general and specific abilities. Scholastic aptitude, often called general intelligence or IQ, is a general ability typically considered to consist of both verbal and numerical aptitudes. Included among the specific abilities are mechanical, clerical, and spatial aptitudes, abstract reasoning ability, and eye/hand/foot coordination. Scholastic aptitude is particularly significant, because it largely determines who will be able to obtain the levels of education required for entrance into the higher-status occupations.

Interestingly, most studies show little direct relationship between measured aptitudes and occupational performance and satisfaction. This does not mean that ability is unimportant, but it does indicate that we must consider other factors in career planning.

Interests

Interest measurement has become popular and is used extensively in career planning. Interests, unlike abilities, have been found to be moderately effective as predictors of vocational success, satisfaction, and persistence. Therefore, vocational planning should give primary consideration to interests. It is important to first determine your areas of vocational interest, then to identify occupations for which these interests are appropriate, and then to determine those occupations for which you have the abilities required for satisfactory job performance. Research evidence indicates only a slight relationship between interests and abilities. In other words, simply because you are interested in a job does not necessarily mean that you have the ability needed for it.

Values

It is important for you to assess, identify, and clarify your values so that you will be able to match them with your career. There is some merit to following the combination of your interests and abilities as primary reliable guides for a general occupational area. After you have considered how your interests and abilities match with possible career choices, it is then helpful to explore your values. For purposes of this discussion, values can be classified in three general areas: (1) spiritual/religious, (2) family/in-terpersonal, and (3) money/material possessions.

Your *work values* pertain to what you hope to accomplish through your role in an occupation. Work values are an impor-tant aspect of your total value system, and knowing those things that bring meaning to your life is crucial if you hope to find a career that has personal value for you. Most career-guidance centers in colleges and universities now offer one or more computer-based programs to help students decide on a career. One popular program is known as the System of Interactive Guidance and Information, or more commonly referred to as SIGI. This program assesses and categorizes your work values. Taking it will aid you in identifying specific occupations that you might want to explore.

You might consider scheduling an appointment in the career-counseling center at your college to participate in a computer-based occupational guidance program. In addition to SIGI, other programs are the Career Information System (CIS), the Guidance Information System (GIS), Choices, and Discover. Each of these programs develops lists of occupations to explore.

2200 words

Write your ending time here: _____

Subtract your starting time: _____

Total time: _____

Check the Rate Chart in the back of the book to find how many words per minute you have read, and then record your score on the Progress Chart.

Step 3: Analyze What You Read—Create a Study Guide

Objective Questions

Go back to the reading and underline what you think might be on a test. Make marginal self-test notes to remember what you have underlined. If you prefer, you may write each self-test note on a flash card and paraphrase the underlining on the back.

Essay/Application Questions

PREDICT ESSAY QUESTIONS   What is the most likely topic for an essay question for this reading?

_____

GRAPHIC ORGANIZER   Fill in the blanks in the following idea map.

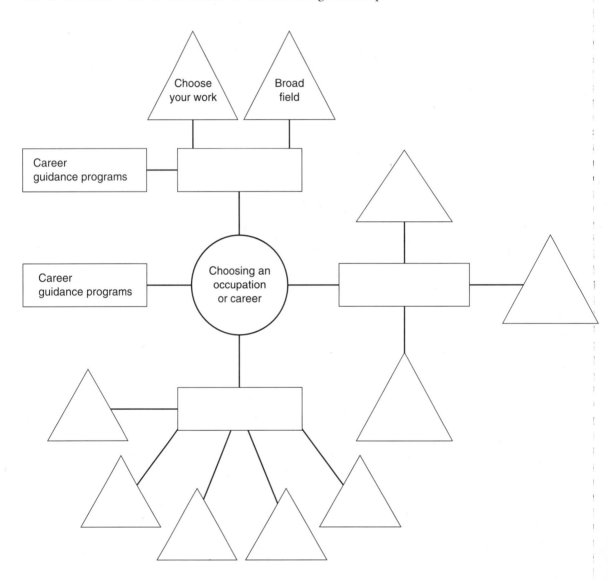

Skill Development: Summarizing

Use your underlining and marginal notes and your graphic organizer to summarize the reading on a separate sheet of paper.

Step 4: Remember What's Important

 Use the marginal notes or flash cards and the graphic organizer for self-testing. Keep testing until you know the material.

Step 5: Make use of What You Read

 When you are ready, complete the Comprehension Check. Do not look back at the reading or the study guide.

Step 6: Evaluate Your Active Critical Thinking Skills

 After your test has been graded, use the checklist on p. 465 to evaluate your skills.

COMPREHENSION CHECK

Multiple Choice

Circle the letter before the best answer to each of the following questions.

1. The first thing to consider in career planning is your
    a. self-concept.
    b. abilities.
    c. interests.
    d. values.

2. By "work values," the author means that your work should be consistent with your
    a. spiritual/religious values.
    b. family/interpersonal values.
    c. values concerning money/material possessions.
    d. all of the above.

3. The author says that choosing a career is
    a. an event that should take place as early as possible.
    b. an ongoing process that takes time.
    c. something that must be done while in college.
    d. the goal of any good college program.

4. How many career changes will a typical worker make in his or her life?
    a. one to three
    b. three to five
    c. five to seven
    d. seven to ten

5. The author would probably
    a. prefer students to get career guidance in high school.
    b. not believe in tests as a way to help in career planning.
    c. like to see more guidance counselors hired at the college level.
    d. encourage students to make a decision and stick to it.

6. The author implies that

   a. most career counselors do a poor job of helping students choose an occupation.

   b. parents, teachers, and counselors are wrong to pressure high school students into choosing a career.

   c. students are more than willing to change majors in college.

   d. students change majors too many times in college.

7. Our attitudes toward certain occupations

   a. are formed before we enter school.

   b. narrow as we grow older.

   c. broaden as we grow older.

   d. are inborn.

Short Answer

What are three dangers to choosing an occupation too soon?

8. _____

9. _____

10. _____

   _____

Essay

Discuss the factors that should be considered in choosing a career. Answer on a separate sheet of paper.

VOCABULARY IN CONTEXT

Write the best word from this list in the blank in each sentence below.

   idealized   attain   socioeconomic   envision   aptitude

1. It is important that you set some goals you can _____ quickly, so that you don't get discouraged.

2. It is sad when a child who loves to sing lacks the _____ for it.

3. During the 1940s, Judy Garland was the _____ image of the wholesome girl, so she could never play a villain or sex symbol in a movie.

4. The _____ status of people in India once varied widely because of their caste.

5. Some writers have the ability to _____ beautiful scenes, while others must write about what they have experienced.

17

Causes of Infection: Pathogens

Vocabulary Preview

prevalent (prev'ə lənt): widely existing

respiratory (res'pər ə tôr'ē): having to do with respiration (breathing)

incubation (in'kyo͞o bā'shən): the phase in the development of a disease between the infection and the first appearance of symptoms

prostration (präs trā'shən): utter mental or physical exhaustion

recurrent (ri kʉr'ənt): appearing or occurring again or periodically

cat, āte, fäther; pen, ēvil; if, kīte; nō, ôr, fo͞od, book; boil, house; up, turn; chief, shell; thick, *the*; zh, treasure; ŋ, sing; ə for *a* in *about*; ' as in *able* (a'b'l)

Step 1: Preread

Preview the following selection by reading the title, the headings, the boldface and italic print, and the illustration. Answer the first two questions without looking back at the reading.

1. What is the subject? _____

2. What is the main idea? _____

3. What is the main idea of the illustration? _____

4. Think about what you know about the causes of infection, what you don't know, and what you might find out from reading this selection. Make up three questions.

    a. _____

    b. _____

    c. _____

Step 2: Read

Read the selection without underlining.

    Write your starting time here: _____

Causes of Infection: Pathogens

Brian K. Williams and Sharon M. Knight

MANY OF THE MICROORGANISMS THAT surround us are beneficial. An example is the bacteria in our intestines, which help in digestion. Here, however, we consider the types of microorganisms that are harmful—namely, pathogens. There are six kinds of pathogens, ranging in size from smallest to largest: *viruses, bacteria, rickettsia, fungi, protozoa,* and *parasitic worms.* (See Figure 1.)

Viruses: The Smallest and Toughest

Viruses may be the smallest of the pathogens, being visible only under an electron microscope. However, they are also the toughest to fight. The reason is that it is difficult to find drugs that will kill a virus without also killing the cell it has taken over. In addition, viruses withstand heat, formaldehyde, and radiation.

A virus is such a primitive form of life that it cannot exist on its own. Indeed, a virus is simply a protein structure containing the nucleic acids DNA or RNA. To survive and reproduce, it must attach itself to a cell and inject its own DNA or RNA. This tricks the cell's reproductive functions into producing new viruses. These new viruses expand the cell until it bursts. The viruses are then set free to seek other cells to take over.

Common characteristics of viruses that are important to know are the following:

- *Viruses are common:* There are many viruses—200 for the common cold alone. This makes them the most prevalent form of contagious disease. **Contagious** means a disease is "catching"—it is easily transmitted from one person (carrier) to another. Viruses include the common cold, influenza (flu), mononucleosis (mono), hepatitis, mumps, chicken pox, measles, rubella, polio, and **HIV,** the human immunodeficiency virus that causes AIDS.

- *Viruses vary in seriousness:* Some viruses cause relatively mild, short-lived illnesses. An example is the 24-hour flu that produces gastrointestinal upset. Other viruses have far more

Viruses: Smallest pathogens.
Typical diseases: Colds, influenza, herpes, rubella, mononucleosis, hepatitis, mumps, chicken pox, HIV.

Bacteria: One-celled pathogens.
Typical diseases: Strep throat, tetanus, bacterial pneumonia, Lyme disease, tuberculosis, scarlet fever, gonorrhea.

Fungi: Plant-like pathogens.
Typical diseases: Athlete's foot, candidiasis ringworm.

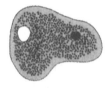

Protozoa: Simplest animal form.
Typical diseases: amebic dysentery, giardia, malaria.

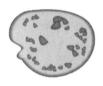

Rickettsia: Virus-like microbes.
Typical diseases: Typhus fever, Rocky Mountain spotted fever.

Parasitic worms: Many-celled.
Typical diseases: Pinworm, elephantiasis.

Figure 1 Pathogens. Examples of each of the six types of pathogens are shown.

serious consequences. These include mononucleosis, hepatitis, polio, or AIDS. The key is which cells the viruses attack. For example, cold viruses attack respiratory cells, which can be replaced. However, the polio virus attacks nerve cells, which cannot be replaced, resulting in paralysis.

- *Viruses are transmitted in different ways:* Some highly contagious viruses are transmitted in the air. When cold sufferers sneeze or cough, they spray extremely fine droplets of virus-bearing mucus and saliva into the environment. Hepatitis A is transmitted by water contaminated by sewage or by another fecal-oral route, as when infected food handlers don't wash their hands. HIV is transmitted by means of infected body fluids through anal, vaginal, or oral sex with an infected partner. It can also be transmitted through sharing drug needles with a person who has the virus, or by an infected pregnant woman to her fetus.

- *Viruses have varying incubation periods:* An **incubation period** is the time lapse between exposure to an organism and the development of symptoms. Cold viruses have short incubation periods, taking perhaps only 24 hours and lasting only 4–5 days. The flu, on the other hand, may develop after 4 days and last about 2 weeks. AIDS may not appear for 10–11 years after infection by HIV and may last 2 or more years.

- *Drug treatment for viruses is limited:* Viruses are hard to reproduce in laboratories. This makes antiviral drug development difficult. Drugs may block viral reproduction for some viruses. For other viruses, drugs may control symptoms but not cure the problem.

    A natural protection against some viruses is **interferon,** a protein substance produced by our bodies. It helps protect healthy cells in their battle with invaders.

Unfortunately, in recent years some old viruses (such as polio) have been causing what seem to be "new" diseases. What seem to be "new" viruses (such as influenza A and B) are also causing old diseases. New viruses and diseases emerge because of several factors. Urbanization and travel help disease travel faster and further afield. Agriculture exposes humans to animal-borne diseases. Organ transplants and blood transfusions can spread undetectable viruses.

Bacteria: The Most Plentiful

Next larger in size to viruses are **bacteria.** These single-celled organisms are visible through a standard microscope. They are the most plentiful of the pathogens. Unlike viruses, many bacteria do not enter cells but thrive on and around the cells. Some bacteria are actually helpful, such as those (*Escherichia coli*) in the digestive tract. However, when people are ill, these bacteria can become harmful. About 100 of the several thousand species of bacteria actually cause disease in people.

The characteristics of bacteria include the following:

- *Bacteria cause a variety of diseases:* Three types of bacteria are spirilla, cocci, and bacilli. Among the types of bacterial infections they cause are strep infections (such as strep throat), staph infections, pneumonia, tuberculosis, scarlet fever, and gonorrhea.

- *Bacteria are transmitted in various ways:* Some bacteria are transmitted through consumption of contaminated water or food. A type of bacteria called chlamydia is largely transmitted by sexual intercourse.

- *Bacteria can harm the body in several ways:* Many bacteria release **toxins,** or poisonous substances. These can lead to diseases such as tetanus, diphtheria, or even that unpleasant traveler's diarrhea sometimes called "Montezuma's revenge."

  Within the body, some bacteria work locally, killing cells near the source of infection. The infection then spreads to other tissue, producing boils, abscesses, and soreness. Other bacteria spread via the bloodstream, causing fever or attacking organs. Some bacteria simply grow until they obstruct vital organs, as in pneumonia.

- *Antibiotics may fight specific bacteria:* **Antibiotics** are bacteria-killing drugs in pill, cream, liquid, or injectable form. One of the most well known antibiotics is **penicillin,** a substance produced from a fungus. (Other antibiotics you may recognize are such drugs as erythromycin, tetracycline, streptomycin, gentamicin, and the cephalosporins.)

  Specific antibiotics work on specific bacteria. No antibiotic, therefore, can be used to treat all bacterial infections. Nor are antibiotics appropriate for treating viral infections. In addition, antibiotics have to be taken properly in order to be effective.

- *Some bacteria are drug-resistant:* Because of inappropriate use and overuse of antibiotics, some antibiotic-resistant strains of bacteria have developed. In addition, some strains of bacteria— for instance, some forms of tuberculosis—are transforming themselves into "superbugs." These bacteria are highly resistant or even invulnerable to some or all antibiotics.

Rickettsia

Rickettsia resemble bacteria but are more complex than viruses. They are disease-causing microorganisms that grow inside living cells. These organisms are generally transmitted by insects such as mites, ticks, and fleas. Rickettsia may cause rashes and fever, such as **typhoid fever (typhus),** a disease characterized by high, disabling fever. Infected ticks transmit **Rocky Mountain spotted fever,** a disease marked by chills, fever, prostration, and pain in muscles and joints.

Fungi: Yeasts, Molds, and the Like

Fungi are single-celled organisms (like yeasts) or multicelled organisms (like molds). Some cause diseases on the skin, mucous membranes, and lungs. The itching, burning, and scaling disorders of the feet and of the scrotal skin known as **athlete's foot** and **jock itch** are caused by a fungus that thrives in moist environments, such as locker-room shower floors. Another kind of fungal disorder is **candidiasis,** a yeast infection of the vagina. Treatment is with antifungal medications.

Protozoa: The Smallest Animals

The smallest animals in existence are **protozoa,** single-celled organisms responsible for many tropical diseases. One example is **malaria,** the severe, recurrent disease borne by mosquitos. It remains one of the most serious and widespread tropical diseases, killing up to 2 million people a year. **African sleeping sickness** is a recurring disease whose chief characteristic is weariness and listlessness. **Amoebic dysentery** is an infection of the intestines.

If you spend time hiking or camping in North America, you need to be particularly careful about drinking unpurified water—even that from mountain streams. It may produce a protozoan infection called **giardia,** characterized by diarrhea, abdominal cramps, and fatigue.

Parasitic Worms

Parasitic worms may be microscopic in size or may range up to 10 feet long. Intestinal parasites, such as the tapeworm or pinworm, cause anal itching in children. They may be contracted by eating undercooked beef or pork. Some of these parasites are more a problem in developing countries than in North America. However, pinworm remains a common problem among school-aged children.

1600 words

Write your ending time here: _____

Subtract your starting time: _____

Total time: _____

Step 3: Analyze What You Read—Create a Study Guide

Objective Questions

Go back to the reading and underline what you think might be on a test. Make marginal self-test notes to remember what you have underlined. If you prefer, you may write each self-test note on a flash card and paraphrase the underlining on the back.

Essay/Application Questions

PREDICT ESSAY QUESTIONS   What is the most likely topic for an essay question for this reading?

_____

MAKE GRAPHIC ORGANIZERS   Fill in the blanks in the following chart. If the answer is not given in the reading, write "not given."

| | Pathogens | | | | | |
	Virus	Bacteria	Rickettsia	Fungi	Protozoa	Worms
Description						
Typical diseases						
Method of transmission						
Treatment						

Skill Development: Summarizing

Use your underlining and marginal notes and your graphic organizer to summarize this reading on a separate sheet of paper.

Step 4: Remember What's Important

 Use the marginal notes or flash cards and the graphic organizer for self-testing. Keep testing until you know the material.

Step 5: Make Use of What You Read

 When you are ready, complete the Comprehension Check. Do not look back at the reading or the study guide.

Step 6: Evaluate Your Active Critical Thinking Skills

 After your test has been graded, use the checklist on p. 465 to evaluate your skills.

COMPREHENSION CHECK

Matching

Write the letter before the pathogen in the space before each disease.

_____ **1.** AIDS   **a.** rickettsia

_____ **2.** tuberculosis   **b.** bacteria

_____ **3.** athlete's foot   **c.** virus

_____ **4.** pinworm   **d.** fungus

_____ **5.** typhoid fever   **e.** protozoa

_____ **6.** amoebic dysentery **f.** parasitic worm

Short Answer

7. Describe the variations in incubation periods for viral diseases.

_____

_____

8. Which pathogen is the most common cause of contagious diseases?

_____

9. What are the problems concerning drug treatments for viral diseases?

_____

_____

10. What are some problems in the treatment of bacterial diseases?

_____

_____

Essay

Describe each pathogen and give at least one method of transmission for each one.

_____

_____

_____

_____

_____

_____

_____

_____

_____

_____

_____

_____

_____

_____

VOCABULARY IN CONTEXT

Write the best word from the following list in the blank in each sentence below.

prevalent   respiratory   incubation   prostration   recurrent

1. Symptoms of heat _____ include dizziness, nausea, low body temperature, and clammy skin.

2. The belief in Santa Claus is very _____ among North American preschool children.

3. Many people have a _____ nightmare in which they have signed up for a class and then forgotten all about it until just before the final exam.

4. Asthma causes such _____ symptoms as wheezing, coughing, and difficulty in breathing.

5. If you get your flu shot during the _____ period of the flu, it will be too late to prevent symptoms.

18

Violence in the Family

Vocabulary Preview

dysfunctional (dis funk′shən əl): abnormally functioning

accessible (ak ses′ə bəl): obtainable

obscure (əb skyo͞or′): to conceal; hide

innuendo (in′yoo en′dō): an indirect remark, gesture, or reference, usually implying something belittling

implicit (im plis′it): suggested or to be understood though not plainly expressed; implied

coercion (ko ur′shən): the use of power to make someone act or think in a certain way

ascertain (as′ər tān′): to find out with certainty

stereotype (ster′ē ə tīp′): a fixed or conventional notion, as of a person, group, idea, etc., held by a number of people, and allowing for no individuality or critical judgment

socialized (sō′shəl īzd): adapted or made to conform to the common needs of a social group

impulsive (im pul′siv): acting or likely to act on impulse, without thinking

cat, āte, fäther; pen, ēvil; if, kīte; nō, ôr, fo͞od, book; boil, house; up, turn; chief, shell; thick, *th*e; zh, treasure; ŋ, sing; ə for *a* in *about*; ′ as in *able* (a′b′l)

Step 1: Preread

Preview the following selection by reading the title, the headings, the two illustrations, and the last paragraph. Answer the first two questions without looking back at the reading.

1. What is the subject?

_____

2. What is the main idea?

_____

3. a. What is the subject of Figure 1 (the graph)?

_____

b. What is the main idea of Figure 1?

_____

_____

4. What is the subject of Table 1?

_____

5. Think about violence among family and acquaintances. Think about what you know, what you don't know, and what you might find out from reading the selection. Make up three questions.

a. _____

b. _____

c. _____

Step 2: Read

Read the selection without underlining.

Write your starting time here: _____

Violence in the Family

GUY LEFRANÇOIS

P ROPHETS AND OTHERS WHO SPECIALIZE IN gloom and related states have been warning us for some time that violence is rapidly becoming a way of life in contemporary societies. And perhaps they are correct. Certainly, police reports indicate that incidence of violent crimes in Western industrialized nations has increased sharply during recent decades, as has international terrorism. However, wife abuse, defined in terms of physical violence by the husband, appears to have decreased by approximately 27 percent between 1975 and 1985.

It might be tempting to assume that violence typically involves strangers and that surrounding ourselves with friends and family will therefore protect us. Sadly, that does not appear to be the case. Indeed, more than 25 percent of all assaults and homicides that are reported to police involve members of the same *family.* And a large percentage of the remainder involve friends or at least acquaintances. More than half of all rapes, crimes that most of us attribute to disturbed strangers in dark parking lots, are committed by acquaintances or relatives—or "dates." One third of all female murder victims are killed by boyfriends or husbands. As Gelles puts it: "We have discovered that violence between family members [is not] a minor pattern of behavior, or a behavior that is rare and dysfunctional. [It] is a patterned and normal aspect of interaction between family members" (see Figure 1).

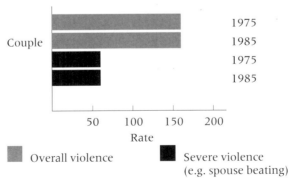

Figure 1 Rate of marital violence per 1,000 couples.

Violence in the family takes a variety of forms. It is perhaps most evident in the observation that more than 9 out of 10 parents admit to using physical force to punish children. It is even more dramatically apparent in instances of child abuse. And it is present, as well, in countless episodes of violence among siblings. Indeed, violence among siblings seems to be highly prevalent among young children, although it diminishes rapidly with increasing age. In a sample of 2,143 families, Straus found that 74 percent of all 3- to 4-year-old children who had siblings occasionally resorted to some form of physical aggression in their interactions. Only 36 percent of those ages 15–17 behaved in similar fashion.

Spouse Battering

Violence in the family is also apparent in instances of wife and husband beating. And surprisingly, the latter is almost as common as the former. In Straus and Gelles's investigation of American families, 3.8 percent of all husbands admitted to activities that the authors define as wife beating. These activities include kicking, biting, hitting with the fist or some other object, threatening with a knife or a gun, or actually using a knife or a gun. And an amazing 4.6 percent of all wives admitted to similar activities with respect to their husbands. However, Straus cautions that wife beating tends to be hidden and secretive more often than is husband beating. Wives are, in fact, far more often *victims* than are husbands.

The picture presented by surveys such as these is probably only a partial sketch, given the privacy of the family. Its affairs are not easily accessible to social science or to law enforcement agencies. In addition, we have an attitude that parents have the *right* to punish their children physically. We tend to think that siblings fighting is normal. Some even believe that a husband has a right to beat his wife. These attitudes tend to obscure the prevalence and seriousness of violence in the family. Shotland and Straw staged a series of events where one individual attacked another. Bystanders almost invariably tried to assist the victim unless the attack involved a man and a woman. When a man attacked a woman, bystanders usually assumed that the couple was married and that they should therefore not interfere.

Why do some husbands beat their wives? There is no simple answer. Some, probably a minority, might be classified as suffering from a psychological disorder. In one study involving 100 battered wives, 25 percent of the husbands had received psychiatric help in the past. And, according to the wives, many more were in need of such help. Many of these husbands came to their marriages with a history of violence. Many had been physically abused and beaten as children. And compared with the general population, more of them were chronically unemployed and poorly educated.

Other factors contribute to violence in the family. These include the high incidence of violence in society, cultural attitudes that accept violence as a legitimate reaction in certain situations, and our predominantly sexist attitudes toward the roles of husband and wife in contemporary marriage.

Sexual Assault

One form of violence that is not restricted to the family, but that occurs there as well, is sexual assault. Sexual assault can range from sexual innuendo and unwanted suggestions to forcible rape. It is an increasingly common problem with a range of sometimes extremely negative consequences.

Rape is ordinarily defined as forcible sexual intercourse with someone *other* than a spouse. In 1989, 89.3 out of every 100,000 American women over the age of 12 were subjected to forcible rape. There was a total of more than 90,000 incidents. This represents an increase of more than 50,000 cases since 1970. At that time the rate per 100,000 women was 46.3 (U.S. Bureau of the Census, 1991).

Note that the legal definition of rape specifically excludes the wife as victim. In this definition is an implicit acceptance of a husband's right to use physical force on his wife. This may explain the reluctance of law enforcement agencies to charge husbands with assault when wives are victims. English common law maintains that a man is still king in his castle, however humble that castle might be.

In many jurisdictions, then, it is legally impossible for a man to rape his wife. He might be guilty of sexual violence variously labeled *sexual aggression, sexual coercion,* or *sexual victimization.* It is *not* legally impossible for a friend, a date, or an acquaintance to rape his partner. In fact, such behaviors are shockingly common. Estimates of instances of what is sometimes called *courtship violence* range from 15 to 25 percent of all women when the violence is restricted to actual or attempted intercourse. Estimates of other forms of courtship violence are much higher.

Rape on Campus

Ward and associates speak of four different kinds of rape that occur on college and university campuses (and elsewhere, too, of course): (1)The *stranger* incident is when the perpetrator attacks an unknown victim. (2) The *party* incident is when victim and perpetrator know each other from a single social function during or after which the assault occurs. (3)The *acquaintance* incident is when the man and woman know each other casually. (4) The *date* incident is when the man and woman have an ongoing relationship.

Prevalence of sexual assault on college campuses is difficult to ascertain, as it is elsewhere. There are problems of definition. There are also problems having to do with underreporting. Koss found that only 58 percent of rape victims reported the incident *to anyone at all.* A mere 5 percent went to the police. Many women are uncertain or ambiguous about the seriousness of the incident. Many think that little or nothing can be done.

A self-report questionnaire survey of 524 women and 337 men on a college campus presents interesting and useful findings about acquaintance rape. During the period covered by the study (less than a year), 34 percent of the women in this group had experienced unwanted sexual contact (kissing, fondling, or touching in a sexual way). Twenty percent had been subjected to attempted sexual intercourse. Ten percent had experienced unwanted completed sexual intercourse. The majority of these episodes occurred with an acquaintance at a party. About three quarters involved alcohol use by the male and one half involved alcohol use by the female. In almost half the cases of unwanted intercourse, no one was told later (see Table 1).

It is perhaps striking that in this sample, men's recollections of sexual incidents were dramatically different from the women's. Only 9 percent of the males recalled having sexual contact with

TABLE 1

Characteristics of "Most Serious" Sexual Incidents

	Type of Experience		
	Contact (N = 176)	Attempted Intercourse (N = 102)	Intercourse (N = 50)
Location			
Dorm	32%	41%	50%
Fraternity	28	10	8
Apartment	29	43	36
Other	11	6	6
Occasion			
Date	9%	8%	14%
Party	68	65	57
Other	24	27	29
Alcohol Use			
Male use	80%	77%	76%
Female use	57	54	65
Relationship			
Stranger	18%	9%	12%
Acquaintance/friend	66	57	47
Boyfriend	14	30	33
Other	2	5	8
Male Tactics			
Just did it	77%	62%	46%
Verbal	15	28	33
Force	8	10	21
Female Response*			
Too frightened	6%	6%	20%
Said no	76	91	70
Cried	5	9	22
Struggled/fought	17	16	28
Other protests	17	7	12
What Resulted*			
Physical injury	0%	3%	10%
Psychological injury	18	30	51
Required counseling	2	2	8
Who Was Told*			
No one	23%	30%	41%
Roommate	41	38	25
Close friend	59	54	41
Counselor	< 1	< 1	4

*Percentages do not add to 100 because of multiple responses.
Source: From Ward, S. K., Chapman, K., Cohn, E., White, S., & Williams, K. (1991). Acquaintance rape and the college social scene. *Family Relations, 40,* 65–71. Copyright 1991 by the National Council on Family Relations. Reprinted by permission.

an unwilling woman. Another 9 percent claimed they had attempted intercourse with an unwilling partner (women reported 34 and 20 percent, respectively). A mere 3 percent of men admitted they had actually completed intercourse (women reported 10 percent).

Attitudes and Violence

Sexual assault is a form of violence that reflects an attitude of male dominance and female passivity. There is an implicit assumption that the man has a right to sexual satisfaction under certain circumstances. In date or acquaintance rape, for example, there is often a misperception of sexual cues coupled with the man's attitude that he is entitled to sex.

Wife battering and child abuse also reflect similar stereotypes of male dominance. The attitudes of men who batter their wives, says Bograd, are more sexist. These men are socialized into power and control over women. Eisikovits and associates report that their sample of wife beaters in Israel had different attitudes about wife beating. They tended to be more impulsive and less self-controlled. They argue that attempts to alleviate the problem need to take into account multiple rather than single contributing factors.

1500 words

Write your ending time here: _____

Subtract your starting time: _____

Total time: _____

Check the Rate Chart in the back of the book to find out how many words per minute you have read and record your score on the Progress Chart.

Step 3: Analyze What You Read—Create a Study Guide

Objective Questions

Go back to the reading and underline what you think might be on a test. Make marginal self-test notes to remember what you have underlined. If you prefer, you may write each self-test note on a flash card and paraphrase the underlining on the back.

Essay/Application Questions

PREDICT ESSAY QUESTIONS   What are the 4 most likely topics for essay questions?

1. _____

2. _____

3. _____

4. _____

MAKE GRAPHIC ORGANIZERS   Following is an outline of the reading. On each blank line, write the missing statistic or other data. The first one has been done for you as an example.

Violence in the Family

I.   Family violence

    A.   Percent of assaults and homicides involving family and friends:

        25% involving family and a lot involving friends

    B.   Percent of rapes by acquaintances: _____

    C.   Percent of female murder victims killed by boyfriends or husbands:

        _____

    D.   Number of parents using physical punishment: _____

    E.   Amount of violence among siblings: _____

        _____

II.   Spouse battering

    A.   Frequency: _____

        _____

    B.   Problems with accuracy of data: _____

    C.   Shotland and Straw study: _____

        _____

    D.   Reasons for wife beating: _____

        _____

    E. Other factors that contribute to family violence: _____

_____

III. Sexual assault

    A. Definitions: _____

    B. Definition of rape: _____

_____

    C. Frequency of rape: _____

_____

    D. Marital rape: _____

    E. Courtship violence: _____

_____

    F. Rape on campus

        1. Four types: _____

        2. Prevalence and problems of underreporting: _____

_____

        3. Questionnaire results for women and men:

_____

IV. Attitude and violence

    A. Attitudes and sexual assault: _____

_____

    B. Attitudes and wife battering and child abuse: _____

_____

    C. Multicultural factors: _____

_____

Skill Development: Summarizing

Use your underlining and marginal notes and your graphic organizer to summarize this reading on a separate sheet of paper.

Step 4: Remember What's Important

 Use the marginal notes or flash cards and the graphic organizer for self-testing. Keep testing until you know the material.

Step 5: Make Use of What You Read

 When you are ready, complete the Comprehension Check. Do not look back at the reading or the study guide.

Step 6: Evaluate Your Active Critical Thinking Skills

 After your test has been graded, use the checklist on p. 465 to evaluate your skills.

COMPREHENSION CHECK

Multiple Choice

Circle the letter before the best answer to each question.

1. The author implies that family violence is considered

    a. abnormal and unacceptable to society.

    b. normal and acceptable to many Americans.

    c. acceptable to social scientists in some forms but not others.

    d. more acceptable than it once was.

2. Between 1975 and 1985, wife abuse appears to have

    a. increased.

    b. decreased.

    c. remained the same.

    d. changed its form.

3. Bystanders will be least likely to help when a

    a. man is attacked by a man.

    b. child is attacked by an adult.

    c. woman is attacked by a woman.

    d. woman is attacked by a man.

4. Factors contributing to family violence include

    a. a high incidence of violence in society.

    b. cultural attitudes that accept violence in certain situations.

    c. sexist attitudes about husbands and wives.

    d. all of the above.

5. Police may be reluctant to interfere in family violence because

    a. they don't think it's a serious crime.

    b. they think the husband has a right to beat his wife.

    c. they can't believe the victim will press charges.

    d. all of the above.

6. Children should be taught how to deal with abusive behavior from

    a. strangers.

    b. friends of the family.

    c. relatives.

    d. all of the above.

7. With regard to husband and wives, English Common Law

    a. tries to be fair.

    b. views women as the husband's property.

    c. gives the wife authority over the children.

    d. presents severe penalties for wife abuse.

8. The author implies that wife beating is most common among the

    a. rich.

    b. poor.

    c. middle class.

    d. foreign born.

Short Answer

9. What are the problems in ascertaining the number of rapes on campus?

    _____

    _____

10. What are the differences in causes of wife battering found by Bograd in the United States and by Eisikovits and associates in Israel?

    _____

    _____

    _____

Essay

Describe the types and the frequency of violent crimes against family members, friends, and acquaintances as they were described in the reading. Answer on a separate sheet of paper.

VOCABULARY IN CONTEXT

Write the best word from this list in the blank in each sentence below.

dysfunctional   accessible   obscure   innuendo   implicit

coercion   ascertain   stereotype   socialize   impulsively

1. Psychologists refer to families that include such behaviors as child abuse,

   alcoholism, and neglect as _____ .

2. In good friendships there is an _____ understanding that you
   can call upon the friend when you are in need.

3. The kinds of off-color jokes told in most offices rely more on

   _____ than on obscenity.

4. When a sexual harasser is in a position that can affect your job, there is an

   element of _____ involved.

5. One of the primary functions of schools is to _____ children so
   that they become functional members of their culture.

6. Hyperactive children can be expected to behave _____ .

7. The _____ of Mom as housecleaner and cook has been changing
   as more mothers have been entering the workforce.

8. Hiding your valuables or keeping them in a safe makes them less

   _____ to burglars.

9. When buying on credit, you should _____ the interest rate and
   find out if there are any other costs.

10. Politicians have the reputation of being dishonest because they usually try to

    say what they think the voters want to hear; they _____ their
    real opinions and intentions.

19

Why We Sleep

Vocabulary Preview

restoration (res'tə rā'shən): a bringing back to health or strength

ordeal (ôr dēl'): difficult, painful, or trying experience

unscrupulous (un skrōō'pyə ləs): unprincipled; not honorable

superimpose (sōō'pər im pōz'): to put on top of something else

circadian (sʉr ka'dē ən): having to do with the rhythms associated with the 24-
    hour cycles of the earth's rotation, such as rhythms of sleeping and waking

**cat, āte, fäther; pen, ēvil; if, kīte; nō, ôr, fōōd, book; boil, house; up,
turn; chief, shell; thick, *the*; zh, treasure; ŋ, sing; ə for *a* in *about*; ' as
in *able* (a'b'l)**

Step 1: Preread

Preview the following selection by reading the title, the headings, and the illustration. Answer the following questions without looking back at the reading.

1. What is the subject? _____

2. What is the main idea? _____

3. What is the subject of the illustration? _____

4. What is the main idea of the illustration? _____

    _____

    _____

5. Think about what you know about why we sleep, what you don't know, and what
    you might find out from reading the selection. Make up three questions.

    a. _____

    b. _____

    c. _____

Step 2: Read

Read the selection without underlining

Write your starting time here: _____

Why We Sleep

James W. Kalat

WE WOULD NOT HAVE BEEN BORN WITH A mechanism that forces us to sleep for 8 hours or so out of every 24 unless sleep did us some good. But what good does it do? Scientists have proposed two theories.

The Repair and Restoration Theory of Why We Sleep

According to the **repair and restoration theory,** the purpose of sleep is to enable the body to recover from the exertions of the day. During sleep the body increases its rate of cell division and the rate at which it produces new proteins. It also digests food. There is no doubt that these and perhaps other restorative processes do occur during sleep. However, nearly all of the same processes also take place when we are awake but sitting quietly. Evidently we do not need sleep in order to rest the muscles or any other tissues, other than perhaps the brain. We have several other reasons to doubt that sleeping is like resting to catch your breath after extensive exercise.

First, if sleep were simply a means of recovering from the exertions of the day, it would resemble the rest periods we have after bouts of activity. But people need only a little more sleep after a day of extreme physical or mental activity than after a day of inactivity.

Second, some people get by with much less than the "normal" 7½ to 8 hours of sleep a day. An extreme case was a 70-year-old woman who claimed that she slept only about 1 hour a night. Researchers who observed her over a number of days confirmed her claim. Some nights she did not sleep at all. Nevertheless, she remained healthy.

Third, some people have intentionally gone without sleep for a week or more. They suffer less severely than we might have expected. In 1965 a San Diego high-school student, Randy Gardner, stayed awake for 264 hours and 12 minutes—11 days—in a project for a high-school science fair. Gardner suffered no serious psychological consequences. On the last night of his ordeal he played about a hundred arcade games against sleep researcher

William Dement. He won every game. Just before the end of the 264 hours he held a television press conference and handled himself well. After sleeping 14 hours and 40 minutes, he awoke refreshed and apparently fully recovered.

You may have heard that unscrupulous people have used sleep deprivation as a means of brainwashing or torturing prisoners. Why would sleep deprivation produce so many more drastic effects on prisoners than it did on, say, Randy Gardner? Two reasons: First, Gardner may have been better able to tolerate sleep deprivation than most other people. After all, we never would have heard about him if he had given up on his project and gone to sleep after 3 days, as most people would have. Second, Gardner knew he was in control of the situation. If he became unbearably miserable, he could simply quit and go to sleep. Tortured prisoners do not have that option. If they stay awake night after night, they do so because of constant prodding, not because of their own decision. For the same reason, rats that have been forced to go without sleep for several days suffer severe health problems that human volunteers seldom experience after similar periods of sleep deprivation.

If you go without any sleep some night—as most college students do at one time or another—you probably will grow very sleep by about 4:00 or 5:00 A.M. But if you are still awake at 7:00 or 8:00 A.M., you will feel much less sleepy than you did before. For the rest of the day you may feel a little strange, but you probably will have little difficulty staying awake and keeping reasonably alert. That night, however, you will feel very sleepy indeed. Apparently, the need to sleep is tied to particular time periods.

In one study, volunteers went without sleep for three nights. An experimenter periodically took their temperature and measured their performance on logical reasoning tasks. Both temperature and logical reasoning declined during the first night and then increased almost to their normal level the next morning. During the second and third nights, temperature and logical reasoning decreased more than they had the first night. But again they improved the following morning (Figure 1). Thus, sleep deprivation produces a pattern of progressive deterioration that is superimposed on the normal circadian cycle of rising and falling body temperature and reasoning ability.

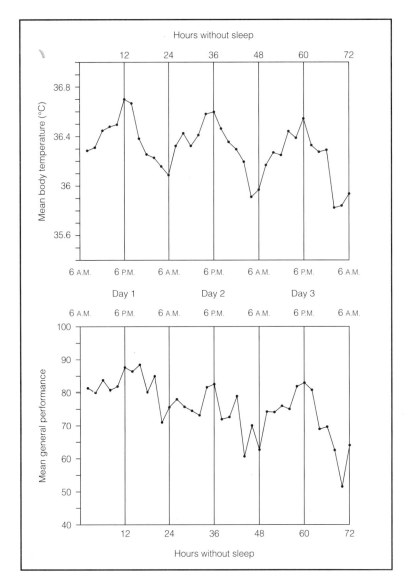

Figure 1 Cumulative effects of 3 days without sleep. Both body
temperature and logical reasoning decrease each night and increase
the next morning. They also deteriorate from one day to the next.

In short, sleepiness apparently depends partly on how long
one has gone without sleep and partly on the time of day (that
is, where one is within the circadian rhythm). Evidently, sleep
contributes to repair and restoration of the body, but that must
not be its only reason for existence.

The Evolutionary Theory of Why We Sleep

Sleep may be a way of conserving energy. If we built a solar-powered robot to explore the planet Mars, we probably would program it to shut down almost all its activities at night in order to conserve fuel and in order to avoid walking into rocks that it could not see.

According to the **evolutionary theory of sleep,** evolution equipped us with a regular pattern of sleeping and waking for the same reason. The theory does not deny that sleep provides some important restorative functions. It merely says that evolution has programmed us to perform those functions at a time when activity would be inefficient and possibly dangerous.

Note, however, that sleep protects us only from the sort of trouble we might walk into. It does not protect us from trouble that comes looking for us! So we sleep well when we are in a familiar, safe place. But we sleep lightly, if at all, when we fear that burglars will break into the room or that bears will nose into the tent.

The evolutionary theory accounts well for differences in sleep among species. Why do cats, for instance, sleep so much, whereas horses and sheep sleep so little? Surely cats do not need five times as much repair and restoration as horses do. But cats can afford to have long periods of inactivity because they spend little time eating and are unlikely to be attacked while they sleep. Horses and sheep must spend almost all their waking hours eating, because their diet is very low in calories. Moreover, they cannot afford to sleep too long or too soundly, because their survival depends on their ability to run away from attackers. (Woody Allen once said, "The lion and the calf shall lie down together, but the calf won't get much sleep.")

Which of the two theories of sleep is correct? Both are, to a large degree. Supporters of the repair and restoration theory concede that the timing and even amount of sleep depend on when the animal is least efficient at finding food and defending itself. Supporters of the evolutionary theory concede that during a time that evolution has set aside for an animal to conserve energy, the animal takes that opportunity to perform repair and restoration functions.

1200 words

Write your ending time here: _____

Subtract your starting time: _____

Total time: _____

Step 3: Analyze What You Read—Create a Study Guide

Objective Questions

Go back to the reading and underline what you think might be on a test. Make self-test notes to remember what you have underlined. If you prefer, you may write each self-test note on a flash card and paraphrase the underlining on the back.

Essay/Application Questions

PREDICT ESSAY QUESTIONS   What is the most likely topic for an essay question?

_____

MAKE GRAPHIC ORGANIZERS   Fill in the spaces in the chart.

Why We Sleep

Theory	Evidence For	Evidence Against
Repair and restoration	1. 2.	1. 2. 3. 4.
Evolutionary	1. 2. 3.	none stated

Skill Development: Summarizing

Use your underlining and marginal notes and your graphic organizer to summarize this reading on a separate sheet of paper.

Step 4: Remember What's Important

 Use the marginal notes or flash cards and the graphic organizer for self-testing. Keep testing until you know the material.

Step 5: Make Use of What You Read

 When you are ready, complete the Comprehension Check. Do not look back at the reading or the study guide.

Step 6: Evaluate Your Active Critical Thinking Skills

 After your test has been graded, use the checklist on p. 465 to evaluate your skills.

COMPREHENSION CHECK

True-False

Mark T or F.

_____ **1.** Sleepiness depends partly on how long you have gone without sleep and partly on the time of day.

_____ **2.** If a person stays up all night, he or she is usually very sleepy around 4 A.M., but less sleepy around 7 A.M.

_____ **3.** You can infer from the reading that scientists don't really know why we sleep.

_____ **4.** It seems that both theories of sleep are correct.

_____ **5.** Logical reasoning is usually better at night than in the morning.

Multiple Choice

Circle the letter before the best answer to each question.

6. The repair and restoration theory of why we sleep does not explain

   a. why resting without sleeping is enough to restore the muscles and other tissues.

   b. why the amount of sleep needed is not much different after a day of extreme activity than after a day of inactivity.

   c. why some people sleep less than others do.

   d. all of the above.

7. According to the reading, human beings

   a. cannot stay awake more than 24 hours.

   b. can go for at least 11 days without sleep.

   c. suffer physical damage if they go more than a week without sleep.

   d. become brainwashed after several days without sleep.

8. You can infer from the reading that the main reason some people can tolerate sleep deprivation better than others is that

    a. people differ in the amount of sleep they need.

    b. people differ in their evolutionary levels.

    c. some people work harder than others.

    d. all of the above are true.

Short Answer

9. Give an example of an animal that sleeps a lot and explain why, according to evolutionary theory.

    _____

    _____

10. Give an example of an animal that sleeps very little and explain why, according to evolutionary theory.

    _____

    _____

Essay

Explain both theories of why we sleep, and give the evidence supporting each one.

_____

_____

_____

_____

_____

_____

_____

_____

_____

_____

_____

VOCABULARY IN CONTEXT

Write the best word from this list in the blank in each sentence below.

restoration   ordeal   unscrupulous   superimpose   circadian

1. Jet lag is caused by disrupting the _____ cycle.

2. The word " _____ " originally referred to a trial in which the accused person was exposed to physical dangers such as being thrown into deep water with weights attached to his body. If he was innocent, he was supposed to be protected by God; if he died, he was guilty.

3. Doctors usually take credit for cures that are really a result of the body's own processes of _____ .

4. If you _____ yellow cellophane over blue cellophane and look through them both, you see green.

5. If you are selling your house it is considered _____ , and in some states illegal, to conceal any known defects from the buyer.

20

Evaluating Reasoning Based on Fallacies

Vocabulary Preview

cite (sīt): quote; mention by way of example, proof, and so on

refute (ri fyo͞ot'): to prove to be false or wrong

geneticist (jə net'ə sist): a specialist in the branch of biology that deals with heredity

authoritative (ə thôr'ə tāt'iv): based on competent authority

alleged (ə lejd'): not actual; so-called; claimed

lauded (lôd'id): praised

cat, āte, fäther; pen, ēvil; if, kīte; nō, ôr, fo͞od, book; boil, house; up, turn; chief, shell; thick, *the*; zh, treasure; ŋ, sing; ə for *a* in *about*; ' as in *able* (a'b'l)

Step 1: Preread

 Preview the following selection by reading the title and the headings as well as words in boldface and italics. Answer the questions without looking back at the reading.

1. What is the subject? _____

2. What is the main idea? _____

3. Think about what you know and don't know about logical fallacies. Make up three questions that might be answered by reading the selection.

   a. _____

   b. _____

   c. _____

Step 2: Read

 Read the selection without underlining.

   Write your starting time here: _____

Evaluating Reasoning Based on Fallacies

Randolph F. Verdeber

IN THIS DISCUSSION, WE LOOK AT several types of specific *fallacies,* mistakes in logical reasoning.

Hasty Generalization

One of the most common thinking fallacies is *hasty generalization.* This fallacy usually occurs when a speaker reasons from example. The problem is a shortage of data; not enough instances are cited. In real-life situations, people often make this error. They make generalizations based on only one or, at most, a few examples. For instance, in support of the argument that teenagers favor legalizing marijuana, a person might cite the opinions of two teenagers who live next door. This sample is too small, and it does not represent a cross section of teenagers. In a speech, the argument might sound good, especially if the speaker dramatizes that one example. But you can refute the argument as a hasty generalization.

Questionable Cause

Another common fallacy is *questionable cause.* This occurs when the alleged cause is not related to, or does not produce, the effect. It is human nature to look for causes for events. If we are having a drought, we want to know the cause. If the schools are in financial trouble, we want to know the cause. If the crime rate has risen during the year, we want to know the cause. In our eagerness to discover causes for behavior we often identify the wrong one.

Think of the people who blame loss of money, sickness, and problems at work on black cats that ran in front of them, or mirrors that broke, or ladders they walked under. We recognize these as superstitions. They are good examples of attributing causes to unrelated events.

Superstitions are not the only examples of questionable cause. Consider a situation that happens every year on many college campuses. One year a coach's team has a winning season, and the coach is lauded for his or her expertise. The next year the team does poorly, and the coach is fired. Has the coach's skill deteriorated that much in one year? It is quite unlikely. But it much easier to point the finger at the coach as the cause of the team's failure than admit that the entire team or the program itself is inferior. The fact is that examples of questionable cause are frequent.

Appeal to Authority

An *appeal to authority* is a fallacy based on the quality of the data. It occurs when people support their arguments with the testimony of an authority. The argument is fallacious when the use of the testimony fails to meet either of two tests: (1) The source is not an authority on the issue, or (2) the content of the testimonial does not agree with other expert opinion.

Consider cases in which the source is not an authority. Advertisers are well aware that because the public idolizes athletes, movie stars, and television performers, people are likely to accept their word on subjects they may know little about. So, when a celebrity tries to get the viewer to buy a car based on the celebrity's supposed "expert" knowledge, the argument is a fallacy.

Although the fallacy of authority may be easy to see in a TV ad, other examples of the fallacy may be harder to recognize. Economists, politicians, and scientists often comment on subjects outside their areas of expertise. Sometimes neither they nor we realize how unqualified they are to speak on such subjects. A scientist's statement is good evidence only in the science in which he or she is an expert. Thus, a geneticist's views on the subject of world food supply may or may not be fallacious. It depends on the point he or she is trying to make.

The other test is whether the content of the testimonial is contrary to other expert opinion. Even when an opinion is relevant to the authority's expertise, it may still be fallacious if it is not supported by the other authorities in that field. If a space biologist claims there must be life similar to ours on other planets, that opinion is no more logical proof than any other opinion if a majority of equally qualified space biologists think otherwise. You can always find someone who has said something in support of even the most foolish statement. Avoid the mistake of accepting any statement as valid support just because some alleged authority is cited as the source.

Appeals Based on Statistics

Fallacies in the use of statistics may be based on the quantity of data, quality of data, or reasoning from data. Statistics are nothing more than a large number of instances. However, statistics sometimes seem to have a bewitching force. Most of us believe that instances presented in statistical form have the weight of authority. Yet there are so many potential fallacies from statistics that we don't have room to discuss them all here. There is truth in the old saying "Figures don't lie, but liars figure." To be safe, look at any statistical proof as potentially fallacious. Even statistics that are used honestly and sincerely may still be fallacious. This is because the clear, logical use of statistics is so difficult.

As you examine arguments supported with statistics, look for the following:

1. *Statistics that are impossible to verify.* You have probably read countless startling statements, such as "Fifteen million mosquitoes are hatched each day in Ontario, Canada" or "One out of every seventeen women in ancient Greece had six fingers." Now, do not quote these—I made them up. But they are no more unlikely than many other examples I have seen. The fact is that we have no way of verifying such statistics. How can anyone count the number of mosquitoes hatched? How can we test whether anyone counted the fingers of ancient Greek women? Statistics of this kind make interesting conversation, but they are fallacious as support for arguments.

2. *Statistics used alone.* Statistics by themselves do not mean much. For example, "Last season the Cincinnati Reds drew approximately 1.7 million fans to their seventy home games." Although this sounds like (and it is) a lot of people, it does not tell much about the club's attendance. Is this figure good or bad? Was attendance up or down? Statistics often are not meaningful unless they are compared with other data.

3. *Statistics used with unknown comparative bases.* Comparisons of statistics do not mean much if the comparative base is not given. Consider the statement "While the Zolon growth rate was dawdling along at some 3 percent last year, Allon as growing at a healthy 8 percent." This statement implies that Allon is doing much better than Zolon. However, if Zolon's

base was larger, its 3 percent increase could be much better than Allon's 8 percent. We cannot know unless we understand the base from which the statistic was drawn.

Ad Hominem Argument

An *ad hominem* argument is a fallacy that occurs with an attack on the person making the argument rather than on the argument itself. For instance, let's say that Bill Bradley, the U.S. senator and former New York Knicks basketball player, presented the argument that athletics are important to the development of the total person. The reply, "Great, all we need is some jock justifying his own existence," would be an example of an ad hominem argument.

Such an attack is often made as a smoke screen to cover a lack of good reasons and evidence. Ad hominem name calling is used to try to encourage the audience to ignore a lack of evidence. It is often used in political campaigns. Ridicule, name calling, and other personal attacks are at times very successful, but they almost always are fallacious.

Although there are many other fallacies, we do not have the space to cover them all here. When someone tries to convince you of something, first identify the point of view. Then identify the arguments that support the point of view. Finally, identify the evidence supporting each argument and analyze it. If reasons are presented, are they logical? If facts are given, are they really factual? Is the testimony given by a real authority? If there are examples, are they numerous enough and representative enough? Even when you can't identify a specific fallacy, you can probably still judge the argument's strengths and weaknesses.

1400 words

Write your ending time here: _____

Subtract your starting time: _____

Total time: _____

Check the Rate Chart in the back of the book to find out how many words per minute you have read and then record your score on the Progress Chart.

Step 3: Analyze What You Read—Create a Study Guide

Objective Questions

Go back to the reading and underline what you think might be on a test. Make self-test notes to remember what you have underlined. If you prefer, you may write each self-test note on a flash card and paraphrase the underlining on the back.

Essay/Application Questions

PREDICT ESSAY QUESTIONS   What is the most likely topic for an essay question?

MAKE GRAPHIC ORGANIZERS   Fill in the following idea map.

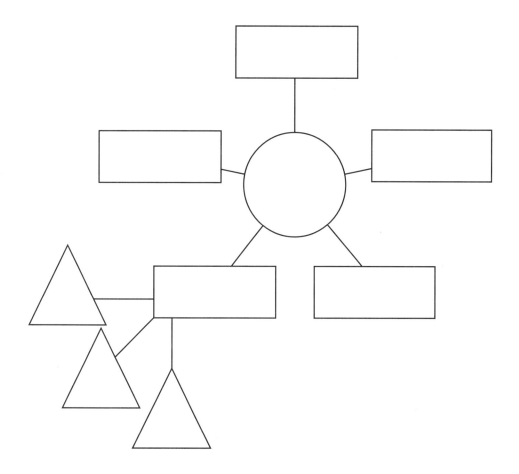

PREDICT APPLICATION QUESTIONS   To prepare for application questions, you will need to be able to identify the fallacies that were discussed. Find or make up at least one new example (not mentioned in the reading) for each type of fallacy. It would help if you could exchange the examples with other members of the class and see if you can identify each other's.

_____

_____

_____

_____

_____

_____

_____

_____

_____

_____

Skill Development: Summarizing

Use your underlining and marginal notes and your graphic organizer to summarize this reading.

_____

_____

_____

_____

_____

_____

_____

_____

_____

_____

_____

Step 4: Remember What's Important

 Use the marginal notes or flash cards and the graphic organizer for self-testing. Keep testing until you know the material.

Step 5: Make Use of What You Read

 When you are ready, complete the Comprehension Check. Do not look back at the reading or the study guide.

Step 6: Evaluate Your Active Critical Thinking Skills

 After your test has been graded, use the checklist on p. 465 to evaluate your skills.

COMPREHENSION CHECK

Matching

Identify the following types of fallacies by writing the appropriate symbol in the blank before each sentence.

AA   appeal to authority (popularity or traditional wisdom)

AH   ad hominem argument

AS   appeal through faulty statistics

HG   hasty generalization

QC   questionable cause

_____ **1.** People who don't agree with me are idiots.

_____ **2.** I got sick last night; it must have been something I ate.

_____ **3.** More school children are losing their ability to distinguish right from wrong. Just look at the vandalism that occurred at Middletown Elementary School.

_____ **4.** There are more bugs in the United States than anywhere else in the world.

_____ **5.** Joe Smoo, the famous basketball player, says that Swiss Mush is the breakfast cereal that makes champions.

_____ **6.** One out of every three people in prehistoric times was killed by a dinosaur.

_____ **7.** Detergent X must be better than detergent Y because it cleaned this stain better.

_____ **8.** The pollution is terrible. See how everyone is coughing?

_____ **9.** Jean Kelley, who plays Dr. Janet Jones on the *Guiding Gift,* says that Aspergrim relieves headaches five times faster than any other aspirin or nonaspirin product.

_____ **10.** The only people who favor eating "health foods" are crackpots and faddists.

Essay

Explain each of the fallacies discussed in the reading.

_____

_____

_____

_____

_____

_____

_____

_____

VOCABULARY IN CONTEXT

Write the best word from this list in the blank in each sentence below.

cite   refute   geneticist   alleged   lauded

1. Consulting a _____ before having children is important for people who have inherited medical problems in their family histories.

2. Tomatoes were once _____ to be poisonous fruits.

3. In term papers, one must _____ sources in footnotes in order to avoid being accused of cheating.

4. General Colin Powell was _____ for his military achievements.

5. Because it's difficult to prove that you *didn't* do something, a false accusation is hard to _____ .

UNIT IV
Critical Reading with ACT

Critical reading means evaluating what an author is saying. Is it true or false? Does it explain what it claims to explain? Does it work? As a college student, you will have to make judgments about what you hear and what you read. Yet many students coming out of high school haven't been taught to do much more than memorize.

In this unit you will read persuasive nonfiction. Authors will try to convince you of their points of view. Persuasion is seen all the time in fields like advertising and politics. However, you will see persuasion in textbooks, too. Here are some examples of issues that call for persuasive writing:

Which theory best explains why we sleep?

Should immigration policies be changed?

When did the universe begin?

You will see persuasive writing in textbooks, in technical or professional writing, and in popular magazines and newspapers. Persuasion can work by fair means or foul. It can use fallacious reasoning and manipulation just as easily as logic and fairness. To be an informed voter or consumer, and a successful student, you must be able to read persuasive writing critically.

In Unit IV you will practice critical reading using five pairs of articles on controversial subjects: health care, sports competition, crime, affirmative action, and euthanasia. Each reading takes an opposing viewpoint. We believe that the goal of critical reading and thinking is to come as close as possible to the truth. The best way of figuring out the truth on any subject is to become familiar with the arguments supporting as many points of view as possible. Everyone is entitled to an opinion on any subject, but it is wrong to hold an opinion because you are ignorant of the arguments on the other side.

You should analyze arguments with an open mind, allowing yourself to be influenced. You should even be open to opinions that appear highly unconventional, because history has shown that majority approval often shifts. For example, at one time "loyal" Americans supported the Vietnam War, but later on those who opposed the war were considered morally correct.

If you can develop an open mind, you will earn higher grades and be more successful in life. You will have better friendships and family relations because you will consider the other person's point of view. You will make better consumer and investment decisions because you will investigate for yourself instead of believing what you are told. You will be a better citizen because you will learn about the issues rather than follow the party line. You will have the sense of confidence that comes from taking charge of your life. Finally, an active critical thinker is rarely either bored *or* boring.

CRITICAL THINKING USING ACT

Critical thinking means (1) identifying the author's point of view, (2) pinpointing the arguments supporting the point of view, (3) identifying the details used to support the arguments, and (4) evaluating the supporting details.

Step 1: Preread

 Before you begin reading, examine your opinions about both sides of the issue. Review the difficult vocabulary that precedes each reading, so that unfamiliar words will not interfere with your comprehension. Then quickly skim the reading to get an understanding of the subject and the author's point of view. Compare your opinions about the subject with the author's. Think about how open you are to what you are about to read.

Step 2: Read

Read the selection without underlining or making notes. Try to understand the author's arguments and support.

Step 3: Analyze What You Read

Go back to the reading and identify the arguments and their support. Support can consist of testimonials from convincing people, logical reasons, statistical or historical facts, or examples. You might want to ask the following questions when evaluating supporting details:

1. *Testimony:* If the author uses testimonials, are his or her sources really experts about the subject? Are they objective or biased? Did the author select the experts who were most qualified or merely those who would support his or her point of view?

2. *Reasons:* If the support consists of reasons, are they logical or is the author using faulty reasoning?

3. *Facts:* If the author uses facts, are they provable or unprovable? Have some facts been included and others omitted in order to support the point of view? You have heard about lying with statistics, but even with good intentions, facts are open to interpretation. Sometimes the author's opinions are disguised as facts.

4. *Examples:* If the author uses examples, are there enough of them? Are they representative enough to support the generalizations the author wants to make?

Loaded Language

Authors can also use loaded language to influence their readers' thinking. For example, supporters of a politician might refer to him or her as a diplomat, strategist, or tactician. Opponents might refer to the same politician as a bureaucrat, influence peddler, power broker—or even as a Macchiavelli. These loaded words can subtly influence our thinking. Another example of the tremendous importance of words occurred when feminists succeeded in changing sexist language like *policeman, fireman, mailman,* and *chairman* to *police officer, firefighter, letter carrier,* and *chairperson.*

Guide for Analysis—Graphic Organizers

As part of this step, you will underline and make notes in the margin to highlight the arguments and supporting details. Then you will make graphic organizers as you did in Units II and III. This means putting the important ideas in visual form so that you can easily understand and remember them. The types of graphic organizers are those you are already familiar with: outlines, idea maps, charts, time lines, diagrams, tables, and graphs.

Step 4: Remember What's Important

 Review your underlining, marginal notes, and graphic organizers until you feel confident that you understand and remember the information.

Step 5: Make Use of What You Read

In college, your instructor will usually guide your use of the information you have prepared: class discussion, a writing assignment, an oral presentation, or a test. In this book we have prepared a Comprehension Check and an exercise on Vocabulary in Context for each reading. At the end of each pair of readings, we provide questions for writing and discussion that you can use to evaluate your understanding of the issue.

Step 6: Evaluate Your Active Critical Thinking Skills

When you receive feedback about your performance in the form of a grade, critique, or other type of evaluation, use the information to build on your strengths and to build up your weaknesses. Use the evaluation chart in the back of the book.

Issue 1: "Three Strikes" Laws

"Three strikes" is a term that refers to laws that give life sentences to criminals convicted of three felonies. The two readings in this section take opposite points of view.

SELF-QUESTIONING

It is important to be aware of your own beliefs and biases when you read. Answering the following questions will help you clarify your views. Write the number from the rating scale that best expresses your opinion. You will take the same survey to reevaluate your views after you have completed Readings 21 and 22.

Rating Scale

1. No

2. Perhaps not

3. No opinion

4. Perhaps

5. Yes

Rate each question from 1 to 5.

_____ 1. Will tougher treatment of criminals reduce crime?

_____ 2. Is it worthwhile to try to reform people convicted of serious crimes?

_____ 3. Can the country afford to keep more people in prison?

_____ 4. Should judges have the power to decide on sentencing?

_____ 5. Are "three strikes" laws a good idea?

21

How Many Prisons Must We Build to Feel Secure?

Vocabulary Preview

rousing (rou′zing): exciting, stirring

ironically (ī rän′ik lē): showing a contrast between what might be expected and what actually occurs

incarcerate (in kar′sə rāt′): to imprison

concede (kən sēd′): to acknowledge, often reluctantly, as being true

predator (pred′ə tôr): one who lives by plundering, robbing, or exploiting others

abduct (ab dukt′): to carry off by force; to kidnap

assailant (ə sāl′ənt): attacker

reaffirm (rē ə furm′): restate; uphold

clemency (klem′ən sē): leniency; mercy

deter (di tur′): to prevent or discourage from acting

cat, āte, fäther; pen, ēvil; if, kīte; nō, ôr, food, book; boil, house; up, turn; chief, shell; thick, *the*; zh, treasure; ŋ, sing; ə for *a* in *about*; ' as in *able* (a′b'l)

Step 1: Preread

Preview the following selection by reading the title, the headings, and the first sentence of each paragraph. Answer the questions without looking back at the reading.

1. What is the subject? _____

2. What is the point of view (the main point the author is trying to make)?

   _____

3. Now take a moment to compare your beliefs about three strikes with the author's. On a scale of 1 (no way) to 5 (definitely), how open is your mind to the author's

   point of view? _____

Step 2: Read

Read the selection without underlining. Just try to understand the author's arguments.

Write your starting time here: _____

How Many Prisons Must We Build to Feel Secure?

Jonathan Simon

P RESIDENT CLINTON RECEIVED ROARS of approval when he rousingly endorsed the "Three Strikes, You're Out" anti-crime proposal during his [1994] State of the Union Address. But now the idea of locking criminals up for life after their third serious felony is being attacked by critics as good politics but bad policy—as a catchy slogan with an expensive price tag that does little to protect people's security and covers too many crimes that aren't serious.

We heard those same concerns voiced in Washington state. But on Election Day [1993], nearly 77 percent of the voters launched the national movement for "three strikes" by approving Initiative 593 to put felons permanently behind bars after their third serious conviction. And ironically, while "three strikes" is under fire in the nation's capital, some opponents of the 1993 initiative now support the new law.

"Sentencing Law Isn't Striking Out" reads the lead editorial in the February 10, [1994], *Spokesman-Review* from [House Speaker] Tom Foley's hometown of Spokane. "We grudgingly admit the new law appears to be working," said the paper, which encouraged a "no" vote on 593. "We felt, and still do," the paper wrote, "that it will add greatly to the increasing cost of incarceration. We also worried that too many small-fry would be caught in the three-strikes net. We didn't want to see relatively harmless felons taking up prison space at age 60, 70 or 80."

"Maybe we've done too much hand wringing," the *Spokesman-Review* conceded, and pointed out that the new law was catching the two kinds of criminals it targeted: "high-profile predators who rape or kill repeatedly; and offenders who terrorize the community with chronic strings of lesser but still serious crimes, such as robbery."

Targeting Career Criminals

Precisely. At present eight criminals are facing the prospect of "striking out" here in Washington state. Three are sex criminals, all of whom have attempted murder (one successfully). Another is a four-time armed robber. The other four are career criminals. One, Larry Fisher, was described in the *New York Times* as a two-time felon. In fact, he has sixteen prior criminal convictions—six felonies, ten misdemeanors and numerous probation violations. Another has five felonies and nine misdemeanors. A third has four previous felonies and fifteen misdemeanors, and the fourth has had fifteen convictions in eight years, five of them felonies. That's sixty-four convictions among four street criminals. Essentially, whenever these fellows weren't in the joint they were out ripping off people's homes and businesses. Our new law locks the revolving door on their careers.

But in the nation's capital, a rehashed version of Washington state's election debate has resulted in a weak White House version of "three strikes" that would not cover six of our eight criminals, including two of the three violent rapists. Philip Heymann, the former number-two official with the Department of Justice, contends that some of the crimes weren't serious enough to be covered by "three strikes," such as second degree robbery, which he characterized as knocking someone down to steal a purse.

That's theory. Here's reality. The first criminal to face the "Three Strikes, You're Out" charge in our state is Cecil Emile Davis. His first strike was second degree robbery back in 1986. But Mr. Davis didn't knock down a lady while snatching her purse. He robbed a convenience store and beat both the clerk and a customer so severely that the judge noted at sentencing his "deliberate cruelty to the victims." So how long did Davis spend behind bars for that attack? Two years. Often, criminals are not charged with a crime or given a sentence that matches the severity of their actual offense, a reality not addressed by the Clinton version of "three strikes."

Davis is charged with abducting a young woman, repeatedly raping her, stabbing her in the throat and throwing her down the recessed stairwell of a church. She managed to survive and has identified Davis as her assailant. If convicted, Davis will "strike out" and be gone for life. Had he committed that crime on government soil, the Clinton bill would not have applied to him.

Other Benefits

As for the costs of incarceration, only 3 percent to 4 percent of most state budgets is spent on corrections, and several studies show that it's much cheaper to lock up a common criminal than allow him to roam free. However, if the governor is convinced that an aging third striker is too old to do harm any longer, our "three strikes" law reaffirms his power to grant pardons or clemency.

Three other benefits to our law should give pause to even its most liberal critics. First, although statistics haven't yet been tabulated, police officers report that the new law is already deterring criminal activity. Second, the tough new penalties are forcing some criminals to seek treatment and counseling they previously refused. Third, the new law is unquestionably driving criminals out of Washington state. In Seattle alone, since "three strikes" passed, seventeen registered sex offenders have moved out of state because their next offense would be their last. That may be good news for people here, but it will only be good for America if lawmakers across the country, including Congress, make the climate for crime as chilly in their states as it now is in Washington state.

900 words

Write your ending time here: _____

Subtract your starting time: _____

Total time: _____

Check the Rate Chart in the back of the book to find out how many words per minute you have read and then record your score on the Progress Chart.

Step 3: Analyze What You Read

Identify the Point of View and Arguments

In the margin of the reading, write POV next to the place the author presents his point of view.

We believe the author presents eight major arguments:

1. The law is catching the types of criminals it targeted.

2. The federal law is too lenient.

3. Clinton's version does not address the problem that criminals are often not charged with a crime or given a sentence that matches the severity of the offense.

4. It's cheaper to lock up a common criminal than to allow him to roam free.

5. There is a way out for third strikers too old to cause harm.

6. Washington state's law seems to be deterring crime.

7. The law is forcing some criminals to seek treatment and counseling.

8. The new law is driving criminals out of state.

Go back to the reading and find each argument. Write Arg. 1, Arg. 2, etc., in the margin next to where each argument appears.

Identify Supporting Details

Following are details that support each argument. They are in random order and they have been paraphrased, so the words are not exactly the same as in the reading. However, the meaning is the same. Go back to the reading and underline each supporting detail. In the blank before each detail, write the number of the argument that the detail is supporting. For example, Detail a is supporting Argument 2, which says that the federal law is too lenient.

Write the most common type of support: facts, examples, testimony, or reasons.

_____ 1. It would not cover six of Washington state's eight criminals.

_____ 2. Seventeen Seattle sex offenders moved out of state.

_____ 3. Emile Davis

_____ 4. The eight criminals facing "striking out"

_____ 5. No support is given

_____ 6. Several studies

_____ 7. Governor can grant pardons or clemency

_____ 8. Police reports

Evaluate Supporting Details

VALID AND INVALID INFERENCES   A valid inference is based on something the author implied. In part a, mark V before each valid inference and I before each one that is invalid. If you mark V, you should be able to point to the place in the reading where it is implied. In part b, indicate the extent to which you agree or disagree with each statement according to the following scale:

1 = disagree

2 = no opinion

3 = agree

_____ **1a.** People convicted of second-degree robbery are actually violent criminals.

_____ **1b.**

_____ **2a.** If left up to judges, sentences would be too lenient.

_____ **2b.**

_____ **3a.** The Washington law is mostly catching drug offenders.

_____ **3b.**

_____ **4a.** The author is concerned about the law catching criminals who really don't deserve life imprisonment.

_____ **4b.**

_____ **5a.** The law contains a process by which a "third striker" can obtain early release for good behavior or other circumstances that indicate he/she is no longer a threat to society.

_____ **5b.**

_____ **6a.** Some criminals have a good chance to be rehabilitated.

_____ **6b.**

_____ **7a.** Criminals who are likely to keep committing serious crimes will move to states without "three-strikes" laws.

_____ **7b.**

_____ **8a.** Liberals generally favor "three-strikes" laws.

_____ **8b.**

Make Graphic Organizers

Fill in the following idea map. Write the point of view in the circle, the arguments in the rectangles, and the supporting details in the ovals.

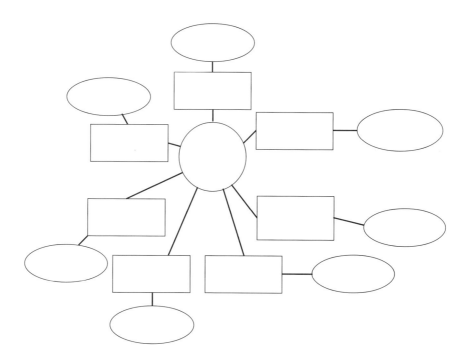

Step 4: Remember What's Important

 Review your marginal notes identifying the point of view and the major arguments. Review the underlining that identified the supporting details. Review the idea map. Test yourself until you are sure that you will remember the material.

Step 5: Make Use of What You Read

When you are ready, complete the Comprehension Check. Do not look back at the reading or the idea map.

Step 6: Evaluate Your Active Critical Thinking Skills

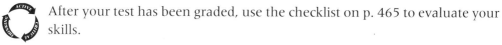 After your test has been graded, use the checklist on p. 465 to evaluate your skills.

COMPREHENSION CHECK

True-False

Mark T or F.

_____ **1.** The Washington state three-strikes law is stronger than the federal government's version.

_____ **2.** The reading discusses the problems with the Washington state law.

_____ **3.** The Washington state law gives the same penalty to three-strikers whether they are robbers or murderers.

_____ **4.** The state version and the federal version cover the same crimes.

Multiple Choice

Circle the letter before the best answer to each question below.

5. The author implies that

   a. as crime in Washington decreases, crime in neighboring states will increase.

   b. judges have the ability to decide when to apply the three-strikes law.

   c. the three-strikes law will not increase the number of prisoners.

   d. all of the above are true.

6. The author implies that

   a. many small-time crooks are caught by the three-strikes law.

   b. the cost of imprisoning the three-strikes offenders is too high.

   c. the Washington state law is catching the right criminals.

   d. new prisons will have to be built to accommodate the three-strikes offenders.

7. The author implies that

   a. the law excludes sex offenders.

   b. only the governor can pardon those who have "struck out."

   c. before the three-strikes law many sentences were too severe, and many were too lenient.

   d. the three-strikes law discriminates racially.

Short Answer

What are three types of offenses the author mentions being targeted by the Washington law?

8. _____

9. _____

10. _____

Essay

Why does the author think the United States should opt for a tough three-strikes law like Washington state's?

_____

_____

_____

_____

_____

_____

_____

_____

_____

VOCABULARY IN CONTEXT

Write the best word from this list in the blank in each sentence below.

rousing   **ironically**   **incarceration**   **concede**   **predatory**

abducted   **assailants**   **reaffirm**   **clemency**   **deters**

1. Supporters of the death penalty say that it _____ people from committing capital crimes.

2. _____ , seizing imported drugs at the borders increases domestic production because it drives the prices up.

3. The returning war hero received a _____ welcome in her hometown.

4. It is usually people with wealthy relatives who are _____ for ransom.

5. With "three-strikes" laws, judges will no longer be able to show

   _____ to offenders who can be rehabilitated.

6. Lions and tigers are _____ animals.

7. When the results of an election are in, the loser is expected to publicly

   _____ .

8. Because they fear revenge, crime victims are sometimes unwilling to identify

   their _____ .

9. _____ of criminals serves several purposes in addition to protecting society: conservatives see it as a means of punishment, and liberals see it as an opportunity for rehabilitation.

10. Some married couples have a second wedding later in life to

   _____ their vows.

22

A Case for Discretion

Vocabulary Preview

discretion (di skresh′ən): freedom of action or judgment

mandatory (man′də tôr′ē): required

sporadic (spə rad′ik): occurring at irregular intervals

culpability (kul′pə bil′ə tē): guilt

mitigate (mit′ə gāt): to make or become less

mete (mēt): to distribute; allot

unsavory (un sā′və rē): morally offensive

relapse (rē′laps): a falling back to a former state; especially after an improvement

integral (in′ti grəl): essential or necessary for completeness

restitution (res′ti too′shən): making good for loss or damage

cat, āte, fäther; pen, ēvil; if, kīte; nō, ôr, fōod, book; boil, house; up, turn; chief, shell; thick, *the*; zh, treasure; ŋ, sing; ə for *a* in *about*; ′ as in *able* (ā′b′l)

Step 1: Preread

Preview the following selection by reading the title and the first sentence of each paragraph. Answer the questions without looking back at the reading.

1. What is the subject? _____

2. What is the point of view? _____

   _____

3. Compare your beliefs about mandatory minimum sentences with the author's. On a scale of 1 (no way) to 5 (definitely), how open is your mind to the author's point

   of view? _____

Step 2: Read

Read the selection without underlining. Just try to understand the author's arguments.

Write your starting time here: _____

A Case for Discretion

Michael Brennan

I STOOD BEFORE FEDERAL DISTRICT COURT JUDGE Kimberly Frankel. The date was May 28, 1995; the place, Portland, Ore. I had just pleaded guilty to five shoplifting charges and one felony count of cocaine possession.

In a similar case in San Diego, Steven White, 32, faced a mandatory sentence of 25 years to life for shoplifting a $130 VCR. He decided instead that a bullet through the brain was the less painful way to go. The suicide note he left offered apologies to his parents for the heartbreak he caused them, but suggested that spending that much time in prison was too high a price to pay for a misdemeanor. The sentence White faced is a result of one of the many federal and state "mandatory minimum" sentencing acts that have been enacted by Congress and various state legislatures since 1986. White's case fell under California's so-called "three strikes you're out" law.

Like me, White had a sporadic history of heroin addiction and nonviolent criminal offenses. His first two strikes—burglary convictions—dated to 1983. His "third strike"—the shoplifting charge, which occurred in 1994—was elevated to a felony by being classed as "petty theft with a prior conviction of theft." Two judges pleaded with prosecutors not to seek the 25-to-life sentence that the recently enacted law called for. They refused.

Many groups oppose mandatory minimum sentences, including the National Association of Veteran Police Officers, the U.S. Sentencing Committee, the American Bar Association and Families Against Mandatory Minimums. Supreme Court Chief Justice William Rehnquist calls mandatory minimums "a good example of the law of unintended consequences."

There are currently 1.2 million people incarcerated in federal and state prisons in this country. The majority of them are up on drug-related crimes, and many are there as a result of mandatory minimum sentences. The average cost of housing a federal prisoner is $20,804 annually. It is ultimately the taxpayer who foots this enormous bill. Furthermore, the hodgepodge of state and federal mandatory drug sentences sometimes leads to violent offenders—Florida's rapists, robbers and murderers, for example—being released early to make room for nonviolent, first-time drug offenders serving lengthy, mandatory-minimum sentences.

Ironically, I came close to being classed as a violent offender. On one of my shoplifting sprees I struggled with a Fred Meyer's department-store security guard as I tried to escape her grasp. If she had described my desperate struggle as resistance and my shoplifting partner's presence as a threat, I could have been charged with robbery 2, which now carried a mandatory five-year sentence under Oregon's Measure 11. But the issue is only partially whether the punishment fits the crime. There are a number of federal prisoners doing life without parole for marijuana sales, for example, while rapists are routinely paroled after only four years.

The more central question, however, is this: is it the American way to remove all discretion from judges and invest prosecutors with an extraordinary degree of power? Are there no circumstances—youth, a previously clean record or varying levels of culpability among codefendants—that might mitigate the degree of punishment that must be meted out? Not under any of the mandatory minimum sentences.

In my case, by the time I appeared before Judge Frankel I had behind me a 15-year on-again, off-again history of heroin addiction that resulted in numerous petty theft convictions, three felony heroin-possession convictions and four stints in county jails.

Judge Frankel was free to weigh this unsavory history against what I had accomplished in the four drug-free years prior to my recent relapse. After my release from jail in 1989 I went from a homeless ex-offender to a working writer. I also initiated and managed a self-help work project in Boston that successfully employed 19 individuals who were dealing with homelessness, AIDS, addiction and mental illness.

The judge, using the discretionary powers that have been an integral part of the American judicial system for 200 years, sentenced me to 30 days in jail, 90 days of work-release, $700 in restitution fees and two years' probation. The work-release program allowed me to pay society back through community-work programs, maintain family connections, earn money at outside work to pay a substantial portion of my incarceration costs and to save funds for post-release living expenses.

Contrast my experience with that of Stephanie Lomax, a former Portland, Ore., resident whose family shared her story with me. Lomax and two codefendants were convicted in Nebraska on conspiracy charges involving crack cocaine. White House drug czar Lee Brown recently stated that crack-cocaine mandatory sentences primarily affect African-Americans, thus adding a racial bias to federal drug laws. He calls crack-cocaine mandatory sentences "bad law" based on "bad information."

Lomas, a 25-year-old pregnant black mother and first-time offender with no previous criminal history, continues to maintain her innocence. She was sentenced to life without parole. This means, literally, that she will die in the same prison system where she gave birth to the child she can no longer hold.

Americans are understandably frightened and frustrated by the impact of drugs and crime on society. One can only hope that our fears have not also destroyed our sense of compassion and justice, and that we can still respond to Stephanie Lomax (and untold thousands like her).

"Does anyone care about what is going on in the system today?" she writes from her cell at the Pleasanton federal prison in California. "I am poor. I have no assets and I'm very much in need of help. Can you help me and my family?"

900 words

Write your ending time here: _____

Subtract your starting time: _____

Total time: _____

Check the Rate Chart in the back of the book to find out how many words per minute you have read and then record your score on the Progress Chart.

Step 3: Analyze What You Read

Identify the Point of View and Arguments

In the margin of the reading, write POV next to the place the author presents his point of view.

We believe the author presents six major arguments:

1. Many knowledgeable people oppose mandatory minimum sentences.

2. The cost of incarcerating so many people, the majority of whom are up on drug-related crimes often as a result of mandatory minimum sentences, is too high.

3. The hodgepodge of state and federal mandatory drug sentences sometimes leads to violent offenders being released to make room for nonviolent, first-time drug offenders serving lengthy, mandatory-minimum sentences.

4. Punishments often don't fit the crime.

5. Some criminals can make valuable contributions to society.

6. Crack-cocaine mandatory minimum sentences primarily affect African-Americans, adding a racial bias to federal drug laws.

Go back to the reading and find each argument. Write Arg. 1, Arg. 2, etc. in the margin next to where each argument appears.

Identify Supporting Details

Following are details that support each argument, listed in random order. Go back to the reading and underline each supporting detail. In the blank before each detail, write the number of the argument that the detail is supporting. Beneath each detail write the type of support: facts, examples, testimony, or reasons.

_____ 1. White House drug czar Lee Brown

Type: _____

_____ 2. National Association of Veteran Police Officers, U.S. Sentencing Committee, American Bar Association, Families Against Mandatory Minimums, Supreme Court Chief Justice William Rehnquist

Type: _____

_____ 3. Florida's rapists, robbers, and murderers

Type: _____

_____ 4. There are currently 1.2 million people incarcerated in federal and state prisons; the average cost of housing a federal prisoner is $20,804 annually.

Type: _____

_____ 5. Steven White; Stephanie Lomax

Type: _____

_____ **6.** Author Michael Brennan

Type: _____

Evaluate the Supporting Details

VALID AND INVALID INFERENCES   If the author implied the statement in the reading, mark V in the blank before part a of each question. If not, mark I. In part b, indicate your agreement or disagreement using the following scale:

1 = disagree

2 = no opinion

3 = agree

_____ **1a.** Mandatory minimum sentences make the judicial system more fair.

_____ **1b.**

_____ **2a.** Stephen White's judges would not have voluntarily imposed the sentence that the prosecutors insisted on.

_____ **2b.**

_____ **3a.** People with three convictions are career criminals.

_____ **3b.**

_____ **4a.** Many sentences are a matter of chance or luck.

_____ **4b.**

_____ **5a.** Judge Frankel made a poor decision.

_____ **5b.**

_____ **6a.** Selling drugs is as serious and harmful as rape.

_____ **6b.**

_____ **7a.** The United States has a bad drug policy.

_____ **7b.**

Make Graphic Organizers

Fill in the following idea map the same way you did in Reading 21.

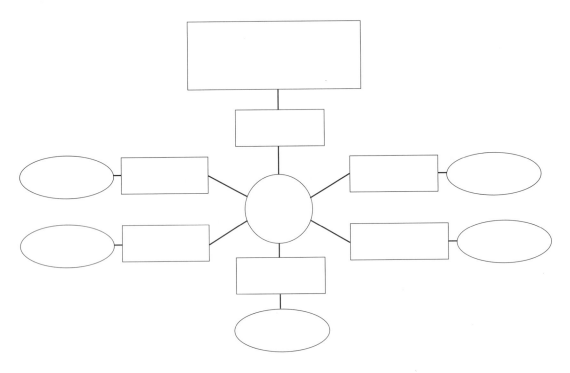

Step 4: Remember What's Important

    Review your marginal notes identifying the point of view and the major arguments. Review the underlining that identified the supporting details. Review the idea map. Test yourself until you are sure that you will remember the material.

Step 5: Make Use of What You Read

    When you are ready, complete the Comprehension Check. Do not look back at the reading or the idea map.

Step 6: Evaluate Your Active Critical Thinking Skills

After your test has been graded, use the checklist on p. 465 to evaluate your skills.

COMPREHENSION CHECK

True-False

Mark T or F.

_____ **1.** Those opposing mandatory minimum sentences such as "three strikes" are groups known to have a liberal bias.

_____ **2.** The author implies that the penalties for nonviolent drug offenses are unreasonable.

_____ **3.** The author implies that allowing judges to use their judgment in sentencing is good for society as well as for the defendants.

_____ **4.** A solution that would have prevented Stephen White's suicide would be to limit "three-strikes" to violent offenders.

_____ **5.** The author implies that we have laws that unfairly penalize African-Americans.

Multiple Choice

Circle the letter before the best answer to each question.

6. The example of Stephen White's suicide supports the argument that

   a. "three-strikes" punishments often don't fit the crime.

   b. violent criminals are often released to make room for nonviolent drug offenders.

   c. suicide costs the taxpayers less than incarceration.

   d. many groups oppose mandatory minimum sentencing.

7. The author implies that

   a. many criminals can be rehabilitated.

   b. rehabilitation is cheaper than incarceration.

   c. judges make better decisions than prosecutors.

   d. all of the above are true.

8. The sentence that the author received from Judge Frankel allowed him to

    a. repay the victims of his crime.

    b. repay society with money and community service.

    c. be supervised by a probation officer.

    d. do all of the above.

Short Answer

9. What points is the author making by using the example of Stephanie Lomax?

    _____

10. What point is the author making by using the example of his own recent trial?

    _____

Essay

Why is the author opposed to mandatory minimum sentences?

_____

_____

_____

_____

_____

_____

_____

_____

VOCABULARY IN CONTEXT

Write the best word from this list in the blank in each sentence below.

discretion   mandatory   sporadic   culpability   mitigate

mete   unsavory   relapse   integral   restitution

1. The good fairy in *Sleeping Beauty* was able to _____ the bad fairy's curse by changing it so that the princess would fall asleep instead of dying.

2. One can never make _____ for a murder.

3. After the flu, you should take care of yourself so you don't have

   a _____ .

4. People in positions of authority over children, such as parents and teachers,

   _____ out rewards and punishments as a way of teaching them how to behave.

5. Most obese people make _____ attempts at dieting, which usually fail.

6. The purpose of a trial is to determine the _____ of the defendant.

7. You should stay away from back alleys that are inhabited by

   _____ characters.

8. Attendance in some classes is _____ ; you will be dropped after a certain number of absences.

9. Taking tests is an _____ part of student life.

10. The saying " _____ is the better part of valor" means that you should use judgment about when to show bravery.

COMPARING VIEWS ON "THREE-STRIKES"

Use the following activities to evaluate your understanding of the issue of "three-strikes" laws. Write your answers on a separate sheet of paper.

1. Summarize each reading. First, write the author's point of view in your own words. Then, in brief form, write each argument and its major support.

2. Evaluate the support for each reading. Consider what each author is implying as well as what he is stating. Is it true? Is it reasonable?

3. Compare the readings. Do you believe that one author's arguments are stronger than the other's? Why?

4. Go back to the self-questioning survey on page 319. Would you change any of your responses after reading the selections? Summarize your opinion on the issue, noting any ways in which your opinion has been affected by your reading.

Issue 2:
Competition in Sports and Games

The two readings take opposing views on the value of competitive sports.

SELF-QUESTIONING

It is important to be aware of your own beliefs and biases when you read. Answering the following questions will help you clarify your views. Write the number from the rating scale that best expresses your opinion. You will take the same survey to reevaluate your views after you have completed Readings 23 and 24.

Rating Scale

1. No

2. Perhaps not

3. No opinion

4. Perhaps

5. Yes

Rate each question 1 to 5.

_____   **1.**   Is participating in sports good for people?

_____   **2.**   Are competitive sports harmful to people who are not good at sports?

_____   **3.**   Are competitive games of chance like "musical chairs" harmful?

_____   **4.**   Can we have the benefits of sports without the competition?

_____   **5.**   Are intellectual competitions like spelling bees harmful to people who lose?

23

No-Win Situations

Vocabulary Preview

counterproductive (koun′tər prə duk′tiv): bringing about effects or results that are contrary to those intended

benign (bi nīn′): harmless

inherent (in hir′ənt): existing in someone or something as a natural and inseparable quality

malicious (mə lish′əs): spiteful; intentionally mischievous or harmful

camaraderie (käm′ə räd′ər ē; kam′-): loyalty and warm, friendly feeling among comrades, comradeship

gloat (glōt): to express malicious pleasure or self-satisfaction

epithet (ep′ə thet′): a descriptive name or title, especially negative

detest (di test′): to dislike intensely; hate

conducive (kən doo′siv): that contributes; tending or leading (to)

aberration (ab′ər ā′shən): a deviation from the normal or the typical

cat, āte, fäther; pen, ēvil; if, kīte; nō, ôr, fo͞od, book; boil, house; up, turn; chief, shell; thick, *the*; zh, treasure; ŋ, sing; ə for *a* in *about*; ′ as in *able* (a′b′l)

Step I: Preread

Preview the following selection by reading the title and the first sentence of each paragraph. Answer the following questions without looking back at the reading.

1. What is the subject? _____

2. What is the author's point of view? _____

_____

3. Compare your beliefs with the author's. On a scale of 1 (no way) to 5 (definitely),

   how open is your mind to the author's point of view? _____

Step 2: Read

 Read the selection without underlining. Just try to understand the author's arguments.

Write your starting time here: _____

No-Win Situations

ALFIE KOHN

I LEARNED MY FIRST GAME AT A BIRTHDAY party. You remember
it: X players scramble for X-minus-one chairs each time the
music stops. In every round a child is eliminated until at the
end only one is left triumphantly seated while everyone else is
standing on the sidelines, excluded from play, unhappy . . .
losers.

This is how we learn to have a good time in America.

Several years ago I wrote a book called *No Contest,* which,
based on the findings of several hundred studies, argued that
competition undermines self-esteem, poisons relationships and
holds us back from doing our best. I was mostly interested in the
win/lose arrangement that defines our workplaces and class-
rooms, but I found myself nagged by the following question: If
competition is so destructive and counterproductive during the
week, why do we take for granted that it suddenly becomes benign and even desirable on the weekend?

This is a particularly unsettling line of inquiry for athletes
or parents. Most of us, after all, assume that competitive sports
teach all sorts of useful lessons and, indeed, that games by definition must produce a winner and a loser. But I've come to believe that recreation at its best does not require people to try to
triumph over others. Quite to the contrary.

Terry Orlick, a sports psychologist at the University of Ot-
tawa, took a look at musical chairs and proposed that we keep
the basic format of removing chairs but change the goal; the
point becomes to fit everyone on a diminishing number of seats.
At the end, a group of giggling children tries to figure out how to
squish onto a single chair. Everybody plays to the end; everybody has a good time.

Orlick and others have devised or collected hundreds of such
games for children and adults alike. The underlying theory is
simple: All games involve achieving a goal despite the presence
of an obstacle, but nowhere is it written that the obstacle has to
be someone else. The idea can be for each person on the field to
make a specified contribution to the goal, or for all the players to

reach a certain score, or for everyone to work with her partners against a time limit.

Note the significance of an "opponent" becoming a "partner." The entire dynamic of the game shifts, and one's attitude toward the other players changes with it. Even the friendliest game of tennis can't help but be affected by the game's inherent structure, which demands that each person try to hit the ball where the other can't get to it. You may not be a malicious person, but to play tennis means that you try to make the other person fail.

I've become convinced that not a single one of the advantages attributed to sports actually requires competition. Running, climbing, biking, swimming, aerobics—all offer a fine workout without any need to try to outdo someone else. Some people point to the camaraderie that results from teamwork, but that's precisely the benefit of cooperative activity, whose very essence is that *everyone* on the field is working together for a common goal. By contrast, the distinguishing feature of team competition is that a given player works with and is encouraged to feel warmly toward only half of those present. Worse, a we-versus-they dynamic is set up, which George Orwell once called "war minus the shooting."

The dependence on sports to provide a sense of accomplishment or to test one's wits is similarly misplaced. One can aim instead at an objective standard (How far did I throw? How many miles did we cover?) or attempt to do better than last week. Such individual and group striving—like cooperative games—provides satisfaction and challenge without competition.

If large numbers of people insist that we can't do without win/lose activities, the first question to ask is whether they've ever tasted the alternative. When Orlick taught a group of children noncompetitive games, two-thirds of the boys and all of the girls preferred them to the kind that require opponents. If our culture's idea of fun requires beating someone else, it may just be because we don't know any other way.

It may also be because we overlook the psychological costs of competition. Most people lose in most competitive encounters, and it's obvious why that causes self-doubt. But even winning doesn't build character: It just lets us gloat temporarily. Studies have shown that feelings of self-worth become dependent on external sources of evaluation as a result of competition; your value is defined by what you've done and who you've beaten. The whole affair soon becomes a vicious circle: The more you compete, the more you *need* to compete to feel good about yourself. It's like drinking salt water when you're thirsty. This process is bad enough for us; it's a disaster for our children.

While this is going on, competition is having an equally toxic effect on our relationships. By definition, not everyone can win a contest. That means that each child inevitably comes to regard others as obstacles to his or her own success. Competition leads children to envy winners, to dismiss losers (there's no nastier epithet in our language than "Loser!"), and to be suspicious of just about everyone. Competition makes it difficult to regard others as potential friends or collaborators; even if you're not my rival today, you could be tomorrow.

This is not to say that competitors will always detest one another. But trying to outdo someone is not conducive to trust—indeed it would be irrational to trust a person who gains from your failure. At best, competition leads one to look at others through narrowed eyes; at worst, it invites outright aggression.

But no matter how many bad feelings erupt during competition, we have a marvelous talent for blaming the individuals rather than focusing on the structure of the game itself, a structure that makes my success depend on your failure. Cheating may just represent the logical conclusion of this arrangement rather than an aberration. And sportsmanship is nothing more than an artificial way to try to limit the damage of competition. If we weren't set against each other on the court or the track, we wouldn't need to keep urging people to be good sports; they might well be working *with* each other in the first place.

As radical or surprising as it may sound, the problem isn't just that we compete the wrong way or that we push winning on our children too early. The problem is competition itself. What we need to be teaching our daughters and sons is that it's possible to have a good time—a better time—without turning the playing field into a battlefield.

1200 words

Write your ending time here: _____

Subtract your starting time: _____

Total time: _____

Check the Rate Chart in the back of the book to find out how many words per minute you have read and then record your score on the Progress Chart.

Step 3: Analyze What You Read

Identify Arguments and Supporting Details

In the margin of the reading, write POV next to the place the author presents his point of view.

For each of the seven arguments in the reading, we have provided supporting details. Fill in the missing argument; if the argument is not clearly stated in the reading, use your own words. Next, write in the type of supporting details (facts, examples, reasons, testimony.)

Argument 1 _____

_____

Detail: Findings of several hundred studies about the workplace and classroom

Type: _____

Argument 2 _____

Detail: They offer a workout and camaraderie.

Type: _____

Argument 3 _____

_____

Detail: How far did I throw? How many miles did we cover?

Type: _____

Argument 4 _____

Detail: Orlich found that two-thirds of the boys and all the girls preferred noncompetitive games.

Type: _____

Argument 5 _____

Detail: Losing causes self-doubt; winning causes gloating; self-worth becomes dependent on external evaluation.

Type: _____

Argument 6 _____

Detail: View others as obstacles; envy winners; dismiss losers; be suspicious; learn aggression

Type: _____

Argument 7 _____

Detail: Cheating and poor sportsmanship

Type: _____

Write Arg. 1, Arg. 2, etc., in the margin of the reading next to the place that each argument appears. Underline the supporting details for each argument.

Evaluate Supporting Details

FACT VERSUS OPINION   Sometimes authors present their opinions as if they were facts. For the purposes of this exercise, a fact is something that can be proved or disproved. An opinion cannot be proved or disproved. Write F in the space before each statement of fact; write O if the statement is someone's opinion.

_____ **1.** "I learned my first game at a birthday party."

_____ **2.** "Several years ago, I wrote a book called *No Contest*. . . ."

_____ **3.** "This is a particularly unsettling line of inquiry for athletes or parents."

_____ **4.** "Orlick and others have devised or collected hundreds of such games for children and adults alike."

_____ **5.** "The underlying theory is simple. . . ."

_____ **6.** "The dependence on sports to provide a sense of accomplishment or to test one's wits is similarly misplaced."

_____ **7.** "When Orlick taught a group of children noncompetitive games, two-thirds of the boys and all of the girls preferred them to the kind that require opponents."

_____ **8.** "There's no nastier epithet in our language than 'Loser!' "

_____ **9.** "And sportsmanship is nothing more than an artificial way to try to limit the damage of competition."

_____ **10.** "The problem is competition itself."

Evaluating Research

Alfie Kohn's book *No Contest,* based on the findings of several hundred studies, concluded that competition undermines self-esteem, poisons relationships, and holds us back from doing our best. Whether or not these conclusions are justified depends on the validity of the research. Below are a few questions that should be answered before we can judge the value of any research.

1. Is the sample representative of the people about whom we want to draw conclusions? In this case, are the people in the studies similar to the whole population of the United States in terms of age, background, and types of competitive activities?

2. Is the sample large enough to draw the conclusions? In this case, is it big enough to predict the effects of competition on people all across the United States?

3. How were the people assigned to groups? For example, were they able to choose the type of competition? If not, could this have been a source of bias?

4. Was the method of measurement adequate? In this case, how could they measure the intensity of the competition, the self-esteem before and after, and the effect of competition in relationships and achievements?

5. Are the results significant? For example, were the differences in self-esteem, relationships, and achievement big enough to warrant the conclusion that competition makes a difference?

A. The following study measures the effect of competition on self-esteem. Two groups of Little League boys were selected. Team 1 had a coach who worked very hard to make the team win. He scheduled a great deal of difficult practice, praised and rewarded the boys who did well and ignored the boys who did not, and kept close track of batting averages and scores. Team 2's coach was more relaxed about practicing, stressed teamwork, and rewarded the entire team for playing, whether they won or lost. After one season, both groups of boys were given a questionnaire that rated their self-esteem in terms of how lovable, how good, how attractive, how intelligent, and how competent they considered themselves. There was a slight difference in that the average boy's score from team 1 was higher. Rate the study on the following scale.

	Yes	No	Can't tell
1. Is the sample representative?			
2. Is the sample big enough?			
3. How were people assigned to groups?			
4. Was the measurement adequate?			
5. Are the results significant?			

B. The following study measures the effects of competitive games on physical aggression in preschoolers. Wadsworth Nursery School, which has ten locations throughout Los Angeles, did a pilot project using all 1,000 of its pupils. The children, who were between 2 and 4 years old, were randomly assigned to one of two groups within their home school for twenty minutes each day. Physical aggression, defined as hitting, pinching, biting, and pushing, was measured for each group, and no significant differences were found. Group A then played competitive games that had clear winners and losers. Group B played games that were participatory and cooperative, without winners and losers. After one month, incidents of physical aggression were again counted. It was found that Group A had twice as many incidents as Group B. Rate the study on the following scale:

	Yes	No	Can't tell
1. Is the sample representative?			
2. Is the sample big enough?			
3. How were people assigned to groups?			
4. Was the measurement adequate?			
5. Are the results significant?			

Make Graphic Organizers

Draw an idea map showing the point of view, the arguments, and their support.

Step 4: Remember What's Important

 Review your marginal notes identifying the point of view and the arguments. Review the underlining that identified the supporting details. Review the idea map. Test yourself until you are sure that you will remember the material.

Step 5: Make Use of What You Read

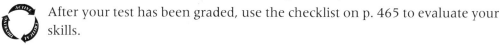 When you are ready, complete the Comprehension Check. Do not look back at the reading or the idea map.

Step 6: Evaluate Your Active Critical Thinking Skills

After your test has been graded, use the checklist on p. 465 to evaluate your skills.

COMPREHENSION CHECK

Multiple Choice

Circle the letter before the best answer to each of the following questions.

1. The writer of the selection wrote a book called

    a. *The Competitive Edge.*

    b. *No Context.*

    c. *No Contest.*

    d. *Don't Compete.*

2. The author believes competition

    a. undermines self-esteem.

    b. poisons relationships.

    c. holds us back from doing our best.

    d. does all of the above.

3. The author talks about Terry Orlick, who is

    a. a famous author.

    b. a sports psychologist.

    c. a professional athlete.

    d. a physical education teacher.

4. When Orlick taught a group of children noncompetitive games

    a. two-thirds of the girls liked them.

    b. two-thirds of all the children liked them.

    c. two-thirds of the boys liked them.

    d. none of the children enjoyed them.

5. From the reading we can infer that the author

    a. believes he is a "loser."

    b. is a coach of a sports team.

    c. believes physical activity is important.

    d. feels that periodic competition such as on the weekend is acceptable.

6. If the author were a member of a school board he would

    a. favor programs that would encourage women to participate in sports.

    b. eliminate all physical education.

    c. favor less competitive physical education programs.

    d. hire only female coaches for team sports.

7. Which activity would the author be most likely to participate in?

    a. volleyball

    b. recreational swimming

    c. tennis

    d. touch football

8. We can infer from the reading that the author would

    a. rather play football than monopoly.

    b. enjoy working in sales.

    c. favor schools that don't have grades.

    d. enjoy being a professional athlete.

Short Answer

9. Give an example of a cooperative activity that offers a physical workout (you may make it up).

    _____   _____

10. Give an example of a cooperative activity that allows us to test our accomplishment (you may make it up).

    _____

Essay

How and why does the author think that we ought to change the types of sports and games that most children participate in?

_____

_____

_____

_____

_____

_____

_____

_____

_____

_____

_____

_____

_____

_____

VOCABULARY IN CONTEXT

Write the best word from this list in the blank in each sentence below.

counterproductive   **benign**   **inherent**   **malicious**   **camaraderie**

gloat   **epithets**   **detest**   **conducive**   **aberration**

1. Because children often _____ spinach, parents are wise to let them watch *Popeye* eat his spinach in the cartoon.

2. The comment was meant to be _____ , but it actually hurt the feelings of several people.

3. It can be _____ to stay up all night to work on a paper, because you make more mistakes when you are tired.

4. Some studies have shown that listening to classical music is more

   _____ to studying than listening to rap music.

5. Children can be very _____ in teasing other children because they have trouble imagining themselves in the other person's place.

6. It is considered poor sportsmanship to _____ after winning a game.

7. Using rude _____ when talking to another person can lead to a fight.

8. The _____ among the co-workers grew stronger after they formed a bowling team.

9. There is an _____ assumption that a clergyman is honest.

10. Having six toes on one foot is an _____ .

24

Who Wins? Who Cares?

Vocabulary Preview

ritualistic (rich'oo wəl is'tik): automatic; prescribed as in a ceremony or custom

pitfalls (pit'fôlz): unanticipated dangers

rapport (ra pôr'): sympathetic relationship; harmony

classically (klas'ik lē): traditionally

tantamount (tant'tə mount'): equal [*to*] in value or effect

connote (kə nōt'): to suggest or convey

empathy (em'pa thē): intellectual or emotional identification with another

eschew (es choo'): to shun; avoid

antagonize (an tag'ə nīz'): to incur the dislike of; make an enemy of

polarize (pō'lə rīz'): to separate into opposed or antagonistic groups

steroid (stir'oid): any of a group of compounds that include the sex hormones, cortisone, and bile acids

succumb (sə kum'): to give way [*to*]; yield

myriad (mir'ē əd): very many

ethical (eth'i k'l): conforming to professional standards of conduct

seductive (si duk'tiv): tempting

ascribe (ə skrīb'): to refer to a supposed cause or source

devastating (dev'ə stāt'ŋ): destroying completely

cliché (klē shā'): an overused expression

intuit (in too'it, -tyoo'-): to know or understand by instinct, without conscious thought

divisive (də vi'siv): causing disagreement or dissension

cat, āte, fäther; pen, ēvil; if, kīte; nō, ôr, food, book; boil, house; up, turn; chief, shell; thick, *the*; zh, treasure; ŋ, sing; ə for *a* in *about*; ' as in *able* (a'b'l)

Step 1: Preread

Preview the following selection by reading the title and the first sentence of each paragraph. Answer the following questions without looking back at the reading.

1. What is the subject? _____

2. What is the author's point of view? _____

3. Compare your beliefs with the author's. On a scale of 1 (no way) to 5 (definitely),

how open is your mind to the author's point of view? _____

Step 2: Read

Read the selection without underlining. Just try to understand the author's arguments.

Write your starting time here: _____

Who Wins? Who Cares?

MARIAH BURTON NELSON

C OMPETITION CAN DAMAGE SELF-ESTEEM, create anxiety and
lead to cheating and hurt feelings. But so can romantic
love. No one suggests we do away with love; rather, we
must perfect our understanding of what love means.

So too with competition. "To compete" is derived from the
Latin competere, meaning "to seek together." Women seem to
understand this. Maybe it's because we sat on the sidelines for so
long, watching. Maybe it's because we were raised to be kind
and nurturing. I'm not sure why it is. But I've noticed that it's
not women who greet each other with a ritualistic, "Who
won?"; not women who memorize scores and statistics; not
women who pride themselves on "killer instincts." Passionate
though we are, women don't take competition that seriously. Or
rather, we take competition seriously, but we don't take winning
and losing seriously. We've always been more interested in
playing.

In fact, since the early part of this century, women have devised ways to make sport specifically inclusive and cooperative.
Physical educators of the 1920s taught sportswomanship as well
as sport skills, emphasizing health, vigor, high moral conduct,
participation, respect for other players and friendship. So intent
were these women on dodging the pitfalls of men's sports that
many shied away from competition altogether.

Nowadays, many women compete wholeheartedly. But we
don't buy into the "Super Bull" mentality that the game is everything. Like Martina Navratilova and Chris Evert, former "rivals"
whose rapport has come to symbolize a classically female approach to competition, many women find ways to remain close
while also reaching for victory. We understand that trying to win
is not tantamount to trying to belittle; that winning is not wonderful if the process of play isn't challenging, fair or fun; and that
losing, though at times disappointing, does not connote failure.
For women, if sports are power plays, they're not about power
over (power as dominance) but power to (power as competence). Sports are not about domination and defeat but caring
and cooperation.

"The playing of a game has to do with your feelings, your emotions, how you care about the people you're involved with," says University of Iowa basketball coach C. Vivian Stringer.

Pam Shriver has said of Steffi Graf, "I hope in the next couple of years that I get to be friends with her because it's just easier. It's more fun. I don't think it affects the competitive side of things."

Friendship has been a major theme of my sporting life as well, along with physical competence, achievement and joy. Though I've competed in seven sports from the high school to the professional level, I have few memories of victories or losses. I don't think winning taught me to be a gracious winner. I don't think losing readied me for more serious losses in life. Rather, my nearly 30 years of competition have taught me how to *play*, with empathy, humor and honesty. If another player challenges me to row harder, swim faster or make more clever moves toward the basket, the games take on a special thrill. But the final score is nearly irrelevant. Chris Evert once said the joy of winning "lasts about an hour."

I'm choosy about whom I compete with, and how. I don't participate in games in which "losers" are no longer allowed to play. Monopoly, poker, musical chairs, and single-elimination tournaments are a few examples. If playing is the point, then exclusion never makes sense. I also eschew competitions that pit women against men; they only serve to antagonize and polarize. I no longer injure myself in the name of victory. Nor, as a coach, will I allow players to get that carried away.

Some women, scarred by childhood exclusion, shamed by early "defeats," or sickened by abuses such as cheating and steroid use, still avoid competition. They're right to be wary. Although these things are more visible in men's sports, female athletes and coaches can also succumb to the "winning is the only thing" myth, committing myriad ethical and personal offenses, from recruiting violations to bulimia, in the name of victory.

But once one understands the spirit of the game, it's not a matter of *believing* that winning and losing aren't important, it's a matter of noticing that they're not. Women seem to notice. Most women can play soccer, golf, or run competitively and enjoy themselves, regardless of outcome. They can play on a "losing" team but leave the court with little or no sense of loss. They can win without feeling superior.

I think it's the responsibility of these women—and the men who remain unblinded by the seductive glow of victory—to share this vision with young players. Children, it seems to me, naturally enjoy comparing their skills: "How far can you throw the ball? Farther than I can? How did you do it? Will you show me?" It's only when adults ascribe undue importance to victory that losing becomes devastating and children get hurt.

Adults must show children that what matters is how one plays the game. It's important that we not just parrot that cliché, but demonstrate our commitment to fair, participatory competition by paying equal attention to skilled and unskilled children; by allowing all children to participate fully in games, regardless of the score; and by caring more about process than results. This way, children can fully comprehend what they seem to intuit: that competition can be a way to get to know other people, to be challenged, and to have fun in a close and caring environment. To seek together.

Some of my best friends are the women and men who share a court or pool or field with me. Together we take risks, make mistakes, laugh, push ourselves and revel in the grace and beauty of sports. Who wins? Who cares? We're playing *with*, not *against* each other, using each other's accomplishments to inspire.

At its best, competition is not divisive but unifying, not hateful but loving. Like other expressions of love, it should not be avoided simply because it has been misunderstood.

1000 words

Write your ending time here: _____

Subtract your starting time: _____

Total time: _____

Check the Rate Chart in the back of the book to find out how many words per minute you have read and then record your score on the Progress Chart.

Step 3: Analyze What You Read

Identify Arguments and Supporting Details

In the margin of the reading, write POV next to the place where the author presents her point of view.

For each of the five arguments in the reading, we have provided supporting details. Fill in the missing argument; if the argument is not clearly stated in the reading, use your own words. Next, write in the type of supporting detail (facts, examples, reasons, testimony).

Argument 1 _____

Detail: . . . it's not women who greet each other with a ritualistic "Who won?"; not women who memorize scores and statistics; not women who pride themselves on "killer instincts."

Type: _____

Argument 2 _____

Detail: Physical educators of the 1920s taught sportswomanship as well as sport skills. . . .

Type: _____

Argument 3 _____

Detail: Martina Navratilova and Chris Evert

Type: _____

Argument 4 _____

Detail: . . . games in which "losers" are no longer allowed to play . . . competitions that pit women against men . . . no longer injure myself in the name of victory . . . allow players to get that carried away.

Type: _____

Argument 5 _____

_____

Detail: . . . demonstrate our commitment to fair, participatory competition by paying equal attention to skilled and unskilled children; by allowing all children to participate fully in games, regardless of the score; and by caring more about process than results.

Type: _____

Write Arg. 1, Arg. 2, etc. in the margin of the reading next to the place that each argument appears. Underline the supporting details for each argument.

Evaluate Supporting Details

FACT VERSUS OPINION: Sometimes authors present their opinions as if they were facts. We have defined a fact as something that can be proved or disproved. An opinion cannot be proved or disproved. Write F in the space before each statement of fact; write O if the statement is an opinion.

_____ **1.** "Competition can damage self-esteem, create anxiety and lead to cheating and hurt feelings."

_____ **2.** "We must perfect our understanding of what love means."

_____ **3.** "'To compete' is derived from the Latin *competere*, meaning 'to seek together.'"

_____ **4.** "Maybe it's because we sat on the sidelines for so long, watching."

_____ **5.** "Passionate though we are, women don't take competition that seriously."

_____ **6.** "Physical educators of the 1920s taught sportswomanship as well as sport skills, emphasizing health, vigor, high moral conduct, participation, respect for other players and friendship."

_____ **7.** "But we don't buy into the 'Super Bull' mentality that the game is everything."

_____ **8.** "For women, if sports are power plays, they're not about power over (power as dominance) but power to (power as competence)."

_____ **9.** "I don't participate in games in which 'losers' are no longer allowed to play."

_____ **10.** "I also eschew competitions that pit women against men. . . ."

EVALUATING RESEARCH   Author Mariah Burton Nelson believes that women engage in a healthier type of competition than men do. Go back to the five questions for evaluating research, which were presented on p. 351. Using the questions as a guide, design a research study to measure whether competition differs in women and in men. You want to be able to draw conclusions to apply to the general population of the United States.

1. How can you make sure your sample is representative?

_____

_____

2. How big a sample do you need?

_____

_____

3. Into what subgroups will you divide your people?

_____

_____

_____

_____

4. How will you decided which people go into which group?

_____

5. How will you measure the differences between your groups concerning your topic?

_____

6. How will you decide whether the results are significant?

_____

_____

_____

Make Graphic Organizers

Draw an idea map showing the point of view, the arguments, and their support.

Step 4: Remember What's Important

 Review your marginal notes identifying the point of view and the arguments. Review the underlining that identified the supporting details. Review the idea map. Test yourself until you can remember the material.

Step 5: Make Use of What You Read

 When you are ready, complete the Comprehension Check. Do not look back at the reading or the idea map.

Step 6: Evaluate Your Active, Critical Thinking Skills

After your test has been graded, use the checklist on p. 465 to evaluate your skills.

COMPREHENSION CHECK

Multiple Choice

Circle the letter before the best answer to each of the following questions.

1. The author calls the highly competitive mentality

   a. "The Superbowl Mentality."

   b. "The Who Wins, Who Cares Mentality."

   c. "The Ends Justifies the Means Mentality."

   d. "The Super Bull Mentality."

2. The author says that

   a. losing does not mean you have failed.

   b. women would rather die than lose.

   c. trying to win is trying to upset the other person.

   d. women don't like to compete.

3. The author doesn't like

   a. losing to anyone when competing.

   b. games that require quick thinking.

   c. games that are not competitive.

   d. games in which "losers" are no longer allowed to play.

4. The author says she

   a. hates losing.

   b. has fond memories of every time she won a game.

   c. has few memories of victories or losses.

   d. thinks losing games as a child prepared her for more serious losses in life.

5. From the reading you can infer that women

   a. are becoming more like men as they enter the job market.

   b. are superior athletes compared to men.

   c. are not raised to enjoy athletic sports.

   d. are better "sports" than men when they lose.

6. From the reading you can infer that most women

   a. would make good coaches of professional sports teams because they would emphasize playing for fun.

   b. would not be respected by male athletes because they are not as talented.

   c. would tend not to make good coaches of professional sports teams because they wouldn't play to win at all costs.

   d. have more difficulty than men trying to make friends with a competitor.

7. From the reading you can infer that

   a. women are inferior athletes.

   b. women should be allowed to play in all professional sports.

   c. if you understand the meaning of competition, winning will not be so important.

   d. women are going to become more like men as time goes on.

8. Who would probably believe in the proverb "It's not whether you win or lose, it's how you play the game"?

   a. gamblers

   b. women

   c. coaches for varsity sports teams

   d. men

Short Answer

Name some bad effects of the "winning is the only thing" myth.

9. _____

10. _____

Essay

Why does the author say that competition can be good?

_____

_____

_____

_____

_____

_____

_____

_____

_____

_____

_____

_____

_____

_____

VOCABULARY IN CONTEXT

Write the best word from each list in the blank in the sentences that follow the list.

Part A

pitfalls	rapport	classically	tantamount	connotes
empathy	eschewed	seductive	ascribed	devastating

1. The student _____ her good grades to studying hard every night.

2. Failing a class can be a _____ experience.

3. To an overeater, a well-stocked refrigerator is very _____ .

4. She was so excited about going to Europe that she forgot to plan for the

   _____ of being a woman traveling alone.

5. Couples in a good relationship develop a _____ that is the envy of their friends.

6. Passing a friend without saying "hello" is _____ to an insult.

7. The word *mother,* besides meaning a female parent, _____ feelings of warmth and caring.

8. The winner and loser had a certain _____ for each other because they understood how much hard work had gone into their training.

9. The alley cat _____ all areas he knew were inhabited by dogs.

10. Jumping in puddles on a rainy day is a _____ childlike behavior.

Part B

antagonize   polarize   steroid   succumb   myriad

ethical   cliché   ritualistic   intuit   divisive

11. Many people _____ to the temptation of chocolate.

12. If you _____ a police officer you are likely to regret it.

13. A _____ is an overused expression.

14. Successful poker players _____ how good a hand their opponents have.

15. Taking sides on an issue can often _____ a community.

16. A _____ of animals can be found in any large zoo.

17. _____ statements can bring disagreement to an otherwise agreeable discussion.

18. Athletes can be disqualified from some competition if illegal _____ use is detected.

19. Lawyers must follow very strict _____ guidelines.

20. A handshake is a _____ greeting in many countries.

COMPARING VIEWS ON COMPETITION IN SPORTS AND GAMES

Use the following activities to evaluate your understanding of the issue of competition in sports and games. Answer on a separate sheet of paper.

1. Summarize each reading. Be sure to include the point of view, the arguments, and their major support.

2. Evaluate the support for each reading. Consider what the author is implying as well as what he or she is saying. Is it true? Is it reasonable?

3. Compare the readings. Do you believe that one author's arguments are stronger than the other's? Why?

4. Go back to the self-questioning survey on page 343. Would you change any of your responses after reading the selections? Summarize your opinion on the issue, noting any ways in which your opinion has been affected by your reading.

Issue 3: Health Care Reform

The two readings take opposing views on what the United States should do about health care.

SELF-QUESTIONING

To help you become aware of your own beliefs and biases about health care, answer the following questions. Write the number for the rating scale that best expresses your opinion. You will reevaluate your views after you have completed Readings 25 and 26.

Rating Scale

1. No

2. Perhaps not

3. No opinion

4. Perhaps

5. Yes

Rate each question 1 to 5.

_____ 1. Do we need to reform our system of health care?

_____ 2. Should we do away with competing health insurance plans and just have one insurer?

_____ 3. Should we have less government control so that competition between plans works better?

_____ 4. Are doctors paid too much?

25

The National Health Care Phobia

Vocabulary Preview

phobia (fō′bē ə): an unreasonable fear

foreordained (fôr′ôr dānd′): determined beforehand

antiquated (an′ti quā tid): out of date

per capita (pər kap′i tə): for each person

leverage (lev′ər ij): power; means of accomplishing something

astute (ə sto͞ot′): shrewd; clever

stupefy (sto͞o′pə fī): to stun or bewilder

incalculable (in kal′kyo͞o lə bəl): too great to be counted

futile (fyo͞ot′'l): useless; hopeless

ostensibly (ä sten′sə blē): seemingly; apparently

munificence (myo͞o nif′ə səns): lavish generosity

advocate (ad′və kit): a person who speaks or writes in support of something

exodus (eks′ə dəs): a departure of a large number of people

queue (kyo͞o): a line or file of persons waiting to be served

anecdote (an′ik dōt′): a short, entertaining account of some happening

adversary (ad′vər ser′ē): opponent; enemy

specter (spek′tər): a haunting or disturbing prospect

antediluvian (an′tē də lo͞o′vē ən): before the biblical flood; very old-fashioned

intubate (in′to͞o bāt′): to insert a tube to administer food, medicine, or gases, or to admit air

affluence (af′lo͞o əns): wealth

cat, āte, fäther; pen, ēvil; if, kīte; nō, ôr, fo͞od, book; boil, house; up, turn; chief, shell; thick, _the_; zh, treasure; ŋ, sing; ə for _a_ in _about_; ' as in _able_ (a′b′l)

Step 1: Preread

Preview the following selection by reading the title, the first paragraph, and the last paragraph. Answer the following questions without looking back at the reading.

1. What is the subject? _____

2. What is the author's point of view? _____

3. Compare your beliefs with the author's. On a scale of 1 (no way) to 5 (definitely),

how open is your mind to the author's point of view? _____

Step 2: Read

Read the selection without underlining. Just try to understand the author's arguments.

Write your stating time here: _____

The National Health Care Phobia

GREGG EASTERBROOK

I N HEALTH REFORM, HARDLY ANYONE IS uttering the most important words on the subject: "national health care." President [Clinton's plan was] based on a new theory widely called "managed competition," though Clinton no longer uses the term. His program [contained] many attractive provisions, such as the beginnings of universal coverage. But in the end, managed competition is an elaborate attempt to avoid facing an obvious fact: national health systems control costs, and market-based systems, no matter how conscientiously designed, do not.

The United States already has the most competitive medicine in the world. It features multiple contending insurance plans, physician advertising in subways, hospital marketing consultancies and more. It is exactly this competition that makes American medicine so expensive. Competition is wonderful in true free markets, but counterproductive in a medical system that operates on the pass-along philosophy of If We Build It, They Must Pay. . . .

National health care is supposedly impossible in the United States. However, it is nearly certain to come to pass soon, perhaps in this decade. Despite the national political phobia, some 88 members of Congress have announced support for the concept. Most Americans sense that a national program is inevitable. And in their hearts, those in the medical industry suspect such a system is foreordained.

Much of the phobia is based on misconceptions about national health care, some of them fostered by various interest groups that benefit from medical cost escalation: that doctors become government employees (they don't in most national systems), that waiting lines are long (they are rare except in Britain), that treatments are antiquated (technology in Germany and France differs little from that in the United States). Most important is the misconception that in national health systems, government always pays. Not so: in some national systems, private insurers pay. But in all national plans, government mandates what medical fees may be. . . .

National health systems suffer an array of problems, not least of which is government involvement in a large economic sector. But the problems afflicting the U.S. pseudomarket system are far worse, beginning with costs so high that even the world's richest nation cannot afford them. Last year health care cost the United States a stunning $832 billion—nearly three times the defense budget, or 13.4 percent of the gross domestic product. Yet that fantastic price fails to produce coverage for millions of Americans. All of the world's other advanced nations, using national plans, devote from 6.6 to 10 percent of GDP to medicine. From that lesser investment they realize universal coverage.

Put more simply, America spends about $2,867 per man, woman and child on health care. Canada spends about $1,915, Germany about $1,659, France about $1,650. Quality of care under the U.S. approach is slightly better in a few categories, like saving premature infants; slightly worse in a few others, like overall infant mortality. On big-picture numbers such as life expectancy, there is no difference between what the U.S. investment buys and what the smaller investments of national health plans buy.

The spread between the GDP percentage of American and French medicine works out to $280 billion a year, roughly the level of the federal deficit in 1991. This suggests that if this country merely achieved the same degree of medical cost discipline already achieved in France, the federal deficit could be wiped out.

Why can't our market-based system control costs? One reason is that physician fees defy textbook dynamics of supply and demand. As the number of physicians has risen their fees have gone up in real terms, though market logic says that under such circumstances fees should decline. Simultaneous increases in doctors and their fees are not an inescapable fact of life. Germany has more physicians per capita than the United States— a greater "doctor glut"—yet real-dollar payments to German physicians have declined over the last two decades.

A second reason is that consumers cannot make informed decisions. Providers of products like cars and news magazines are under constant pressure from consumers who keenly understand the cost-benefit ratios of various offerings. No such pressure exists in health care, where patients have little bargaining leverage, and even the most astute consumers rapidly become stupefied.

Third, there is the complexity of the American approach. Studies show that America spends about 20 percent of its medical costs on administration. Canada spends about 10 percent. That is: the government-run Canadian system has low costs for bureaucratic overhead, while the market-run American system has high bureaucratic costs. What could better show that in health care market logic is stood on its head, and thus medical competition will have the reverse of the desired effect? The high-end estimates for red tape in American medicine come to a breathtaking $167 billion a year. That figure represents roughly what France and Germany combined spend annually on their entire health-care systems.

But the most important reason medical competition does not cut expenditures is that in medicine there is no relationship between the cost of a service and its value. Market systems function by price signals. In medicine, price signals don't work. A $10 hypo of antibiotic delivered to a child may be worth an incalculable sum, saving the entire span of the child's life. A $100,000 bone-marrow transplant for a late-stage cancer patient may provide nothing more than a few extra days of suffering and billings for more futile procedures. How can a system designed to run on price signals make sense of that?

In 1990 the *New England Journal of Medicine* published a study that concluded: "Higher [health] expenditures in the U.S. are explained entirely by higher fees; the quantity of physicians' services is actually lower in the United States than in Canada [but] U.S. fees for procedures are more than three times as high as in Canada." High pricing of medical services is best reflected in physician incomes. Most American doctors are skilled, hard-working and high-minded. But the mean income of a self-employed American physician is $170,000, about six times the typical family income. U.S. physician incomes have risen well ahead of earnings generally for some 20 years.

Physician fees alone represent a fifth of U.S. medical expenditures. More important, doctors issue the orders that result in hospital admissions, tests and procedures. If the tone set by doctors is one of craving for gain regardless of what society can afford, the system will reflect that example. Chief executives of large hospitals, even some that are ostensibly "nonprofit," average $236,000 a year. The CEOs of the largest pharmaceutical companies pulled down an average $6.6 million last year; those of the largest health insurers, $1.2 million. Although physicians and executives in national health-care systems are well paid—German doctors earn a median $110,000 annually—nothing like the level of American medical munificence exists in other nations.

Recently the General Accounting Office estimated that switching to a national health system could save $67 billion annually. This figure was dismissed in many quarters as "only $67 billion." Saving $67 billion with a national health plan, Congressional Budget Office director Robert Reischauer told a House hearing, would "only" wipe out a year's increase in medical spending at the current unrestrained rate.

Forget for a moment that $67 billion is a sum greater than federal spending for education and foreign aid combined. The GAO estimate was solely for savings on paperwork. The study assumed that under a national health-care plan physicians, hospital presidents and drug-company CEOs would continue to be paid at their current rates.

If instead a national health system lowered medical fees to approximately the level of those in the former West Germany, the savings might sustain high technology and offer universal care without . . . tax increases. . . . Wishful thinking? Let's examine an American city where this has already happened.

Imagine a place where physicians are well paid and self-employed. Patients choose their doctors. Insurance premiums are the same for all, whether sick or healthy, big business or mom-and-pop. No one is denied coverage for switching jobs or having a preexisting condition. Medical costs are 34 percent lower than the U.S. average. Yet services are rendered without waiting periods. The technology is first-class. This is not health-care heaven, it's Rochester, N.Y. "You don't practice in this community to get rich," says Dr. Philip Bonanni, a Rochester internist. "But doctors here practice medicine as every good physician dreams of, at a high standard, without worrying about whether the patient can pay, without being interfered with."

For decades Rochester has run what amounts to a guerrilla insurrection in health-care reform. City leaders devised a system that combines the cost control of national health care with the best of market-driven medicine. Medical technology is up to date, the area having about the same proportion of magnetic resonance imaging (MRI) machines as New York or Los Angeles. Yet care is delivered at a price that equates to 9 percent of GDP. If Rochester's cost levels were extended nationwide, U.S. health-care expenditures would decline by $285 billion per year.

The city's approach begins with a dominant insurer, Rochester Blue Cross, covering about 80 percent of the population. Decades ago executives of Kodak, Rochester's largest employer, concluded that only a dominant insurer would have the clout to keep medical prices low. Kodak persuaded other Rochester employers to support this concept.

Rochester Blue Cross is in effect a "single payer," something advocates of national medicine call the key to cost control. If one large underwriter pays medical bills, that payer can compel providers to lower fees. Doctors and other care providers in Rochester grumble about this, but there has been no exodus from the city, because even at lower prices health care continues to confer abundance upon most practitioners. For instance, the national average for an "intermediate" pediatrician visit is $40; in Rochester the price is $33.37. In most cities an MRI scan costs $1,500. In Rochester it costs about $800.

Arthur Aspengren, president of a Rochester council that helps employers coordinate health-care policy, notes that "Kodak cameras and Xerox copiers are better than they used to be yet also cheaper in real dollars. Why can't health care get better and cost less, like any other product? Everybody assumes that health care can only get more expensive. In Rochester we find that is not necessarily so."

The success of Rochester medicine is widely credited to progressive behavior by local employers like Kodak and Xerox. That helps, but the willingness of Rochester physicians to work for less is the driving factor, both reducing costs and setting a virtuous example that spreads through the system.

Rochester is hardly immune from cost concerns. As its population ages, medical expenses have been increasing, though since the increases start from a lower level, total costs remain well below the national figure. . . .

But aren't there horrible queues in national health systems? There are in the United Kingdom, the source of most clammy anecdotes about national plans. France, Germany, Sweden and other countries offer rapid access. All of them, for instance, have more hospital beds per capita than the United States. And don't national health systems deny patients the freedom to choose doctors? Again, this is mainly true of the British system. France, Germany, Sweden and other nations afford considerable choice. Today a Canadian has more freedom in choosing a physician than an American, since in Canada the fine print on insurance policies is never an issue. Some 47 percent of Americans already have restricted choice because of enrollment in various managed-care plans, while the 15 percent lacking insurance have no say about who, if anyone, treats them. In Canada anyone may go to any doctor. If the United States converts to national health care, it can avoid some of the problems of other national health systems by benefiting from their experience. The United States should, for example, shun the sort of mega-HMO structure that plagues Britain. The health-maintenance organization is a fine idea on paper, but in practice it can create a financial incentive to deny treatment. It is worth noting that Physicians for a National Health Program, a group of mainly liberal doctors, opposes the trend toward HMOs. Its Dr. David Himmelstein, a Boston internist, says HMOs "render doctors the financial adversaries of their patients."

"Fee for service will always be the best relationship between doctor and patient," says Dr. John Berryman, a Washington, D.C., obstetrician. "It's just that the fees should be lower." In the Canadian, French, German and Swedish national systems, doctors are privately employed and bill according to how much work they do. They simply bill for less than American physicians, and they need less since they do not require large accounting staffs to deal with unending insurance disputes. . . .

The United States could also profit from the lessons of national health-care systems in the area of medical education. French and German physicians do not graduate from med school with debts of $50,000 or more; tuitions are government-paid. Conversion to this system would add a line item to the federal budget. But society's net health expenditures might fall. As Jules Cohen, a professor at the University of Rochester medical school, points out, the specter of graduating with crushing debt pushes young doctors into specialist tracks, where they can earn money faster to pay off their loans. In turn, the oversupply of specialists makes American medicine much more expensive. In other Western nations up to 40 percent of physicians are specialists; in the United States the figure nears 80 percent. Each year countless young physicians ending their residencies lament that they would like to perform community-oriented medicine but must join a profit-maximizing practice to service med-school debts.

Finally, the United States can implement a national system that leaves in a little fat. There is value in obtaining medical procedures on demand, value in investing in research into new pharmaceuticals and medical gadgets, even if some turn out to be frills. America could cut costs and still retain a cushion that ensures frontline technology without waiting. Suppose the United States cut its health share of GDP to 11.7 percent, halfway between present U.S. expenditures and spending in Canada, the nation with the world's second most expensive medicine. That would still yield a saving of "only" $89 billion a year.

Is it cast in stone that the political system would oppose national health care? The antediluvian American Medical Association would; it practically must be intubated whenever the words "national health" are mentioned. But the AMA represents the lowest common denominator of the medical world. An important cultural clue: these days when young doctors meet journalists, one of the first things most say is, "I'm not a member of the AMA." Groups such as the American College of Physicians have expressed willingness to endorse aspects of national health, such as lower fees, in return for reforms such as reduced malpractice pressure. Polls suggest a solid majority of Americans favor a national health plan.

At the center of the question will be, as always, doctors. A more modest, publicly fixed fee system, of the type used in Rochester and in national-health-care countries, would reduce doctors' incomes somewhat but remove from their lives the worry that others are charging more, the pressures of being a business manager rather than a healer, the predatory insurers looking over their shoulders.

A national health approach, modified to incorporate the strong points of American medicine, could offer doctors a more pleasant life and offer patients quality care at affordable costs. . . .

Someday, when some form of national health care has come to the United States, we will look back . . . and say: why didn't we just get it over with then? Private-sector market forces are the foundation of American affluence. But there is no shame in admitting that in the special case of medical care, such forces backfire.

2700 words

Write your ending time here: _____

Subtract your starting time: _____

Total time: _____

Check the Rate Chart in the back of the book to find out how many words per minute you have read and then record your score on the Progress Chart.

Step 3: Analyze What You Read

Identify Arguments and Supporting Details

In the margin of the reading, write POV next to the place the author presents his point of view.

Following are the major arguments from the reading. Fill in the supporting details.

1. Competition does not work in the United States health care system.

Reason: _____

2. National health care is inevitable.

Fact 1: _____

Fact 2: _____

Fact 3: _____

3. Much of the resistance to national health care is based on misconceptions.

Example 1: _____

Example 2: _____

Example 3: _____

Example 4: _____

4. Countries with national health care systems provide universal coverage and similar quality care at lower cost than the system we are now using.

    Example 1: _____

    Example 2: _____

    Example 3: _____

5. The savings from national health care could wipe out the budget deficit.

    Fact: _____

    _____

6. The market-based system cannot control costs.

    Reason 1: _____

    Reason 2: _____

    Reason 3: _____

    Reason 4: _____

7. If a national health system lowered medical fees to approximately the level of those in the former West Germany, the savings might sustain high technology and offer universal care.

    Example: _____

8. If the United States converts to national health care, it can avoid some of the problems of other national health systems by benefiting from their experience.

    Example: _____

9. The United States should pay medical school tuitions.

    Reason: _____

10. The United States should implement a national system that leaves in a little fat.

    Reason 1: _____

    Reason 2: _____

11.   Opinion is changing in favor of national health care.

Fact 1: _____

Fact 2: _____

12.   A publicly fixed fee system would benefit doctors.

Reason 1: _____

Reason 2: _____

Reason 3: _____

Write Arg. 1, Arg. 2, etc. in the margin of the reading next to the place that each argument appears. Underline the supporting details for each argument.

Evaluate Supporting Details

PROVABLE VERSUS UNPROVABLE   Evaluate the following ideas from the reading. If the statement is provable, write P in the space. If it is unprovable, write U in the space. One has been done for you as an example.

Example: ___**U**___ In their hearts, those in the medical industry suspect such a system is foreordained.

_____ **1.**   In all national plans, government mandates what medical fees may be.

_____ **2.**   The problems afflicting the U.S. pseudomarket are far worse (than those of national systems).

_____ **3.**   The spread between the GDP percentage of American and French medicine works out to $280 billion a year.

_____ **4.**   As the number of physicians has risen their fees have gone up in real terms.

_____ **5.**   All other advanced nations have universal coverage.

_____ **6.** Most American doctors are skilled, hardworking, and high-minded.

_____ **7.** Nothing like the level of American medical munificence exists in other nations.

_____ **8.** In Rochester, everyone pays the same for health care.

_____ **9.** Rochester Blue Cross is in effect a "single payer."

_____ **10.** The AMA represents the lowest common denominator of the medical world.

LOADED LANGUAGE   The words that authors choose can also be used to support their point of view. For each of the following phrases from the reading, write the implication that the underlined words have. One is done for you as an example.

Example: The national health care phobia

Implication: The U.S. has irrational fears about national health care.

1. . . . a medical system that operates on the pass-along philosophy of If We Build It, They Must Pay

Implication: _____

2. . . . the U.S. pseudomarket system.

Implication: _____

3. . . . large hospitals, even some that are ostensibly "nonprofit"

Implication: _____

4. . . . nothing like the level of American medical munificence exists in other nations

Implication: _____

5. "But doctors here practice medicine as every good physician dreams of, at a high standard, without worrying about whether the patient can pay.

Implication: _____

6. For decades Rochester has run what amounts to a guerrilla insurrection in health-care reform.

Implication: _____

7. The success of Rochester medicine is widely credited to <u>progressive behavior</u> by
    local employers.

    Implication: _____

8. . . . the source of most <u>clammy anecdotes</u> about national plans

    Implication: _____

    _____

9. The <u>antediluvian</u> American Medical Association. . . .

    Implication: _____

10. . . . the <u>predatory</u> insurers

    Implication: _____

Make Graphic Organizers
Draw an idea map showing the point of view, the arguments, and their support.

Step 4: Remember What's Important
 Review your marginal notes identifying the point of view and the arguments.
Review the underlining that identified the supporting details. Review the idea
map. Test yourself until you can remember the material.

Step 5: Make Use of What You Read
 When you are ready, complete the Comprehension Check. Do not look back at
the reading or the idea map.

Step 6: Evaluate Your Active Critical Thinking Skills

 After your test has been graded, use the checklist on p. 465 to evaluate your skills.

COMPREHENSION CHECK

True-False

Mark T or F.

_____ **1.** The author believes that the United States has a true free market in medical care.

_____ **2.** The author believes that many of the false ideas about national health care were planted by those who benefit from rising costs of medical care.

_____ **3.** The author admits that the United States has more advanced medical care than most European countries.

_____ **4.** The author supports the trend toward more HMOs.

Multiple Choice

Circle the letter before the best answer to each of the following questions.

5. The author says "national health care is supposedly impossible in the U.S." because

    a. most Americans oppose it.

    b. we cannot afford it.

    c. the medical industry opposes it.

    d. all of the above are true.

6. In all national health care systems

    a. doctors become government employees.

    b. waiting lines are long.

    c. treatments are outdated.

    d. government controls what fees may be charged.

7. The reason that the United States has been unable to control medical costs is that

    a. physician fees keep rising.

    b. people are not given enough information to make informed decisions about health care.

    c. we have a complex health care bureaucracy.

    d. all of the above are true.

8. The key element in the success of the Rochester model is

   a. a single payer.

   b. lower physician fees.

   c. progressive employers.

   d. all of the above.

Short Answer

Why should a national system leave in a little fat?

9. _____

10. _____

Essay

Why does the author think the United States should adopt a national health care system? Answer on a separate sheet of paper.

VOCABULARY IN CONTEXT

Write the best word from each list in the blank of the sentences that follow the list.

Part A

   phobias   foreordained   antiquated   per capita   leverage

   astute   stupefied   incalculable   futile   ostensible

   1. The "big one," the earthquake all Californians fear, will do _____ damage wherever it strikes.

   2. She was so completely unprepared that she just stood there

      _____ when she was served with divorce papers.

   3. Politicians' _____ motives are to serve their constituents, but their real motives often involve doing what will best promote their careers.

   4. Parents' attempts to fight for control of teenagers' behavior are

      _____ because teenagers are biologically programmed to resist, and they have more time, energy, and determination than parents do.

5. _____ income is higher in Beverly Hills than in St. Louis.

6. In a survey of common _____ , public speaking came out on top, ahead of the fear of death.

7. After the spread of computer word processing programs, typewriters became

   _____ .

8. Workers once banded together to form labor unions in order to gain

   _____ in bargaining with employers.

9. Some _____ investors have made billions of dollars in the stock market.

10. The Prince of Wales is _____ to become King of England, but Prince Charles may be an exception because of his marital problems.

Part B

munificence   advocates   exodus   queues   anecdote

adversaries   specter   antediluvian   intubated   affluent

11. Hamlet saw the _____ of his dead father, who charged him to avenge his murder.

12. _____ of capital punishment argue that executions reduce the chances that other people will commit crimes that carry the death penalty.

13. People who have anorexia nervosa, an eating disorder, sometimes must be

   forcibly _____ to keep them from starving themselves to death.

14. The biblical _____ referred to the mass departure of Israelites from Egypt.

15. Historically, unrestrained capitalism has conferred _____ on a few at the top and poverty on all the rest.

16. Unless we control the national budget deficit, which transfers our bills to

   future generations, our children can expect to be less _____ than we are.

17. Until "no-fault" divorce became available, the husband and wife were forced to

be _____ in court.

18. Permitting registration for classes by mail can prevent long

_____ at the beginning of the semester.

19. The beginning of the Old Testament refers to _____ times.

20. A good way to capture your audience's interest at the beginning of a speech is

to tell a joke or an interesting _____ .

26

Government=Quack Rx

Vocabulary Preview

farcical (fär′si kəl): absurd; ridiculous

languish (lan′gwish): to continue in a state of neglect

magnitude (mag′nə tōōd′): size; importance

resurrect (rez′ə rekt′): to raise from the dead; bring back to life

egregious (ē grē′jəs): remarkably bad; flagrant

cat, āte, fäther; pen, ēvil; if, kīte; nō, ôr, fōōd, book; boil, house; up, turn; chief, shell; thick, *the*; zh, treasure; ŋ, sing; ə for *a* in *about*; ' as in *able* (a′b′l)

Step 1: Preread

 Preview the following selection by reading the title, the first sentence of each paragraph, and the last paragraph. Answer the following questions without looking back at the reading.

1. What is the subject? _____

2. What is the author's point of view? _____

    _____

3. Compare your beliefs with the author's. On a scale of 1 (no way) to 5 (definitely), how open is your mind to the author's point of view? _____

Step 2: Read

 Read the selection without underlining. Just try to understand the author's arguments.

Write your starting time here: _____

Government = Quack Rx

Malcolm S. Forbes Jr.

A CHILLING TRAGEDY OVERSEAS AND an almost farcical mistake here underscore how much of a nonsolution socialized medicine is for our health care cost crisis.

In France four high-ranking government officials and three
former ministers are on trial. In the mid-1980s they decided
against testing blood supplies for the AIDS virus. They did so
with the full knowledge of the possible consequences. Several
hundred hemophiliacs have already died because of tainted
transfusions. The death toll could reach 2,000.

Why would well-educated, responsible officials do something like this? Testing the blood would have meant overturning
established, bureaucratic procedures. Because the procedures
were invented in the U.S. and not in France, officials apparently
believed that nothing should be done until a French method was
developed. The scandal languished for years as the government
did its best to hush it up. Despite the magnitude of their murder-
ous act, the maximum jail time for any of the four officials, if
found guilty, will be four years.

France has long considered its nationalized health system to
be the world's best.

At home, Mittie Hearns has been fighting for six months to
prove to Medicare that she is not dead. Thanks to a computer
error, a hospital discharge form for the woman was mismarked
so the computer picked her up as having died. Despite phone calls
and personal appearances, Medicare was unable to resurrect her.

All-powerful bureaucracies are less accountable, less responsive to consumers than companies operating in an open, free-
enterprise system.

Egregious, scandalous behavior occurs in open markets, but
the forces of competition and the inability to use the power of the
State for cover-ups bring the bad out into the open sooner and
often reduce the likelihood of its happening in the first place.

The most vivid modern example is pollution. The worst,
longest running abuses took place in socialist countries. So what
is the answer to our own health problems of rapidly rising prices,
growing controls and the inability of millions to get insurance?

Free enterprise. We don't have it in medical care finance. Insurance premiums are fully tax deductible for companies but not for individuals. That ought to be switched. Let consumers pay directly for their health insurance and get the tax credits that currently go to corporations. The credits can be geared so that even unemployed or low-income people can get basic coverage.

By such a tax code change, tens of millions of Americans would police this $800 billion industry instead of employers, insurance companies and bureaucrats. Buyers would choose the kind of insurance they actually want. Many people, for example, would opt for a big deductible. The price of insurance would drop sharply since the buyer would be paying routine bills and still have comprehensive coverage for major accidents and illnesses.

Imagine what would happen to the cost of your auto insurance, which is high enough, if you filed insurance claims every time you bought gasoline or changed the tires.

The most remarkable change resulting from such a reform would be that health care providers, particularly hospitals, would suddenly have to make their pricing comprehensible. Consumers would actually be able to compare costs of one institution with those of another.

Nationalized medicine doesn't work. Countries with such systems are introducing free-enterprise elements to keep them from collapsing. In Canada health care costs have been rising faster than those in the U.S.

Moreover, socialized medicine destroys research and development, particularly for less well known diseases: There are not many votes to be had by devoting government money to afflictions that don't afflict many people. That's why most of the pharmaceutical breakthroughs come from the U.S. rather than Europe, Japan or Canada.

So-called play-or-pay solutions advocated by . . . Clinton and others are simply a way station to a national health care system. (Under this program, companies must either pay for health insurance for their employees or pay a major tax to a government health insurance fund.)

Free markets work for such basics as housing, food, transportation. It can work in health care as well.

600 words

Write your ending time here: _____

Subtract your starting time: _____

Total time: _____

Check the Rate Chart in the back of the book to find out how many words per minute you have read and then record your score on the Progress Chart.

Step 3: Analyze What You Read

Identify Arguments and Supporting Details

In the margin of the reading, write POV next to the place the author presents his point of view.

Following are the major arguments from the reading. Fill in the supporting details.

1. Bureaucracies are less accountable, less responsive to consumers than companies operating in an open, free-enterprise system.

   Example 1: _____

   Example 2: _____

2. The forces of competition and the inability to use the power of the state for cover-ups bring the bad out into the open sooner and often reduce the likelihood of its happening in the first place.

   Example: _____

3. We should bring free enterprise to health care finance by making health insurance premiums deductible by individuals.

   Reason 1: _____

   Reason 2: _____

4. Consumers would be able to compare costs of one institution with those of another.

   Reason: _____

5. Nationalized medicine doesn't work.

   Fact 1: _____

   Fact 2: _____

Fact 3: _____

6. Play-or-pay is not a good idea.

Reason: _____

Write Arg. 1, Arg. 2, etc. in the margin of the article next to the place that each argument appears. Underline the supporting details for each argument.

Evaluate Supporting Details

PROVABLE VERSUS UNPROVABLE   If the statement can be proved (or disproved), write P. If it is unprovable, write U.

_____ 1. All-powerful bureaucracies are less accountable, less responsive to consumers than companies operating in a free-enterprise system.

_____ 2. The worst, longest-running abuses (in pollution) took place in socialist countries.

_____ 3. Cover-ups are less likely under free enterprise than in a bureaucracy.

_____ 4. Insurance premiums are fully tax deductible for companies but not for individuals.

_____ 5. Most of the pharmaceutical breakthroughs come from the United States rather than Europe, Japan, or Canada.

_____ 6. Free markets work for such basics as housing, food, transportation.

_____ 7. In Canada health care costs have been rising faster than those in the United States.

_____ 8. Making health insurance tax deductible for individuals would lower the price of insurance.

_____ 9. So called play-or-pay solutions are a way station to a national health care system.

_____ 10. If individuals paid for health insurance, they could choose the kind of insurance they actually want.

LOGICAL REASONING   Several of the author's statements contain logical errors or insufficient explanations. This leaves his arguments open to criticism. For each of the following ideas, write the criticism that would be presented by someone taking the opposing point of view in a debate.

1. The kind of problem the French had with the tainted blood is more likely to occur in a bureaucracy (run by government) than in a free-enterprise system (run by business).

   Criticism: _____

   _____

2. Having individuals rather than employers pay for health insurance would cause prices to drop.

   Criticism: _____

   _____

3. Tax credits can be geared so that even unemployed or low-income people can get basic coverage.

   Criticism: _____

   _____

4. Socialized medicine destroys research and development.

   Criticism: _____

   _____

5. Free markets work for such basics as housing, food, transportation.

   Criticism: _____

   _____

LOADED LANGUAGE   For each of the following phrases, write the implication that the underlined words have.

1. Government = Quack Rx

   Implication: _____

2. . . . how much of a nonsolution socialized medicine is for our health care cost crisis

   Implication: _____

Make Graphic Organizers

Draw an idea map showing the point of view, the arguments, and their support.

Step 4: Remember What's Important

Review your marginal notes identifying the point of view and the arguments. Review the underlining that identified the supporting details. Review the idea map. Test yourself until you can remember the material.

Step 5: Make Use of What You Read

When you are ready, complete the Comprehension Check. Do not look back at the reading or the idea map.

Step 6: Evaluate Your Active Critical Thinking Skills

After your test has been graded, use the checklist on p. 465 to evaluate your skills.

COMPREHENSION CHECK

True-False

Mark T or F.

_____ **1.** The author is probably a Republican.

_____ **2.** Trading big deductibles for lower insurance premiums is easier for the poor than for the rich.

_____ **3.** The author seems to care primarily about the problems of the poor.

_____ **4.** The author is a strong advocate of universal health coverage.

Multiple Choice

Circle the letter before the best answer to each question below.

5. The author's proposed solution would work best for

    a. the poor who do not pay taxes.

    b. the rich who can use tax deductions.

    c. the middle class who may or may not need tax deductions.

    d. everyone equally.

6. The author uses the French decision not to test for the AIDS virus to illustrate

    a. the problems of bureaucracies.

    b. the arrogant attitude typical of the French.

    c. the fact that a government can get away with murder.

    d. the fact that public officials are not held accountable for what they do.

7. According to the author, free enterprise works because

    a. business is more caring than government about individuals.

    b. competition drives down prices and keeps people honest.

    c. it takes advantage of the tax system.

    d. all of the above are true.

8. According to the author, we don't have free enterprise in health care because

    a. the government pays for Medicare and Medicaid.

    b. "play-or-pay" is a step toward nationalization.

    c. Insurance premiums are fully deductible for employers but not for individuals.

    d. all of the above are true.

Short Answer

List two criticisms the author makes of countries that have national health insurance.

9. _____

10. _____

    _____

Essay

Why does the author say that free enterprise is a better solution to our health care problems than government intervention?

_____

_____

_____

_____

_____

_____

_____

_____

_____

_____

VOCABULARY IN CONTEXT

Write the best word from this list in the blank in each sentence below.

farcical   **languish**   **magnitude**   **resurrect**   **egregious**

1. Because Medicare does not cover long-term custodial care, old people can

    bankrupt their families if they _____ for years in nursing homes.

2. When beautiful young women marry very old, very rich men, their show of

    grief at the funeral can seem _____ .

3. Modern medicine has been able to _____ some people who have
    been dead for a short while.

4. If you make an _____ error on your income tax return, you are
    likely to be audited by the IRS.

5. A cure for cancer would be a breakthrough of the first _____ .

COMPARING VIEWS ON HEALTH CARE REFORM

Use the following activities to evaluate your understanding of the issue. Answer on a separate sheet of paper.

1. Summarize each reading, including the point of view, the arguments, and the major support.

2. Evaluate the support for each reading. Are the examples good ones, are the reasons logical, are the facts provable, does loaded language degrade the message?

3. Compare the readings. Do you believe that one author's arguments are stronger than the other's? Why?

4. Go back to the self-questioning survey on p. 374. Would you change any of your responses after reading the selections? Summarize your opinion on the issue, noting any ways in which your opinion has been affected by your reading.

Issue 4: Euthanasia

The two readings take opposing views on euthanasia (mercy killing).

SELF-QUESTIONING

To help you become aware of your own beliefs and biases about euthanasia, answer the following questions. Write the number from the rating scale that best expresses your opinion. You will reevaluate your views after you have completed Readings 27 and 28.

Rating Scale

1. No

2. Perhaps not

3. No opinion

4. Perhaps

5. Yes

Rate 1 to 5.

_____ 1. Does a human being have the right to take his or her own life?

_____ 2. Do we have the right to kill for political reasons (in war)?

_____ 3. Do we have the right to kill criminals (capital punishment)?

_____ 4. Do we have the right to abort a fetus?

_____ 5. Do we have the right to help another person die if he or she is suffering terribly with no hope of recovery?

_____ 6. Would you "pull the plug" on a relative who was never going to regain consciousness?

_____ 7. If your parent left a "living will" asking to die if there were no hope of recovery, would you follow his or her wishes?

27

Acting to End a Life Is Sometimes Justified

Vocabulary Preview

intercede (in'tər sēd'): to make an appeal on behalf of another

welter (wel'tər): confusion; turmoil

salient (sāl'yənt): outstanding; striking

euthanasia (yōō'thə nā'zhə): act of causing a painless death so as to end suffering

elicit (i lis'it): to draw forth; to evoke (a response)

qualified (kwôl'i fīd): modified, limited

intercurrent (in'tər kur'ənt): occurring during another disease

gradation (grā dā'shən): a stage or step

compos mentis (käm'pəs men'tis): of sound mind; sane

squeamishness (skwēm'ish nəs): ease with which one becomes nauseated or shocked

humanitarian (hyōō man' ə ter'ē ən): person devoted to promoting the welfare of humanity, especially through the elimination of pain and suffering

hypocritical (hip'ə krit'i k'l): pretending to feel what one does not

arbiter (är'bə tər): judge

theological (thē'ə läj'i k'l): having to do with the study of God or religion

glibly (glib'lē): smoothly (spoken), often too smoothly to be convincing

cat, āte, fäther; pen, ēvil; if, kīte; nō, ôr, fōōd, book; boil, house; up, turn; chief, shell; thick, *the*; zh, treasure; ŋ, sing; ə for *a* in *about*; ' as in *able* (a'b'l)

Step 1: Preread

Preview the following selection by reading the title and the first sentence of each paragraph. Answer the following questions without looking back at the reading.

1. What is the subject? _____

2. What is the author's point of view? _____

_____

3. Compare your beliefs with the author's. On a scale of 1 (no way) to 5 (definitely),

how open is your mind to the author's point of view? _____

Step 2: Read

 Read the selection without underlining. Just try to understand the author's arguments.

Write your starting time here: _____

Acting to End a Life Is Sometimes Justified

Christiaan Barnard

WHETHER LIFE ENDS WITH A BANG OR A WHIMPER, the end is a private moment. No one can share the last fears or hopes at the bedside, and no one can intercede in a confrontation that concerns only the dying and the approach of death.

Certainly, the concept of "death with dignity" has become an increasing focus of debate, not the least because of medical progress that has brought about demographic changes and a major increase in the number of retired and aged persons. The issue has generated a welter of legislation, much of which confuses rather than clarifies a salient question in euthanasia: Who will pull the plug?

Possibly one of the more useful outlines of the problem was put forward by Dr. Joseph Fletcher, a professor of medical ethics at the University of Virginia, in a paper given at a 1974 Euthanasia Conference in New York City. He listed eight levels of attitude and opinion on the human initiatives that can be exercised in the case of a patient dying of an incurable disease, as follows:

1. An absolute refusal to elicit any human initiative in the death or the dying. Life must always be considered as the ultimate human value.

2. A qualified refusal, in that the doctor can refrain from employing extraordinary means of preserving life but would nevertheless do whatever possible by ordinary means to keep life going.

3. Declining to start treatment in a patient who has an incurable disease and is suffering from a curable intercurrent illness (for example, the terminally ill cancer patient with pneumonia). The doctor refuses to initiate treatment for the lung infection that can be cured and in this way may actually hasten death.

4. Stoppage of treatment, with consent, where it is the patient's wish not to be treated any further.

5. Stoppage of treatment, without consent, when the attending physician feels that further treatment can only prolong suffering.

6. Leaving the patient with an overdose of narcotic or sedative, thus assisting the dying person to take his own life.

7. Prior permission is given by the patient to the doctor to administer an injection, under certain circumstances, from which the patient will not recover.

8. Without consent, and on his own authority, the doctor ends the patient's life with an overdose of drugs.

It is clear that the second, third, fourth and fifth situations are gradations of passive euthanasia. In none of these does the doctor take the initiative in ending the patient's life. The sixth, seventh and eighth describe grades of active participation.

There is thus a distinct difference between passive—or indirect—euthanasia, where death is induced by suspension of treatment, and the so-called active or direct euthanasia, where death is brought about by a definite act.

In general, the layman's view of euthanasia is one of "mercy killing," or active intervention to end life, with little or no concept of the possibility of a passive form.

I make no excuses and ask no forgiveness for admitting that I have practiced passive euthanasia for many years. In fact, I gave instructions to the doctor attending my own mother in her last illness that she should receive no antibiotics nor be tube fed. At that stage, she was in her 98th year, suffering from her third stroke and unconscious with pneumonia.

I have never practiced active euthanasia, a deed that in my country is regarded as murder and could merit the death penalty. But I do believe that in the clinical practice of medicine, active euthanasia has a definite place. I also believe that we should not be afraid to discuss its place in the scheme of things and to explore the possibilities in this approach to the terminally ill.

I cannot accept the simple statement that a doctor does not have the right to take life; furthermore, I believe the greatest difficulty is to define life. I myself have defined it as joy in living. Given the absence of this quality, without hope of restitution, the request of the suffering person—if conscious and compos mentis—and the satisfaction of other criteria such as good faith on the part of those caring for the person and the completion of legal requirements, there is no ethical reason why active medical euthanasia may not be administered.

Indeed, I have always wondered at the kind of person who would mercifully end the life of a suffering animal, yet would hesitate to extend the same privilege to a fellow being. It may be that in all of us there lurks a sense of guilt—and what more guilt-making burden can we assume than that of responsibility for another's death?

The error, perhaps, is one of category—that of regarding squeamishness as mercy.

As a scientist and a humanitarian, I find society's attitude toward the different ways of causing the death of an individual both hypocritical and illogical. Consider that, for as long as man has inhabited the earth, he has accepted with few reservations the right to kill and be killed on the battlefield, even when this leads to not only his own but multiple deaths.

I have talked to legal, ethical and medical authorities in many parts of the world on the need for active euthanasia, the problems that would confront the doctor in such situations and the safeguards required. Again and again the same questions came up:

Who will decide when a life is to be terminated and how can mistakes be avoided?

Would doctors perhaps misuse the right to take life by getting rid of the people they do not like?

Would the medical profession not lose a lot of the trust that is placed in it if doctors were given the right to take a life?

Does a doctor have the right to play God?

Must God be the final arbiter on the taking of life?

If it is feared that a doctor is playing God when he terminates a life, it can just as readily be argued that he is playing the same role when he prolongs the life of a terminally-ill patient. And surely, when the terminally-ill person develops an intercurrent infection that will cause death if not treated, are we not also interfering with God's will by instituting treatment and preventing the patient from dying of the infection?

Generally, these same questions can be raised about war, capital punishment and abortion. I maintain that if doctors are given the right to practice active euthanasia, and all the necessary safeguards are developed, then most of these objections would fall away.

And at the risk of finding myself out on a theological limb, I say that if it is playing God to reduce human suffering, then I do not believe that the God of mercy and compassion would mind if we mere mortals play God under such circumstances. When we glibly bracket talk of terminating life with mention of the Deity, what in fact do we know of God's interpretation of life?

1150 words

Write your ending time here: _____

Subtract your starting time: _____

Total time: _____

Check the Rate Chart in the back of the book to find out how many words per minute you have read and then record your scores on the Progress Chart.

Step 3: Analyze What You Read

Identify Arguments and Supporting Details

In the margin of the reading, write POV next to the place where the author presents his point of view.

For each supporting detail, fill in the argument. Some of the arguments are not stated directly; you will have to infer and paraphrase. Then fill in the type of supporting detail (facts, examples, reasons, testimony).

Argument 1: _____

Detail: Eight gradations

Type: _____

Argument 2: _____

Detail: Joy in life

    Type: _____

    Argument 3: _____

Detail: We are willing to end the life of a suffering animal but not of a suffering human.

    Type: _____

    Argument 4: _____

    _____

Detail: People don't mind killing other people in wars.

    Type: _____

    Argument 5: _____

    _____

Detail: Treating intercurrent infections.

    Type: _____

    Argument 6: _____

Details: War, capital punishment, and abortion

    Type: _____

    Argument 7: _____

Details: God may have mercy and compassion; we don't know His will.

    Type: _____

Write Arg. 1, Arg. 2, etc., in the margin of the reading next to the place where each argument appears. Underline the supporting details for each argument.

Evaluate Supporting Details

FACT VERSUS OPINION   Write F in the space before each statement of fact; write O if the statement is someone's opinion.

_____   1.   "I gave instructions to the doctor attending my own mother in her last illness that she should receive no antibiotics nor be tube fed."

_____   2.   "He [Fletcher] listed eight levels of attitude and opinion on the human initiatives that can be exercised in the case of a patient dying of an incurable disease. . . ."

_____   3.   "In the clinical practice of medicine, active euthanasia has a definite place."

_____   4.   "I have never practiced active euthanasia, a deed that in my country is regarded as murder and could merit the death penalty."

_____   5.   "There is no ethical reason why active medical euthanasia may not be administered."

_____   6.   "I find society's attitude toward the different ways of causing the death of an individual both hypocritical and illogical."

_____   7.   "I have talked to legal, ethical, and medical authorities in many parts of the world on the need for active euthanasia. . . ."

_____   8.   "If doctors are given the right to practice active euthanasia, and all the necessary safeguards are developed, then most of the objections would fall away."

_____   9.   The God of mercy and compassion wouldn't mind if we reduced human suffering through euthanasia.

_____ 10.   In passive euthanasia the doctor does not take the initiative in ending the patient's life.

AUTHOR'S CREDIBILITY: BACKGROUND AND REPUTATION   When judging the credibility of a speaker or writer it is valuable to know the background of the person. Here are some facts about Dr. Christiaan Barnard, whose opinions are key to the discussion of euthanasia in Reading 27.*

Use this scale to rate each fact on whether it increases or decreases credibility.

*The information on Christiaan Barnard is excerpted from *Current Biography Yearbook, 1968.* (New York: The H. W. Wilson Company, 1969), pp. 45–48.

Greatly increases	Increases	Neither increases nor decreases	Decreases	Greatly decreases
1	2	3	4	5

_____ 1. Christiaan Barnard was born in 1923 and was raised in Cape Town, South Africa.

_____ 2. He conducted the first successful human heart transplant operation in medical history in December 1967.

_____ 3. Louis Washkansky, the first transplant recipient, died eighteen days after the transplant.

_____ 4. He teaches surgery at University of Cape Town Medical School and directs surgical research at the school's Groote Schuur Hospital.

_____ 5. His father was a Dutch Reformed minister.

_____ 6. Barnard and his three brothers grew up in conditions bordering on poverty.

_____ 7. He received his MD degree in 1953.

_____ 8. He did all his early research on animals.

_____ 9. He came to the United States and studied at the University of Minnesota Medical School under the renowned surgeon Dr. Owen H. Wangensteen.

_____ 10. At first he supported himself by mowing lawns, washing cars, and doing other odd jobs.

_____ 11. He was able to complete all the work for a PhD degree within two years.

_____ 12. In 1960 he attracted international attention in scientific circles by transplanting a second head onto a dog.

_____ 13. In the early 1970s, he retired from surgery because of severe arthritis in his hands.

_____ 14. He has two daughters.

_____ 15. His temper can be short and sharp.

Make Graphic Organizers

Draw an idea map showing the point of view, the arguments, and their support.

Step 4: Remember What's Important

 Review the marginal notes identifying point of view and arguments. Review the underlining that identifies the supporting details. Review the idea map. Test yourself until you can remember the material.

Step 5: Make Use of What You Read

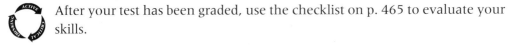 When you are ready, complete the Comprehension Check. Do not look back at the reading or the idea map.

Step 6: Evaluate Your Active Critical Thinking Skills

After your test has been graded, use the checklist on p. 465 to evaluate your skills.

COMPREHENSION CHECK

Circle the letter before the best answer to each question.

1. An example of passive euthanasia is
   a. giving the patient an overdose of drugs.
   b. giving the patient an injection that will kill him or her.
   c. leaving an overdose of drugs with the patient, in case the patient wants to kill himself or herself.
   d. stopping treatment of the patient.

2. Barnard defines life as
   a. having a heartbeat.
   b. having brainwaves.
   c. breathing.
   d. having joy in living.

3. Barnard states that euthanasia has become an increasing focus of debate because
   a. more doctors are quietly practicing it.
   b. it has caused a large number of malpractice suits.
   c. there have been medical breakthroughs that can prolong life artificially.
   d. many doctors have been arrested for practicing it.

4. To those who believe that God is against euthanasia, Barnard says that
   a. a merciful God would approve of it.
   b. prolonging life artificially is also playing God.
   c. we do not know how God interprets life.
   d. all of the above are true.

5. Barnard seems to believe that doctors
   a. cannot prolong life.
   b. never practice euthanasia now.
   c. should accept some responsibility for their patients' lives.
   d. should prolong life, hoping for new medical breakthroughs for the terminally ill.

6. Barnard suggests that people who are against euthanasia are really

   a. ethical.

   b. cowardly.

   c. vicious.

   d. brave.

7. After reading the selection, one might conclude that Barnard

   a. has practiced active euthanasia without admitting it.

   b. would not practice passive euthanasia even if it were legal.

   c. wouldn't practice active euthanasia in any situation.

   d. would practice active euthanasia if it were legal.

8. Barnard feels that the public

   a. is naive about euthanasia.

   b. believes in active euthanasia.

   c. is convinced that active euthanasia occurs constantly.

   d. should sign statements telling their doctors not to administer life-prolonging treatment in terminal cases.

Short Answer

What are the two main types of euthanasia discussed in the reading?

9. _____

10. _____

Essay

Why does the author support active euthanasia?

_____

_____

_____

_____

_____

_____

_____

_____

_____

_____

_____

_____

_____

_____

VOCABULARY IN CONTEXT

Write the best word from this list in the blank in each sentence below.

intercede   welter   salient   euthanasia   elicit   qualified

intercurrent   gradations   compos mentis   squeamishness

humanitarians   hypocritical   arbiter   theological   glib

1. Veterinarians have been practicing _____ on people's pets for many years.

2. The most _____ feature of the blue whale is its enormous length, which can equal three Greyhound buses.

3. Discussions about sex, politics, and religion can be relied on to

   _____ strong feelings.

4. A plea of insanity will not stand up if the court has ruled the accused

   _____ .

5. A baseball umpire is the _____ in close decisions during a game.

6. Becoming a clergyman takes many years of _____ study.

7. It is _____ for a politician who claims to believe in family values
   to divorce his wife for a younger, prettier woman.

8. Used-car salespeople often appear _____ in TV commercials.

9. Examples of famous _____ are Albert Schweitzer, Mother
   Teresa, Mahatma Ghandi, and Martin Luther King.

10. Parents often give their _____ consent when teenagers start
    dating. They have to know where they are, whom they are with, and when
    they will be home.

11. An example of an _____ infection is when a terminal cancer
    patient dies of pneumonia.

12. The intensity of most colors comes in many _____ , from very
    pale to very dark.

13. _____ is not a good quality in a doctor or nurse.

14. People who _____ when a husband and wife are arguing often
    lose the friendship of both.

15. The _____ of outdated laws still on the books includes one that
    makes it illegal to hunt camels in Arizona.

28

In Crisis, She Rejected Plea to Expedite Dying

Vocabulary Preview

expedite (ek′spə dīt′): to speed up or make easy

inexplicable (in eks′pli kə bəl): cannot be explained or understood

hypothetical (hī′pə thet′i k′l): speculative; not based on actual events

obliged (ə blījd′): compelled by moral, legal, or physical force

affirmative (ə fur′mə tiv): positive; confirming

objets d'art (äb′zhā där′): small objects of artistic value

salutary (sal′yoo ter′ē): beneficial; healthful

recoiling (ri koil′iŋ): drawing back, as in fear

predecease (prē′dē sēs′): to die before (someone else)

commonweal (käm′ən wēl): public good; general welfare

cat, āte, fäther; pen, ēvil; if, kīte; nō, ôr, food, book; boil, house; up, turn; chief, shell; thick, *th*e; zh, treasure; ŋ, sing; ə for *a* in *about*; ' as in *able* (a′b′l)

Step I: Preread

Preview the following selection by reading the title and the first sentence of each paragraph. Answer the following questions without looking back at the reading.

1. What is the subject? _____

2. What is the point of view? _____

    _____

3. Compare your beliefs with Elisabeth Kubler-Ross's. On a scale of 1 (no way) to 5 (definitely), how open is your mind to her point of view?

    _____

Step 2: Read

 Read the selection without underlining. Just try to understand the arguments.

Write your starting time here: _____

In Crisis, She Rejected Plea
to Expedite Dying

DEREK GILL

IN THE EARLY SUMMER OF 1967, Elisabeth and Manny Ross moved for the fifth time. They now felt comfortably settled in Chicago and, assuming they would be living and working there for the foreseeable future, they bought a home a few blocks away from the house they had been renting.

Elisabeth and Manny had decided to postpone their annual summer vacation and instead take a holiday at Christmas in order, as they had just explained to their 7-year-old son, Kenneth, to give him and his little sister, Barbara, "a real Swiss Christmas" with sleigh bells and festivals.

Suddenly, and apparently without stimulus or prompting, Elisabeth felt a deep and inexplicable concern about her mother's wellbeing. She turned to Manny and told him she had to fly to Switzerland immediately—tomorrow, if they could get plane reservations. She admitted that her impulsive decision sounded crazy, but there was some very important reason—a purpose she did not yet understand—why she should be with her mother as quickly as possible. A week later, she and the two children arrived in Zurich. There they boarded the train for Zermatt, where Mrs. Kubler and other members of Elisabeth's family were staying.

Zermatt was the ideal place for a restful vacation and for what Elisabeth called "a time for old-fashioned happiness." Mrs. Kubler looked in the pink of health and had, on the day the Ross family arrived, been on an eight-mile hike with Elisabeth's older brother, Ernst, and her fraternal triplet, Eva (her identical triplet, Erika, could not be there).

On the last evening at the resort where they were all staying, when the sun was setting over the peaks, Mrs. Kubler sat with Elisabeth on the balcony of her bedroom where Kenneth and Barbara, exhausted after the day's outing, were fast asleep.

Mother and daughter sat through a long silence and watched shadows move like ragged fingers across the green valleys far below. Then Mrs. Kubler turned to face Elisabeth and said, "I want your solemn promise that you'll do something for me. I want you to promise that, when I become incapable, when I become a human vegetable, you'll help me to die." She spoke with an uncharacteristic urgency.

Elisabeth was taken aback, both by the appeal and by its timing. She reacted not as an expert on dying, not as a teacher who instructed others to be alert for symbolic language, but as a shocked daughter. She replied too quickly, "What nonsense is this! A woman who is in her 70s and who can hike miles every day in the mountains is sure to die very suddenly. Mother, you're the last person to become a human vegetable."

Mrs. Kubler continued to speak as if she had not heard her. She again asked for a promise that, when she became incapable of caring for herself, Elisabeth would help her to die.

Elisabeth looked at her mother with astonishment and again protested that the question was purely hypothetical. In any case, she said firmly, she was totally opposed to mercy killing, if that was what her mother was talking about. In her opinion, no physician had the right to give a patient an overdose to relieve suffering. She could not promise her mother—or, for that matter, anyone else—to expedite dying. In the unlikely event that her mother did in fact become physically incapable, all that she could promise was that she would help her to live until she died.

Mrs. Kubler began to cry softly. It was only the second time in her life that Elisabeth had seen her mother shed tears.

Mrs. Kubler rose from her chair and went inside. For a while, Elisabeth sat alone and thought about her mother's request, her own response to it and her attitude toward euthanasia. It was tempting to avoid the issue. She remembered some lines of Erich Fromm, the psychiatrist-philosopher: "There is no such thing as medical ethics. There are only universal human ethics applied to specific human situations."

There were times, she was obliged to admit, when it was wrong to keep someone alive—but such a time would occur when a patient was clearly beyond medical help, when organs were kept functioning only with machines. So long as there was a meaningful life, so long as a patient could express and receive feelings, it had to be wrong to "play God" and decide arbitrarily whether a patient should live or die. Surely, though, it was not to answer this hypothetical question that she had changed the family's vacation plans and come to Switzerland.

Next day, when Mrs. Kubler accompanied Elisabeth and the children to the train station, both women were tense and uncomfortable. However, when the train came in, Elisabeth turned to her mother, hugged her and said, "All I can promise you is that I will do for you what I do for all my patients. I promise I will do my best to help you live until you die."

Mrs. Kubler appeared to understand now what Elisabeth was saying. She nodded, wiped her eyes, smiled and said, "Thank you."

Those were the last words Elisabeth heard her mother speak. Hardly had the family arrived back in Chicago when a cable came from Eva. It read, "Mother has had a massive stroke."

Three days later Elisabeth was back in Switzerland.

At the hospital Elisabeth found her mother unable to speak, unable to move anything except her eyelids and, very feebly, her left hand. It was obvious, however, from the expression in her eyes, that Mrs. Kubler understood what was said to her.

They devised a method of communicating. Her mother would use her eyelids and her slightly mobile left hand to indicate affirmative or negative answers to questions put to her. One blink of the eyelids or one squeeze of the hand would signify an affirmative and two blinks or two squeezes would mean a negative response.

Using this form of communication, Mrs. Kubler made it very clear that she did not want to remain in the hospital. Elisabeth confronted her mother with the impossibility of her returning home, where she would require round-the-clock nursing attention. It was Eva who came up with the solution.

She knew of an infirmary, more a rest home than a hospital, in Riehen, a few miles outside of Basel. Set in spacious well-tended grounds, it was run by a dedicated group of Protestant nuns.

Immediately after taking her mother to the infirmary, Elisabeth spent a couple of painful days quite alone at the Klosbachstrasse apartment. She sorted clothes, furniture and objets d'art; she took down pictures and curtains and labeled everything for subsequent distribution according to her mother's expressed wishes.

Elisabeth now believes that in closing down the family home in Zurich, she was given a new and important understanding about life and death. Life, she now sees, is a series of losses, and every loss is a "little death." In the hour or so before she finally left the home on Klosbachstrasse she had gone through the five identifiable stages of dying: denial, anger, bargaining, depression and acceptance.

Each "little death"—and this was one of hers—was a salutary and perhaps essential preparation for death itself. But every ending was also a new beginning.

Another lesson, long and difficult, now focused on the infirmary at Riehen. Mrs. Kubler, paralyzed and unable to speak, held on to life—not just for the few weeks that Elisabeth and her sisters had anticipated, not for months, but for four years. She had clearly foreseen the manner of her dying and, recoiling at the prospect, had pleaded with Elisabeth for mercy killing.

For Elisabeth, the issue of euthanasia was no longer a hypothetical one, no longer an intellectual debating point, but a question of the heart and conscience. There were times when she was ready to change her views, moments when she wondered agonizingly whether she should have given her mother the promise she had asked for; but these doubts stalked her only when she was far away from Switzerland.

For when she was with her mother, her conviction remained that neither she nor anyone else had the right to take the life of someone who could still express and receive feelings. Mrs. Kubler was not a human vegetable. She needed no machines to keep her heart beating or her lungs breathing.

Today, Elisabeth Kubler-Ross sees her prime task as helping people to live a full life without being burdened by their "negativities," helping people to take care of "unfinished business" before they die.

She claims that the evidence of patients who have had near-death encounters with spiritual guides and relatives who have predeceased them supports her belief that physical existence—with all its pain, stress, struggle and challenge—is, in effect, "a learning experience and a growth period" for an ongoing journey.

She is convinced that the only thing of value that man carries with him through the "transition" is the record of how much he contributed to the commonweal—"how much he cared and how much he loved."

1400 words

Write your ending time here: _____

Subtract your starting time: _____

Total time: _____

Check the Rate Chart in the back of the book to find out how many words per minute you have read, and then record your score on the Progress Chart.

Step 3: Analyze What You Read

Identify Arguments and Supporting Details

This reading has only one argument and one piece of support. Fill in the blanks below.

Point of view: _____

_____

Argument: _____

Supporting detail: _____

Type of support (facts, examples, testimony, reasons): _____

In the margin of the reading, write POV next to the place the author presents the point of view, and ARG next to where the argument is presented. Underline the supporting detail.

Evaluate Supporting Details

FACT VERSUS OPINION   Write F in the space before each statement of fact; write O if the statement is someone's opinion.

_____ **1.** "There were times . . . when it was wrong to keep someone alive. . . ."

_____ **2.** "Three days later Elisabeth was back in Switzerland."

_____ **3.** "Each 'little death'. . . was a salutary and perhaps essential preparation for death itself."

_____ **4.** "They devised a method of communicating."

_____ **5.** "Physical existence . . . is . . .' a learning experience and a growth period' for an ongoing journey."

_____ **6.** "The only thing of value that man carries with him through the
'transition' is the record of how much he contributed to the commonweal. . . ."

_____ **7.** "She needed no machines to keep her heart beating or her lungs
breathing."

_____ **8.** "She had clearly foreseen the manner of her dying. . . ."

_____ **9.** "So long as there was a meaningful life, so long as a patient could
express and receive feelings, it had to be wrong to 'play God' and
decide arbitrarily whether a patient should live or die."

_____ **10.** "Those were the last words Elisabeth heard her mother speak."

AUTHOR'S CREDIBILITY: BACKGROUND AND REPUTATION   When judging the credibility of a speaker or
writer it is valuable to know the background of the person. Here are some facts about
Dr. Elisabeth Kubler-Ross, whose opinions are key to the discussion of euthanasia in
Reading 28.*

Use this scale to rate each fact on whether it increases or decreases credibility.

Greatly increases	Increases	Neither increases nor decreases	Decreases	Greatly decreases
1	2	3	4	5

_____ **1.** Elisabeth Kubler-Ross was born on July 8, 1926, in Zurich, Switzerland.

_____ **2.** She weighed barely two pounds at birth.

_____ **3.** During her own critical illness from pneumonia at the age of five,
Elisabeth Kubler was taken to a children's hospital and kept in isolation for weeks.

_____ **4.** Before going to medical school she worked as a cook, a mason, and a
roofer.

_____ **5.** She is a psychiatrist.

*The information on Elisabeth Kubler-Ross is excerpted from *Current Biography Yearbook, 1980.* (New York:
The H. W. Wilson Company, 1981), pp. 191–194.

_____ **6.** She is known for her pioneering work in counseling terminally ill patients.

_____ **7.** She was the first doctor to describe the stages a terminally ill patient goes through: denial, anger, bargaining, depression, acceptance.

_____ **8.** Her books have brought generous praise from medical colleagues and laypeople and earned her a reputation as a scientist of courage and compassion.

_____ **9.** Her later research has been directed toward verifying the existence of life after death.

_____ **10.** She has said, "I know for a fact that there is life after death."

_____ **11.** In recent years she has met with growing skepticism from the medical community.

_____ **12.** She obtained her MD degree in 1957.

_____ **13.** She became an assistant professor of psychiatry at the University of Chicago Medical School.

_____ **14.** In 1973, she became the medical director of Family Services and Mental Health Center of South Cook County, Chicago Heights.

_____ **15.** She has a son, Kenneth Lawrence, and a daughter, Barbara Lee.

Make Graphic Organizers

Draw an idea map showing the point of view, the arguments, and their support.

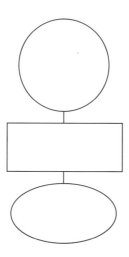

Step 4: Remember What's Important

Review the marginal notes identifying point of view and arguments. Review the underlining that identifies the supporting details. Review the idea map. Test yourself until you can remember the material.

Step 5: Make Use of What You Read

When you are ready, complete the Comprehension Check. Do not look back at the reading or the idea map.

Step 6: Evaluate Your Active Critical Thinking Skills

After your test has been graded, use the checklist on p. 465 to evaluate your skills.

COMPREHENSION CHECK

Circle the letter before the best answer to each question.

1. Kubler-Ross went to Switzerland in early summer because
   a. her mother had sent a telegram saying she was ill.
   b. her mother hadn't seen her grandchildren in years.
   c. it was a planned vacation.
   d. she was concerned about her mother.

2. When Kubler-Ross arrived in Switzerland, she found that her mother was
   a. dying.
   b. dead.
   c. in fine health.
   d. depressed.

3. Closing down the family home made Kubler-Ross
   a. reconsider her mother's request.
   b. deny that her mother was dying.
   c. afraid of death.
   d. understand life and death better.

4. After Mrs. Kubler had her stroke, she could
   a. use sign language with her hands.
   b. talk with great difficulty.
   c. not communicate at all.
   d. blink her eyes and barely use her left hand.

5. The reading implies that Kubler-Ross
   a. is skeptical of extrasensory perception.
   b. believes in extrasensory perception.
   c. went to a psychic about her mother.
   d. saw a ghost.

6. Mrs. Kubler's relationship with Elisabeth seemed

    a. impersonal and cold.

    b. warm and close.

    c. not so warm as with her other daughters.

    d. abnormal for a mother and daughter.

7. The last time Kubler-Ross saw her mother before her mother's stroke she thought

    a. they were arguing.

    b. they parted on good terms.

    c. her mother was becoming senile.

    d. her mother was in poor health.

8. If Kubler-Ross were to develop an illness similar to her mother's, she would probably

    a. request euthanasia.

    b. change her mind about euthanasia.

    c. see her illness as a valuable experience.

    d. go to Switzerland, where euthanasia is legal.

Short Answer

Elisabeth Kubler-Ross believed that people should be kept alive as long as two criteria were met. They are

9. _____

10. _____

Essay

Why does Kubler-Ross take the position she takes on euthanasia?

_____

_____

_____

_____

_____

_____

VOCABULARY IN CONTEXT

Write the best word from this list in the blank in each sentence below.

expedite   inexplicable   hypothetical   obliged   affirmative

objets d'art   salutary   recoiling   predecease   commonweal

1. Before you give an _____ answer to a request for a loan, be sure you clarify when it will be repaid.

2. When somebody does you a favor, you may feel _____ to them.

3. To _____ solving criminal cases, the police look for eyewitnesses.

4. Priceless _____ are found in museums around the world.

5. The increase in crime is a problem affecting the _____ .

6. Your will should have additional beneficiaries in case your children

   _____ you.

7. People start thinking about the supernatural when _____ events occur.

8. A proper diet is _____ .

9. Before you give an _____ answer to a request for money, be sure you know all the facts.

10. _____ when someone startles you is a natural defense mechanism.

COMPARING VIEWS ON EUTHANASIA

Use the following activities to evaluate your understanding of the issue.

1. Summarize each reading, including the point of view, the arguments, and the major supporting details.

2. Evaluate the support for each reading. Are the examples good ones, are the reasons logical, are the facts provable, does loaded language degrade the message?

3. Compare the readings. Do you believe that one author's arguments are stronger than the other's? Why?

4. Go back to the self-questioning survey on page 406. Would you change any of your responses after reading the selections? Summarize your opinion on the issue, noting any ways in which your opinion has been affected by your reading.

_____

_____

_____

_____

_____

_____

_____

_____

_____

_____

_____

Issue 5:
Affirmative Action

The two readings take opposing views on affirmative action.

To help you become aware of your own beliefs and biases about affirmative action, answer the following questions. Write the number from the Rating Scale that best expresses your opinion. You will reevaluate your views after you have completed Readings 29 and 30.

Rating Scale

1. No

2. Perhaps not

3. No opinion

4. Perhaps

5. Yes

Rate 1 to 5.

_____ **1.** Is the reason that women and minorities are underrepresented in the work force that they are not as qualified or competent as white males?

_____ **2.** If affirmative action were removed, would most companies go back to hiring mostly white males?

_____ **3.** Do you believe that we have achieved the goal of equal opportunity for everyone?

_____ **4.** Do we need affirmative action now?

_____ **5.** Is "reverse discrimination" against white males a serious problem?

29

The Dream, the Stars and Dr. King

Vocabulary Preview

affirmative action (ə fʉrm'ə tiv ak'shən): a policy or program for correcting the effects of discrimination in the employment or education of members of certain groups, such as women and minorities

commemorate (kə mem'ə rāt'): to honor the memory of

suppress (se pres'): to keep from appearing or being known

legacy (leg'ə sē): something handed down, as from an ancestor

squander (skwan'dər): to spend or use wastefully or extravagantly

pander (pan'dər): to help satisfy the immoral or vicious ambitions, vices, or desires of another

intractable (in trak'tə bəl): hard to manage or change

eradicate (ē rad'i kāt'): to wipe out; remove

seminal (sem'ə nəl): of essential importance

apartheid (ə pär'tīd'): strict racial segregation and economic and political discrimination

cat, āte, fäther; pen, ēvil; if, kīte; nō, ôr, fo͞od, book; boil, house; up, turn; chief, shell; thick, *the*; zh, treasure; ŋ, sing; ə for *a* in *about*; ' as in *able* (a'b'l)

Step 1: Preread

Preview the following selection by reading the title and the first sentence of each paragraph. Answer the following questions without looking back at the article.

1. What is the subject? _____

2. What is the point of view? _____

    _____

3. Compare your beliefs with Jesse Jackson's. On a scale of 1 (no way) to 5 (definitely),

    how open is your mind to his point of view? _____

Step 2: Read

 Read the selection without underlining. Just try to understand the arguments.

Write your starting time here: _____

The Dream, the Stars and Dr. King

JESSE JACKSON

L AST WEEK IN MEMPHIS, WE COMMEMORATED the death of Dr. Martin Luther King. He was struck down 27 years ago—not a dreamer, but a man of action. We have come a long way since then, in part as a fruit of his labors.

In less than 30 years, as schools opened and ceilings lifted, a large African American middle class has been created. High school graduation rates, even intelligence test results, grow closer between whites and blacks with each passing year.

The civil-rights movement that Dr. King led also helped women lift the shackles on their opportunity. The same laws that guarantee equal opportunity for African Americans apply to women, to other minorities, to the disabled. Our society benefits as fewer of its people have their genius suppressed or their talents wasted.

We have come a long way—but we have far to go. Commission after commission, report after report, show that systematic discrimination still mars our country.

African Americans have more difficulty obtaining business loans, buying homes, getting hired. Schools and housing patterns are still largely separate and unequal. Women still face glass ceilings in corporate offices. Ninety-seven percent of the corporate CEOs of the Fortune 500 are white men. That does not result from talent being concentrated among males with pale skin.

Today, Dr. King's legacy—the commitment to take affirmative actions to open doors and opportunity—is under political assault. Dr. King worked against terrible odds in a hopeful time. America was experiencing two decades of remarkable economic growth and prosperity. It was assumed, as the Kerner Commission made clear, that the "growth dividend" would enable us to reduce poverty and open opportunity relatively painlessly. But the war on poverty was never fought; instead, the dividend and the growth were squandered in the jungles of Vietnam.

Three decades later, the country is more prosperous but the times are less hopeful. Real wages for working people have been declining for 20 years. People are scared for good reason, as lay-offs rise to record levels even in the midst of a recovery.

In this context, political predators flourish, feeding on old hates, pandering to old fears. What else could explain the remarkably dishonest assault on affirmative-action programs that seek to remedy intractable patterns of discrimination?

House Speaker Newt Gingrich, a history professor, sets the tone by simply eradicating history. The Washington Post reported: "Gingrich dismissed the argument that the beneficiaries of affirmative action, commonly African Americans, have been subjected to discrimination over a period of centuries. 'That is true of virtually every American,' Gingrich said, noting that the Irish were discriminated against by the English, for example."

As Roger Wilkins writes in a seminal essay in the Nation magazine, this is breathtakingly dishonest for a history professor. Blacks have been on the North American continent for nearly 375 years. For 245 of those, the country practiced slavery. For another 100 or so, segregation—legal apartheid—was enforced throughout the South and much of the North, often policed by home-grown terrorists. We've had only 30 years of something else, largely the legacy of the struggle led by Dr. King.

The media plays up the "guilt" African Americans supposedly suffer about affirmative action. I can tell you this. Dr. King felt no guilt when special laws gave us the right to vote. He felt no guilt about laws requiring that African Americans have the opportunity to go to schools, to enter universities, to compete for jobs and contracts. This supposed guilt is at best a luxurious anxiety of those who now have the opportunity to succeed or fail.

If Dr. King were alive today, he would be 66, younger than Sen. Bob Dole (R-Kan.) who suggests that discrimination ended "before we were born." Unlike Dole, Dr. King would be working to bring people together, not drive them apart.

Modern-day conservatives haven't a clue about what to do with an economy that is generating greater inequality and reducing the security and living standards of more and more Americans. So they seek to distract and divide.

Now, as the Republican "contract with America" fizzles into an ad campaign, Dole reaffirmed his abandonment of affirmative action. Sen. Phil Gramm (R-Tex.) called for more cuts from the poor.

As we head into this coyote time, we would do well to re-member Dr. King's legacy. No matter how desperate things were, no matter how grave the crisis, no matter how many times his dreams were shattered, Dr. King refused to grow bitter. Men and women, he taught, "have the capacity to do right as well as wrong, and [our] history is a path upward, not downward. It's only when it is truly dark that you can see the stars."

800 words

Write your ending time here: _____

Subtract your starting time: _____

Total time: _____

Check the Rate Chart in the back of the book to find out how many words per minute you have read, and then record your score on the Progress Chart.

Step 3: Analyze What You Read

Identify Arguments and Supporting Details

In the margin of the reading, write POV next to the place the author presents his point of view.

Following are eight arguments. Fill in the supporting details and the type of supporting details for each one.

1. We have come a long way in less than 30 years.

Support: _____

_____

Type: _____

2. Society benefits from affirmative action.

Support: _____

Type: _____

3. Systematic discrimination still mars our country.

Support: _____

_____

_____

Type: _____

4. Affirmative action is under political assault.

Support: _____

_____

Type: _____

5. Opponents of affirmative action are dishonest.

Support: _____

Type: _____

6. African American guilt is not an important issue.

Support: _____

Type: _____

7. Bob Dole is using dishonesty to drive people apart.

Support: _____

Type: _____

8. We should not grow bitter.

Support: _____

Type: _____

Write Arg. 1, Arg. 2, etc. in the margin of the article next to the place that each argument appears. Underline the supporting details for each argument.

Evaluate Supporting Details

PROVABLE VERSUS UNPROVABLE   If the statement can be proved (or disproved), write *P.* If it is unprovable, write *U.*

     _____ **1.** A large African American middle class has been created.

     _____ **2.** Dr. King's civil-rights work has also helped women, other minorities, and the disabled.

     _____ **3.** African Americans have more difficulty obtaining business loans.

     _____ **4.** Women still face glass ceilings.

     _____ **5.** 97% of corporate CEOs of Fortune 500 companies are white men.

     _____ **6.** Newt Gingrich knows he isn't telling the truth.

     _____ **7.** An expansion of opportunities for African Americans began about 30 years ago.

     _____ **8.** Bob Dole is intentionally trying to divide people along racial lines.

     _____ **9.** Modern-day conservatives don't know what to do to solve the problem of reduced security and living standards.

     _____ **10.** Times will get better.

LOADED LANGUAGE   Write the implied meaning of the underlined words in the following statements:

a. "... also helped women lift the shackles on their opportunity."

    Implication: _____

b. "... political predators flourish ..."

    Implication: _____

c. "As we head into this coyote time ..."

    Implication: _____

_____

VALID AND INVALID INFERENCES   For each idea you think was implied by the author, write *V*. If you don't think it was implied, write *I*. If you write *V*, also write the sentence from the article in which it was implied.

     _____ **1.** Without affirmative action, white males would be preferred for jobs.

Sentence: _____

_____

_____ **2.** The percent of African Americans living in poverty has reduced since the civil-rights movement.

Sentence: _____

_____ **3.** School segregation still exists.

Sentence: _____

_____ **4.** African Americans have had the same problems with discrimination that other groups of immigrants have had.

Sentence: _____

_____ **5.** Intelligence tests accurately measure intelligence.

Sentence: _____

_____ **6.** Dr. King's civil-rights work has helped all Americans.

Sentence: _____

_____

_____ **7.** Newt Gingrich minimizes the effects of slavery on African Americans.

Sentence: _____

_____ **8.** Reverse discrimination is a serious problem.

Sentence: _____

_____ **9.** Republicans are purposely raising false issues.

Sentence: _____

_____

_____ **10.** Democrats have a better political platform than Republicans.

Sentence: _____

Make Graphic Organizers

Draw an idea map showing the point of view, the arguments, and their major support.

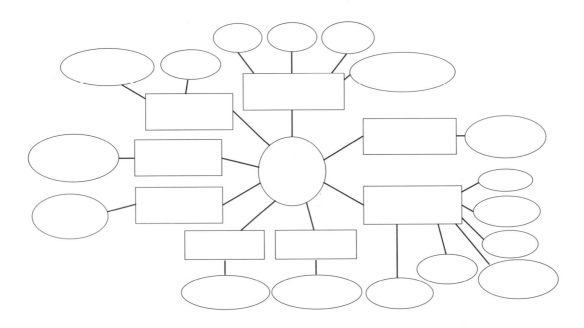

Step 4: Remember What's Important

 Review your marginal notes that identified the point of view and the arguments. Review the underlining that identified the supporting details. Review the idea map. Test yourself until you remember the material.

Step 5: Make Use of What You Read

 When you are ready, take the Comprehension Check. Do not look back at the article or the idea map.

Step 6: Evaluate Your Active Critical Thinking Skills

After your test has been graded, use the checklist on p. 465 to evaluate your skills.

COMPREHENSION CHECK

True-False

Mark T or F.

_____ **1.** Affirmative action has been a failure.

_____ **2.** According to the author, conservatives have a plan to solve the country's economic problems.

_____ **3.** The author implies that liberals know how to solve the country's economic problems.

_____ **4.** Conservatives seek to distract and divide Americans.

Multiple Choice

Circle the letter before the best answer to each question below.

5. The war on poverty was never fought because
   a. conservatives opposed it.
   b. we spent the money on the war in Vietnam.
   c. the amount of poverty was just too great.
   d. Dr. King was killed.

6. The American economy is
   a. increasing the gap between rich and poor.
   b. making people feel less secure.
   c. reducing the living standards of more and more Americans.
   d. doing all of the above.

7. Compared to the 1960s the country is
   a. poorer.
   b. more optimistic.
   c. more racist.
   d. less hopeful.

8. According to the author, Newt Gingrich and Bob Dole are

    a. ignorant of history.

    b. lying about history.

    c. addressing important economic issues.

    d. trying to unite the country.

Short Answer

9. What does Jesse Jackson mean when he says that "political predators flourish, feeding on old hates, pandering to old fears"?

    _____

    _____

10. What are the historical facts about opportunities for African Americans in the United States?

    _____

    _____

Essay

Why does Jesse Jackson think about affirmative action programs and about the current attack on them? Use a separate piece of paper.

VOCABULARY IN CONTEXT

Write the best word from this list in the blank in each sentence below.

> **affirmative action   commemorate   suppress   legacy**
>
> **squandering   pander   intractable   eradicate   seminal**
>
> **apartheid**

1. The word _____ comes from a word that means "separate" in Afrikaans, a language of South Africa.

2. _____ programs included giving preference to equally qualified women and minorities in hiring, in college admission, and in awarding business contracts.

3. We now have a national holiday to _____ Dr. Martin Luther King.

4. Censorship of the press exists to _____ opinions or language the people in power don't like.

5. Nearly everyone wishes we could _____ poverty, ignorance, and suffering.

6. Charles Darwin was a _____ thinker in the field of evolution.

7. Allowances should be given to train children to manage their money instead of

   _____ it on candy and videogames.

8. The antique clock was a _____ from my grandmother.

9. Opponents of gambling argue that state lotteries _____ to the fantasies of people too ignorant to understand the odds against winning, usually the poor.

10. Ethnic hatred has proven an _____ problem, leading to bloodshed in areas such as Ireland, Bosnia, and parts of Africa.

30

Spiral of Silence

Vocabulary Preview

appease (ə pēz'): to quiet, esp. by giving in to the demands of

subverted (sub vɐr'tid): undermined

Orwellian (ôr wel'ē ən): like the works of George Orwell, who wrote *1984*, a novel about a totalitarian society

prima facie evidence (prī'mə fā'shē): evidence adequate to establish a fact or presumption of fact unless refuted.

craven (krā'vən): very cowardly

litigation (lit'i gā'shən): lawsuit

diffuse (di fyo͞oz'): spread out

acquiesce (ak wē es'): to agree or consent quietly without protest, but without enthusiasm

inhibitions (in'hi bish'ənz): mental or psychological processes that restrain or suppress an emotion, thought, or action

latent (lāt''nt): hidden and undeveloped

judicious (jo͞o dish'əs): showing sound judgment; wise and careful

fanatical (fə nāt'ik'l): unreasonably enthusiastic

ideological (ī'dē ə läj'i kəl): based on the ideas or opinions or way of thinking of an individual, class, or group

intimidating (in tim'ə dāt'iŋ): causing fear or timidity

defection (de fek'shən): abandonment of loyalty

cat, āte, fäther; pen, ēvil; if, kīte; nō, ôr, fo͞od, book; boil, house; up, turn; chief, shell; thick, *the*; zh, treasure; ŋ, sing; ə for *a* in *about*; ' as in *able* (a'b'l)

Step I: Preread

Preview the following article by reading the title and the first sentence of each paragraph. Answer the following questions without looking back at the article.

1. What is the subject? _____

2. What is the point of view? _____

3. Compare your beliefs with the author's. On a scale of 1 (no way) to 5 (definitely),

how open is your mind to his point of view? _____

Step 2: Read

Read the article without underlining. Just try to understand the arguments.

Write your starting time here: _____

Spiral of Silence

PETER BRIMELOW

"I HAVE ALREADY GIVEN TWO COUSINS to the war, and I stand prepared to sacrifice my wife's brother rather than the rebellion be not crushed."

Humorist Artemus Ward's joke during the Civil War applies today, says Claremont McKenna College sociologist Frederick R. Lynch to the American political elite's attempt to appease minority and feminist groups by imposing "affirmative action" quotas against white, often younger and blue-collar males.

Government-imposed quotas were explicitly banned in the 1964 Civil Rights Act. Nevertheless they immediately spread through the economy. For most of that time, they received eerily little media and even less academic attention. Of some 1,300 papers given at a recent American Sociological Association conference on Race and Ethnic Relations, the topic attracted only one.

The result: the situation summarized in the title of Lynch's new paperback, *Invisible Victims: White Males and the Crisis of Affirmative Action*. The ideal of merit hiring has been subverted by politicized hiring, with white men unable to defend themselves against open discrimination. But quotas bring other problems, including conflict among the "protected classes" they benefit, and growing racial polarization, particularly as the articulate middle class begins to suffer.

Lynch just laughs at the suggestion, recently made by a columnist in a business weekly, that affirmative action, while a regulatory burden, is not massive in scale.

"Race-norming [adjusting test scores to produce racially proportionate results] alone affected millions of people," he says. "Many state and local governments did it with their GATBS [General Aptitude Test Batteries, taken by job seekers and supplied to potential employers]. And private testing agencies did it to protect their clients against lawsuits—they called it "EEO-proofing." (The federal Equal Employment Opportunity Commission muscles business into quotas.)

But Lynch is not surprised at the blunder. "There's incredible denial," he says. He cites California Democratic representative Don Edwards, a mouthpiece of the civil rights establishment, claiming on the *New York Times* Op Ed page that quotas did not exist—within weeks of three Supreme Court decisions about them. And, using similar Orwellian doublethink, supporters insisted that the 1991 Civil Rights Act did not impose quotas, although its key point was to override the Supreme Court and make work force racial imbalance prima facie evidence of employer discrimination.

Corporate America's craven terror of litigation and political punishment makes research into quotas extremely difficult. "We're not letting you anywhere near our program," a Kmart executive told Lynch recently.

It's understandable—in a way. Sears, Roebuck & Co. spent 15 years and perhaps as much as $20 million to defeat an EEOC discrimination suit. Sears prevailed largely because it was able to show it had a voluntary quota program. Corporations cling to such programs as a defense in court, even if it means putting up with some unqualified or incompetent workers. They hate white male employees moaning about quotas—and, above all, suing to expose reverse discrimination's legal inconsistencies.

The white male victims of affirmative action are diffused through the population and hard to track down. After finding and interviewing a sample, Lynch has identified several reasons for their helplessness.

"Affirmative action has been an administrative revolution imposed by judges and bureaucrats," he says. It is not easily opposed, particularly because much of it is implemented informally and orally. Recently, the secrecy has in part been a response to the increasingly unstable legal situation as the influence of the Reagan-Bush judicial appointments is felt. But Lynch says some affirmative action personnel openly tell him they intend to get around any law.

A few of Lynch's male victims were political liberals who felt obliged to rationalize their fate. But most acquiesced with varying degrees of anger; some changed jobs. Usually totally isolated, these men felt that no one would help them.

They were right. The older generation of white male managers has compromised, Lynch argues, because they think quotas will fall only on the younger, baby-boom generation. And the EEOC discourages white male discrimination complaints about corporations with approved, i.e., anti-white male, affirmative action plans. Litigation, for the tiny group that tried it, proved expensive, exhausting, chancy and immensely time-consuming —one case remains unsettled after more than six years.

A further factor in this male paralysis: the peculiar male psychology itself. These victims seem really to have believed that real men don't cry. A considerable number did not even mention their disappointment to friends, relatives or fellow workers.

Their wives almost always felt no such inhibitions. "My wife is mad as hell; she's angrier than I am," said a victim. Some wives absolutely insisted on being interviewed for Lynch's study. One woman made a telling point: Discrimination against white males injures not only the men themselves but their wives and families. "This 'hidden' or latent conflict generated by affirmative action between career women versus homemaker wives has gone virtually unnoticed in the affirmative action literature," Lynch notes judiciously.

"Karl Marx insisted that for any sort of class consciousness to arise, there must be communication of a common sense of oppression," Lynch writes. "With the mass media and the social sciences rarely recognizing the phenomenon, much less portraying it sympathetically, white males have been easily and silently victimized one by one."

Lynch's survey of the media indicates that quotas have been basically ignored. Thus he was unable to find one TV show portraying a white male being damaged by affirmative action.

Partly the media were able to ignore the issue because neither conservatives nor liberals raised it. For example, the likelihood that Robert Bork would find quotas unconstitutional spurred the civil rights establishment's fanatical resistance to his Supreme Court nomination. But White House lobbyists said nothing.

Partly, however, the media's motive is ideological. From J. Anthony Lukas' bestseller about busing, *Common Ground*, Lynch quotes a *Boston Globe* reporter: "If they [the Boston Irish] don't like integration, we'll shove it down their throats."

All of which, Lynch argues, has induced a classic "spiral of silence," whereby people assume their doubts are not shared and suppress them, thus mutually intimidating each other. But in fact opinion polls show quotas are overwhelmingly unpopular, even with the "protected classes" themselves. And when the Democratic Party asked pollster Stanley Greenberg to investigate blue-collar defection in the 1984 presidential election, quotas emerged as the crucial factor. The party promptly tried to stifle Greenberg's report.

Lynch is now researching his next book on "diversity management"—the use of quotas, with no pretense that they are remedial or temporary, for the current beneficiaries of affirmative action and the ongoing wave of nonwhite immigrants. This is the new frontier for affirmative action professionals. However, Lynch reports that they receive his research on white males with much interest.

"They're worried about 'The White Male Problem,' white males resisting their work," he says. "They just can't understand it."

1150 words

Write your ending time here: _____

Subtract your starting time: _____

Total time: _____

Check the Rate Chart in the back of the book to find out how many words per minute you have read, and then record your score on the Progress Chart.

Step 3: Analyze What You Read

IDENTIFY THE ARGUMENTS AND SUPPORTING DETAILS   The point of view of this article is implied rather than stated in one place in the article. Look back at the point of view you identified in Step 1. You may or may not want to change it. In any case, write what you now believe to be the point of view:

_____

In the following exercise, arguments are in the left column; supporting details are in the right column. Go back to the article and find which details support which arguments. Write the letter of the detail in the blank before the argument it supports. There may be more than one piece of support for some arguments. Other arguments may not have any support. In that case, write *none* in the blank.

ARGUMENTS

_____ 1. Affirmative action quotas are an attempt by the political elite to appease minority and feminist groups.

_____ 2. Affirmative action imposes quotas against white males.

_____ 3. Government-imposed quotas are illegal.

_____ 4. Quotas have received eerily little media or academic attention.

_____ 5. Affirmative action has subverted the ideal of merit hiring.

_____ 6. Quotas cause conflict among "protected classes."

_____ 7. Quotas cause racial polarization.

_____ 8. Affirmative action is massive in scale.

_____ 9. There is denial.

_____ 10. Using workforce racial imbalance as prima facie evidence of employer discrimination is a way of imposing quotas.

_____ 11. Research into quotas is difficult.

_____ 12. To avoid litigation, employers cling to voluntary quotas.

DETAILS

a. The media's motive is partly ideological.

b. Affirmative action personnel just can't understand the white male's problem.

c. "We're not letting you anywhere near our program" a Kmart executive told Lynch recently.

d. Quotas were explicitly banned in the 1964 Civil Rights Act.

e. Don Edwards claimed that quotas did not exist.

f. Race-norming affected millions.

g. Supporters insisted that the 1991 Civil Rights Act did not impose quotas.

h. Affirmative action is not easily opposed because much of it is informal and oral.

i. Stanley Greenberg's research

j. Politically liberal victims feel obliged to rationalize their fate.

k. Opinion polls

l. Male psychology that real men don't cry

m. Most felt that no one would help.

n. Of some 1,300 papers given at a recent American Sociological Assn. conference, there was only one on reverse discrimination.

_____ **13.** Voluntary quotas mean putting up with some unqualified or incompetent workers.

_____ **14.** White male victims of affirmative action are helpless.

_____ **15.** Discrimination against white males also injures their wives and families.

_____ **16.** Affirmative action causes hidden conflict between career women and homemakers.

_____ **17.** There is little communication of a common sense of oppression among white males.

_____ **18.** The media ignore quotas.

_____ **19.** A "spiral of silence" exists.

_____ **20.** Quotas are unpopular.

_____ **21.** "Diversity management" is the new frontier for affirmative action personnel.

_____ **22.** Affirmative action personnel have started to worry about white male resistance.

o. Corporate America is afraid of lawsuits and political punishment.

p. Older white male managers think quotas will only fall on younger workers.

q. Lynch was unable to find one TV show portraying a white male being damaged by affirmative action.

r. Litigation is expensive, exhausting, chancy, and time-consuming.

s. EEOC discourages white male complaints against companies with anti-white male affirmative action plans.

t. Sears prevailed largely because it was able to show it had a voluntary quota program.

u. The mass media and social science rarely recognize the problem, and do not portray it sympathetically.

v. The media were able to ignore the issue because nobody raised it.

Go back to the reading selection and write the number of each argument (Arg 1–Arg 22) in the margin next to where it appears. Underline the supporting details.

Evaluating Supporting Details

TYPE OF SUPPORTING DETAILS   Go back to the 22 supporting details listed above. For each one, identify how it is used to support the argument (fact, testimony, example, reasons) and fill in the blanks below.

a. _____   l. _____

b. _____   m. _____

c. _____   n. _____

d. _____   o. _____

e. _____   p. _____

f. _____   q. _____

g. _____   r. _____

h. _____   s. _____

i. _____   t. _____

j. _____   u. _____

k. _____   v. _____

PROVABLE VERSUS UNPROVABLE   If the statement can be proved or disproved, write *P.* If it cannot be proved or disproved, write *U.*

_____   **1.**   The 1964 Civil Rights Act explicitly banned quotas.

_____   **2.**   The ideal of merit hiring has been subverted by politicized hiring.

_____   **3.**   White men are unable to defend themselves against discrimination.

_____   **4.**   Affirmative action increases racial polarization.

_____   **5.**   There's incredible denial.

_____   **6.**   The 1991 Civil Rights Act imposes quotas.

_____   **7.**   Clinging to voluntary quota programs means putting up with some unqualified or incompetent workers.

_____ **8.** The EEOC discourages white male discrimination complaints about corporations with approved, i.e., anti-white male, affirmative action plans.

_____ **9.** Affirmative action causes a conflict between career women and homemaker wives.

_____ **10.** He was unable to find even one TV show portraying a white male being damaged by affirmative action.

LOADED LANGUAGE   Write the implied meaning of the underlined words in the following statements.

1. . . . they received <u>eerily</u> little media attention . . .

Implication: _____

2. . . . California Democratic Representative Don Edwards, a <u>mouthpiece</u> of the civil rights establishment . . .

Implication: _____

3. . . . using <u>Orwellian doublethink</u>, supporters insisted that the 1991 Civil Rights Act did not impose quotas . . .

Implication: _____

4. Corporate America's <u>craven terror</u> of litigation . . .

Implication: _____

5. . . . corporations with approved, <u>i.e., anti-white male</u>, affirmative action plans. . . .

Implication: _____

6. . . . the civil rights establishment's <u>fanatical resistance</u> to his Supreme Court nomination. . . .

Implication: _____

7. . . . the federal Equal Employment Opportunity Commission <u>muscles</u> business into quotas. . . .

Implication: _____

VALID AND INVALID INFERENCES   For each idea that you think was implied in the article, write *V.* If you don't think it was implied, write *I.* If you write *V,* also write the sentence from the article in which it was implied.

_____ **1.** Hiring on the basis of merit would produce a higher proportion of white males than we have now.

Sentence: _____

_____

_____ **2.** White males are more frequently married to homemakers than to career women.

Sentence: _____

_____

_____ **3.** Affirmative action always involves quotas.

Sentence: _____

_____

_____ **4.** The only reason employers have voluntary affirmative action programs is fear of litigation.

Sentence: _____

_____ **5.** Affirmative action often requires employers to hire less qualified or competent employees.

Sentence: _____

_____

_____ **6.** The reason for underrepresentation of women and minorities is that they are not qualified or competent as are white males.

Sentence: _____

_____

_____ **7.** Companies have affirmative action programs because of cowardice.

Sentence: _____

_____

_____ **8.** If white males united, they could get rid of affirmative action.

Sentence: _____

_____

Make Graphic Organizer

Because there are 22 aguments, use a separate piece of paper large enough to make an idea map showing all of them. Show the point of view, the arguments, and the major supporting details.

Step 4: Remember What's Important

 Review your marginal notes, underlining, and idea map. Test yourself until you can remember the material.

Step 5: Make Use of What You Read

 When you are ready, take the Comprehension Check. Do not look back at the article or the idea map.

Step 6: Evaluate Your Active Critical Thinking

 After your test has been graded, use the checklist on p. 465 to evaluate your skills.

COMPREHENSION CHECK

True-False

Mark T or F.

_____ **1.** Lynch views white males as helpless victims of discrimination.

_____ **2.** Lynch implies that racial imbalance in the workforce is not necessarily evidence of employer discrimination.

_____ **3.** Lynch is opposed to "diversity management."

_____ **4.** Lynch believes that affirmative action involves putting up with unqualified or incompetent workers.

Multiple Choice

Circle the letter before the best answer to each question.

5. The reason most white males put up with affirmative action is that
   a. they feel that no one will help them.
   b. they don't have the resources to litigate.
   c. the EEOC discourages them.
   d. all of the above are true.

6. The reason white males lack a class consciousness is that
   a. the mass media ignores their problem.
   b. the social sciences ignore their problem.
   c. nobody is sympathetic to their problem.
   d. all of the above are true.

7. Most people who read Lynch's books are likely to be
   a. conservatives.
   b. liberals.
   c. social scientists.
   d. in the media.

8. Lynch believes that affirmative action requires

    a. quotas.

    b. reverse discrimination.

    c. race-norming.

    d. all of the above.

Short Answer:

9. What does Lynch mean by a "spiral of silence"?

_____

_____

10. What is meant by the following statement: "A further factor in this male paralysis: the peculiar male psychology itself."?

_____

Essay

How does the author explain affirmative action and the white male response to it? Answer on a separate sheet of paper.

VOCABULARY IN CONTEXT

Write the best word from the list in the blank in each sentence below.

appease	subverted	Orwellian	prima facie evidence	craven
litigation	diffused	acquiesce	inhibitions	latent
judiciously	fanatical	ideological	intimidating	defect

1. During the days of the Soviet Union, ballet dancers and other artists who went on tour would regularly _____ to the West.

2. "Henpecked husbands" in cartoons give in to _____ their nagging wives.

3. Parents must use punishment _____ , or it will lose its effect.

4. Lawyers earn a living from _____ .

5. The reason cocktail parties are popular is that drinking alcohol lowers our

_____ and makes socializing much easier.

6. Having a large, muscular person give you a hostile stare is very

_____ .

7. Republicans and Democrats in Congress must overcome some of their

_____ differences in order to do their jobs and pass legislation.

8. A child with a _____ talent in music should be encouraged to develop it.

9. She was so _____ about her diet that she refused to take a bite of her own wedding cake.

10. The feathers all over the cat's face was _____ that he ate the bird.

11. If your child asks you to take over his paper route while he has the flu, you will

probably _____ reluctantly.

12. The ideal of social justice has been _____ by people who will sell out for money.

13. Lying to avoid facing the consequences of your action is a _____ response.

14. The toxic chemicals got into the groundwater and _____ throughout the city.

15. The Soviet Union under Stalin was an _____ society in which individual rights were not important.

COMPARING VIEWS ON AFFIRMATIVE ACTION

Use the following activities to evaluate your understanding of the issue.

1. Summarize each article, including the point of view, the arguments, and the major supporting details.

2. Evaluate the support for each article. Are the examples good ones, are the reasons logical, are the facts provable, does loaded language degrade the message?

3. Compare the articles. Do you believe that one author's arguments are stronger than the other's? Why?

4. Go back to the self-questioning survey on p. 435. Would you change any of your responses after reading the articles? Summarize your opinion on the issue, noting any ways in which your opinion has been affected by your reading.

APPENDIX A

Evaluation Checklist

1. Score on Comprehension Check _____

2. Which section was your weakest: objective or essay?

   _____

3. Objective section:

   a. Do you understand why your wrong answers were wrong? _____

   b. Did your underlining and marginal notes cover the correct information?

   _____

   c. Did you review them enough to remember them? _____

4. Essay/application:

   a. Do you understand why you got the score you did? _____

   b. Did your graphic organizer(s) cover the correct information? _____

   c. Did you review them enough to remember them? _____

5. Test-taking skills:

   a. Did you use the time available to maximize your score? _____

   b. Did you follow the directions? _____

   c. Did you answer the easy questions first? _____

   d. If you changed any answers, did it improve your score? _____

   e. Did you leave anything blank? _____

Reading Efficiency

INCREASING READING FLEXIBILITY

Because they have to read so much, efficient reading is crucial for college students. But if your response is to say "I read _____ words per minute," you do not understand a basic principle of efficient reading. Good readers are flexible; they adjust their reading speeds. They read a textbook more slowly than the newspaper. They read Shakespeare more slowly than *Newsweek*.

The most important thing to keep in mind is the purpose of your reading. If you are trying to read and memorize textbook material for a test, you read much more slowly than if you are relaxing with a detective story or looking through the newspaper.

TYPES OF READING

There are four basic types of reading: study reading, rapid reading, skimming, and scanning. Each type is suited to a particular type of reading material and reading purpose, and each should be practiced at different speeds.

Use **study reading** on difficult textbook or technical material when your purpose is thorough understanding and/or memorization. Study reading rates usually do not exceed 250 words per minute. (Study reading is discussed in Unit III.)

Rapid reading should be used when your purpose is to get a general idea of what you read and when the material is not extremely complicated. Types of materials suitable for rapid reading include newspapers, magazines, novels, and light nonfiction.

Skimming is quickly looking over a selection to get the general idea rather than reading every word. It is used (1) when surveying a chapter or article, (2) when all you need is a general overview, and (3) when reviewing something you once read to refresh your memory. To give you an example of skimming, we have emphasized some words in the following article. Read the bold print only; then, without looking back, answer the questions that follow the article.

If you are seriously interested in a **car,** you should **haggle with the dealer** over the price. The sticker price on the window of a car is there because the law says it must be, but only a naive buyer accepts the sticker price as any-

	Study Reading	Rapid Reading	Skimming	Scanning
Speed	Up to 250 wpm	250–800 wpm	Up to thousands of wpm	Up to thousands of wpm
Purpose	Thorough under-standing and recall	Recreation, information, light reading	Survey, over-view, review	Locating specific information
Types of Material	Textbooks, tech-nical materials	Newspapers, magazines, novels	Any type	Any type

thing but a starting point for negotiations. Shop around, shop carefully, and **never pay the asking price.**

You can easily **learn the dealer's cost for a new car** (invoice price) by buying an inexpensive guide titled **Edmund's New Car Prices,** available at bookstores and newsstands. Total the dealer's cost including options, and then **offer $125 to $200 above** this cost. You should aim to settle for **no more than $200 to $500 over** the dealer's cost for an **American** car, **or $500 for a foreign** car.

A **good time to close** a deal is often **late Sunday night** (or the last night of the week the dealer is open) **or at the end of the month.** (Many dealer-ships offer bonuses to the person who has the best sales record at the end of the week or month.) It is good to **deal directly with the sales manager or assistant** manager, because this person is authorized to agree on a price.

When you have settled on the car you want and have agreed with the salesperson on a price, you should **have the dealer put the agreement in writing before** you make a **deposit.** The order form for this agreement should **include a statement of the precise car** being bought, the **acces-sories** agreed on (if any), the **sales tax, registration fee,** and the **value of the trade-in** (if any). In addition, an **officer of the firm must sign** the order form or it has no legal value. The salesperson's signature means noth-ing; you may find that when the time comes to close the deal, you have been low-balled (promised a better deal than you are actually able to get) or high-balled (offered more on your trade-in than you will actually get). A person might be both high-balled and low-balled during the course of the negotiations. Both practices are very common among car dealers.

1. What is the article about? _____

2. What is the main idea? _____

3. How much should you pay for a new foreign car? _____

4. Who should you try to deal with? _____

The answers are (1) buying a car; (2) you can get a better deal if you know what you're doing; (3) no more than $500 over the dealer's cost; (4) manager or assistant manager.

Scanning is locating specific information, such as a name, a place, or a date. For example, when you look up something in the dictionary or in the telephone book, you are scanning. You run your eyes over the page and read only the information surrounding what you are looking for. You may also use scanning in textbooks—for example, when you are looking for a particular name or date in a chapter.

FACTORS IN THE READER

In addition to your purpose and the type of material you are reading, factors in yourself also affect the rate at which you read.

One cause of slow reading is a small vocabulary. If you encounter many unfamiliar words, your thought processes will be interrupted. This will interfere with both speed and comprehension.

Another factor that influences reading rate is your comprehension skills. The ability to quickly identify the author's organization (subject, main ideas, and support) is essential to grasping the overall picture that he or she is trying to get across.

Your speed and comprehension will also increase if you have some familiarity with the concepts you will be reading about. Your background knowledge also affects your level of interest and, therefore, your ability to concentrate.

Finally, the way you read affects your speed and comprehension. Phrase reading—grouping words into meaningful phrases—allows you to read faster. Poor readers read word by word.

Poor | readers | read | like | this.

Good readers | read like this.

One way of overcoming word-by-word reading is to practice drawing lines between thought units, as in the second example. After you have drawn lines, you can practice reading by looking at each unit rather than each word. Phrase reading also reduces some other common bad reading habits, such as habitually looking back at what you have just read.

RATE CHART

To find your reading rate, first look in the left-hand column of the chart on the next page to find the time it took you to read the article. Then look along that line until you come to the column headed by the number of words you read. Where the two lines cross, you will find a number indicating how many words per minute you have read. For example, if you read 1200 words in five minutes, you have read 240 WPM.

To find your reading rate for timings that do not appear on the chart, first compute your time in seconds. (Multiply the number of minutes by 60 and add the number of remaining seconds.) Then divide the number of words read by your time in seconds. Multiply the result by 60 to get back to minutes and seconds.

PROGRESS CHART

At the bottom of the chart on page 471, enter the date, your reading rate (in words per minute), and your comprehension score for each article you read. Then construct a graph by putting a dot in the square closest to your reading rate for each article. Make the graph by connecting the dots.

Your goal is to show improvement in rate with no loss in comprehension. A score of 80 percent comprehension is considered adequate for most purposes. However, even if you stay at the same reading rate for all 30 articles, you are still showing improvement. This is because the articles get harder in each section of the book. Don't worry if you see some dips as well as increases in your reading rate. Articles vary in difficulty because of the content, the vocabulary, your familiarity with the subject matter, and your level of interest. More difficult material should be read more slowly. However, if your reading rate appears to be dropping, you should discuss the problem with your instructor.

$$\text{WPM} = \frac{\text{Words read}}{\text{Time in seconds}} \times 60$$

Reading Time Min.	Sec.	600	800	900	1000	1150	1200	1300	1400	1500	1600	1700	2200	2700	3250
0	40	900	1200	1350	1500										
0	50	720	960	1084	1200	1380	1440								
1	00	600	800	900	1000	1150	1200	1300	1400	1500					
1	10	514	685	769	855	983	1026	1114	1200	1285	1371	1457			
1	20	450	600	677	752	865	902	975	1050	1125	1200	1275			
1	30	400	533	600	667	767	800	867	933	1000	1067	1133	1467		
1	40	360	480	539	599	689	719	780	840	900	1066	1020	1320		
1	50	327	436	492	546	628	656	709	764	818	958	927	1200		
2	00	300	400	450	500	575	600	650	700	750	800	850	1100	1350	1625
2	10	276	369	415	461	530	553	600	646	692	738	785	1015	1246	1477
2	20	257	342	386	429	494	515	557	600	643	685	729	942	1157	1392
2	30	240	320	360	400	460	480	520	560	600	640	680	880	1080	1300
2	40	225	300	337	375	431	449	487	525	562	600	637	825	1012	1219
2	50	212	282	318	353	406	424	458	494	529	565	600	776	953	1147
3	00	200	267	300	333	383	400	433	467	500	533	567	733	900	1083
3	20	180	240	270	300	345	360	390	262	450	480	510	660	810	975
3	40	163	218	245	272	313	327	371	382	409	436	463	600	736	886
4	00	150	200	225	250	287	300	325	350	375	400	425	550	675	813
4	30	133	192	200	222	256	267	289	311	333	355	377	489	600	722
5	00	120	160	180	200	230	240	260	280	300	320	340	440	540	650
5	30	109	145	164	189	209	218	236	254	273	290	309	400	491	591
6	00	100	133	150	167	192	200	217	233	250	267	283	367	450	542
7	00		114	129	143	164	171	186	200	214	229	243	314	386	464
8	00		100	113	125	144	150	162	175	187	200	212	275	337	406
9	00			100	111	128	133	144	156	167	178	189	245	300	361
10	00				100	115	120	130	140	150	160	170	220	270	325
11	00					105	109	118	127	136	145	155	200	245	295
12	00						100	108	117	125	133	142	183	225	271
13	00							100	108	115	123	131	169	208	250
14	00								100	107	114	121	157	193	232
15	00									100	107	113	147	180	217
16	00										100	106	137	169	203

WPM

WPM	Pretest	1	2	3	4	5	6	7	8	9
1,000										
950										
925										
900										
850										
825										
800										
750										
725										
700										
675										
650										
625										
600										
575										
550										
525										
500										
475										
450										
425										
400										
375										
350										
325										
300										
275										
250										
225										
200										
175										
150										
125										
100										
Article	Pretest	1	2	3	4	5	6	7	8	9
Rate (WPM)										
Comprehension Score										
Date										

WPM

	10	11	12	13	14	15	16	17	18	19	20
1,000											
950											
925											
900											
850											
825											
800											
750											
725											
700											
675											
650											
625											
600											
575											
550											
525											
500											
475											
450											
425											
400											
375											
350											
325											
300											
275											
250											
225											
200											
175											
150											
125											
100											
Article	10	11	12	13	14	15	16	17	18	19	20
Rate (WPM)											
Comprehension Score											
Date											

WPM

WPM											
1,000											
950											
925											
900											
850											
825											
800											
750											
725											
700											
675											
650											
625											
600											
575											
550											
525											
500											
475											
450											
425											
400											
375											
350											
325											
300											
275											
250											
225											
200											
175											
150											
125											
100											
Article	21	22	23	24	25	26	27	28	29	30	Posttest
Rate (WPM)											
Comprehension Score											
Date											

Word Parts

Most of the difficult words in English come from Latin, or from Greek through Latin. Following are 60 common prefixes and 150 common roots. You already know many of them, and learning the rest will greatly improve your vocabulary.

Here are some suggested ways to learn them:

As you look at each word part, read the meaning and the examples. Then try to think of another word that comes from the same word part. If you can think of another word, check it in a dictionary that gives the etymology of each word, to make sure that it does come from the same word part. Some pocket-size dictionaries save space by omitting the etymology. If your dictionary doesn't have etymologies, you can use a dictionary in a library. If you can't think of another word, try to find one by looking in the dictionary.

To memorize the word parts you don't already know, you can put them on flash cards. Put the word part on the front. Put the meaning and some examples on the back. Examples that you have made up yourself will be easier to memorize than ones that came from our list or from the dictionary. Then test yourself until you have memorized the word part. The average person takes seven self-testing sessions to learn a new word part. Following is a sample flash card:

Front	Back
mem (men, mn, min)	mind, memory remind memorial demented remember memento reminisce mnemonic

60 COMMON PREFIXES

Prefix	Meaning	Examples
a (an)	not	anonymous, atypical
ab (a)	away, from, down	absence, amoral

Prefix	Meaning	Examples
ad (ac, af, ag, an, ap, ar, as, at)	to	admit, accept, affect, aggravate, annex, appeal, arrange, assess, attract
ambi (amphi)	both	ambidextrous, amphibian
ante (ant)	before	antecedent, anterior
anti (ant)	against	antisocial, antonym
auto	self	autobiography, autocrat
bene	good	benediction
con (com, co, col, cor)	with, together	concurrent, communicate, cooperate, collate, correspond
contra	against	contradict, contraband
de	from, away, down	derail, descend
dia	through, across	diameter, diaphanous
dis (dif)	apart, not	discontinue, different
epi	upon, over, among	epidermis, epidemic
eu (ev)	good	eulogy, evangelical
ex (extra, e, ec, ef)	out, former, beyond	exit, ex-wife, extraordinary, emit, eccentric, effect
hetero	different	heterogenous, heterosexual
homo	same	homogenize, homosexual
hyper	over, beyond	hyperactive, hypersensitive
hypo	under	hypodermic, hypoallergenic
in (il, im, ir, en, em)	not, into, very	inaction, insight, invaluable, illogical, immobile, implicit, irregular, encompass, embrace
inter	between	interrupt, intercollegiate
intra (intro)	into, within	intramural, introduce
mal	bad, wrong, ill	malicious, malfunction
mega	big	megaphone, megalopolis
micro	small	micrometer, microbe
mis	wrong	misspell, misgivings
multi	many	multiply, multimillionaire
non (n)	not	nonprofit, neither
ob (oc, of, op, o)	against	obstruct, occasion, offend, oppose, omit
omni	all	omnivorous, omnipotent
pan	all	pan-African, panacea
para	alongside, beyond	paragraph, paraphrase
per	through, by, thorough	per annum, perspective

Prefix	Meaning	Examples
peri	around	perimeter, peripheral
poly	many	polygon, polyester
post	after	posterity, posterior
pre	before	preliminary, prevent
pro (pur)	before, forward, for	prospect, pursuit
re (retro)	again, back	reenter, retroactive
se	apart	secede, secret
sub (suc, suf, sup, sus)	under, below	submarine, succumb, suffer, suppress, suspect
super (sur)	above, beyond	superior, surpass
tele	distance	telegraph, telepathy
trans	across	transatlantic, transfer
ultra	beyond, extremely	ultrasonic, ultraviolet
un	not, reverse of an action	unwise, undo

Numbers

Prefix	Meaning	Examples
uni, mono	one	unison, unit, monotone
du (di), bi	two	duo, dioxide, biennial
tri	three	tripod, triple, trilogy
quater (quadr), tetra	four	quartet, quadrangle, tetrahedron
quint, penta	five	quintuplet, pentagon
sex (hex)	six	sexagenarian, hexagon
sept (hept)	seven	September,* heptagon
oct	eight	octopus, October*
nov (non)	nine	November,* nonagenarian
dec	ten	decade, December*
hemi (semi, demi)	half, partial	hemisphere, semicircle, demigod
kilo, mil	thousand	kilowatt, milligram, mile
cent	hundred	century, bicentennial

Note that prefixes for the months are based on their place in the Roman calendar.

150 COMMON ROOTS

Root	Meaning	Examples
act (agi)	drive, do	activate, agitate

Root	Meaning	Examples
aer (aero)	air	aerial, aerodynamics
al (alt)	other	alien, altruist
am (amat, amour)	love	amicable, amateur, paramour
anim	mind, soul	inanimate, animal
ann (enn)	year	annual, biennial
anthro (anthrop)	man, human	anthropology, misanthrope
aqu	water	aquatic, aqueduct
arch	chief, ruler	monarchy, anarchist
aster (astr)	star	asterisk, astronomy
aud (audit)	hear	audible, audition
biblio	book	bibliography, bible
bio	life	biology, biography
cad (cas, cid)	fall	cadence, cascade, coincidence
cap (cep, ceive)	hold, seize	capacity, reception, deceive
capit (cap, chap, chief)	head	caption, captain, chapter, chief
cav	hollow	cavity, cavern
cede (ceed, cess)	go	secede, succeed, process
chrom(e)	color	chromatic, monochrome
chron	time	chronicle, anachronism
cide (cis)	cut, kill	matricide, scissors
cir, cycl	round	circular, cyclone
cit (civ)	government	citizen, civil
claus (close, clus, clude)	shut	claustrophobia, foreclose, cluster, exclude
cline (clim)	slope	incline, climax
corp	body	corporate, corpulent
crat (cracy)	rule	democratic, aristocracy
cre (crease, cres)	grow	increment, increase, crescent
cred	believe	credible, credit
cult	develop	cultivate, acculturate
cur (cour)	run	recurrent, recourse
cur (sur)	care	manicure, curator, insure
dem	people	democratic, epidemic
dent (dont)	teeth	denture, orthodontist
derm	skin	dermatologist, hypodermic
dic (dict, dit)	say, speak	indicate, dictate, edit
doc (dox)	opinion, belief	doctrine, orthodox
duc	lead	conductive, aqueduct
dynam	power	dynamic, dynamo

Root	Meaning	Examples
ego	self	egotistical, egocentric
equa (equi)	equal	equanimity, equilibrium
fac (fec, fic)	make, do	facilitate, effect, fiction
fal (fals)	deceive	fallacy, falsify
fend (fens)	against, from	defendant, offensive
fer	carry	prefer, ferry
fic (fig)	form	fiction, figure
fid	faith	confidant, infidel
fin	limit	infinite, finish
fix	stationary	prefix, fixate
flect (flex)	bend	inflection, reflex
flu	flow	fluid, influential
fort (forc)	strong	fortress, reinforce
fract (frag)	break	fraction, fragment
fund (fuse, found)	pour or melt	refund, fusion, profound
gamy	marriage	bigamy, misogamy
gen (gin)	birth, origin, race	genetic, origin, genocide
geo	earth	geology, geography
grad (gress)	go, walk, step	graduate, progress
gram (graph)	write	telegram, graphics
grat (grac)	pleasing, thanks, favor	gratis, ingrate
her (hes)	stick	inherent, adhesive
hydr (hydro)	water	dehydrate, hydroelectric
jac (ject)	throw	jacket, reject
jud (jus, jur)	right	judicial, justice, injure
jug (junc, just)	join	conjugate, juncture, adjust
kine (cine)	move	kinetic, cinema
labor	work	collaborate, laboratory
lect (leg)	gather, read, law	collect, legal
libr (liber)	book, free	library, liberal
lic	permit, allure	license, elicit
liter	letter	literate, literature
loc	place	location, allocate
log (logy, ology)	word, speech, study of	logo, logic, genealogy
luc (lum, lus, lun, lux)	light	lucid, luminous, illustrate, lunar, luxury
magna (max)	great	magnify, maximum
man	hand	manual, emancipate
mania	madness	kleptomania, manic

Root	Meaning	Examples
mater (matr)	mother	alma mater, matriarch
mem (men, mn, min)	mind, memory	memo, mental, amnesia
meter (metr)	measure	thermometer, metric
mis (mit)	send	emissary, emit
mort	die	mortal, mortuary
mob (mot, mov)	move	mobile, motivate, remote, remove
nat (nai, neo, nov)	new, born	prenatal, naive, neoclassic, novel
naut, nav	water	astronaut, navigate
nomos, onym	name	nomenclature, synonym
ocle (ocul, opt)	eye	monocle, binocular, optical
pac (pact)	peace	pacify, pact
par (part)	equal, share	disparity, compartment
pass (path)	feel, disease	passion, antipathy, pathology
pater (patr)	father	paternal, patriotic
ped	child	pediatrician, pedagogy
ped (pod)	foot	pedal, podiatrist
pel (puls)	drive	compel, repulsive
pend (pens, pond)	hang, weight, pay	pending, expense, ponder
pet (peat)	seek, request	perpetual, repeat
phil	love	philanthropy, philologist
phobia	fear	claustrophobia, hydrophobia
phon	sound	phonograph, symphony
photo (phos)	light	photographic, phosphorus
pict (pig)	paint	depict, pigment
plac (plea)	please, calm	placate, implacable, please
plic (plex, ply)	bend, fold	implicate, perplex, reply
polis (polit)	city, citizen	cosmopolitan, politician
port	carry	porter, opportune
pose (posit, pound)	put	dispose, deposit, impound
press (prim, print)	squeeze, press	pressure, reprimand, imprint
psych	mind, soul	psyche, parapsychology
punct (pung, point, pug)	prick	punctuate, pungent, appoint, pugnacious
quer (ques, quir, quis)	ask, seek	query, question, inquiry, inquisition
reg (rect, right)	straight, direct	irregular, erect, forthright
rog	ask, seek	derogatory, interrogate
rupt	break	interrupt, rupture
scope	see	telescope, microscope

Root	Meaning	Examples
scrib (script)	write	inscribe, manuscript
sens (sent)	feel, think	sensitive, sentiment
sequ (secut, suit)	follow	sequence, persecute, pursuit
sid (sed, sess)	sit	reside, sediment, session
sign	mark, signal	insignia, designate
sim (sym, syn, syl)	together, same	simulate, sympathy, synonym, syllable
sol	alone	solo, solitude
solv (solu)	loosen, explain	solvent, solution
son (sound)	sound	sonar, resound
spec (spect, spic, spis)	see, look	speculate, inspect, despicable, despise
spir	breathe	respiration, expire
stat (stan, sist, stit)	stand	static, stand, resist, constitute
struct	build	construct, structure
tact (tag, tang, ting)	touch	contact, contagious, tangible, tinge
temp	time, heat	contemporary, tempo, temperature
ten (tain, tin)	hold	contain, retention, pertinent
tend (ten)	stretch	tendon, extensive
ter (terr)	earth	interment, terrestrial
text	weave, construct	textile, texture
theo (the)	god	theology, atheist
therm	hot, warm	thermos, thermometer
thesis	put, place	synthesis, hypothesis
tom (tomy)	cut	atom, tonsillectomy
torq (tort)	twist, wind	torque, contort
tract	draw, pull	subtract, traction
urb	city	urbane, suburban
vac (void)	empty	vacuum, evacuate, void
val (valu)	worth, strength	ambivalent, evaluate
ven (vent)	come	intervene, adventure
verb	word	adverb, verbatim
vers (vert, verg)	turn	versus, avert, verge
vic (van, vinc)	conquer, change	vicarious, vanquish, invincible
vid (vis, view)	see	video, visual, review
vita (viv)	life	vital, vivacious
voc (vok)	call	vocal, revoke
volv (volu)	roll, will	revolve, voluntary

Credits